REUSING OCL
IN THE DEFINITION OF
IMPERATIVE LANGUAGES

Fabian Büttner

Vom Fachbereich Mathematik und Informatik
der Universität Bremen zur Verleihung
des akademischen Grades eines Doktors
der Ingenieurwissenschaften (Dr.-Ing.)
genehmigte Dissertation

Gutachter: Prof. Dr. Martin Gogolla
                    Prof. Dr. Hans-Jörg Kreowski

Kolloquium: 26. Oktober 2010

Bibliografische Information der Deutschen Nationalbibliothek

Die Deutsche Nationalbibliothek verzeichnet diese Publikation in der
Deutschen Nationalbibliografie; detaillierte bibliografische Daten sind
im Internet über http://dnb.d-nb.de abrufbar.

ISBN 978-3-8325-2811-9

Logos Verlag Berlin GmbH
Comeniushof, Gubener Str. 47,
10243 Berlin
Tel.: +49 (0)30 42 85 10 90
Fax: +49 (0)30 42 85 10 92
INTERNET: http://www.logos-verlag.de

Abstract

The Object Constraint Language (OCL) has proven to be a valuable ingredient for the specification of UML models. It allows to formulate logical propositions for models that typically cannot be expressed in the visual modeling paradigms of UML. A similar textual ingredient is required for the imperative specification of behavior in certain applications of UML, most prominently Executable UML models and model transformation. There is no such imperative language in the UML standard, but there are several candidates for such a language that are based on OCL for expressions. One of them is ImperativeOCL, which is part of the OMG Query, Views, Transformations (QVT) standard. However, the embedding of OCL into several of these languages is what we call a non-modular embedding. Such a non-modular embedding results in problems w. r. t. to language semantics and/or sets up obstacles for the reuse of existing OCL tools and instruments. In our work we therefore define requirements for a modular embedding of OCL into an imperative language. We introduce our language SOIL (Simple OCL-based Imperative Language) which embeds OCL in a modular way. We provide an informal description of SOIL as well as a formal definition of the language syntax and semantics, and prove its consistency and type safety. We describe applications of our approach in two fields: first, the extension of the UML-based Specification Environment (USE) by an imperative language and, second, the development of the model transformation tool XGenerator2 that has been successfully applied in several eGovernment projects. Our work makes three major contributions. First, we provide a critical review of the embedding of OCL into existing programming languages. Second, we provide a simple but already useful OCL-based imperative language with a sound and formal semantics that can be implemented out of the box using existing OCL engines. Third, our work contributes a general guideline for a safe embedding of OCL into other languages.

Acknowledgements

I am very grateful to my supervisor Martin Gogolla for several fruitful discussions and helpful comments. I also like to express my gratitude to my co-supervisor Hans-Jörg Kreowski for accepting the task of examining this thesis. Furthermore, I want to thank my colleagues Lars Hamann, Mirco Kuhlmann, Arne Lindow, Oliver Radfelder, and Paul Ziemann for a lot of invaluable feedback on my work and for the exceptional working atmosphere. I really enjoyed working with you in our research group. My special thanks goes to Mirco who took the burden of reviewing the formal parts of my work. I also want to thank Daniel Gent who put a lot of effort in the USE implementation of SOIL. While working on my thesis, I had the chance to discuss several of my research contributions at the UML/MODELS conferences and workshops and I am grateful for all the stimulating discussions and comments I took from there. Last but most important I want to thank my wife Gesa for her patience and never-ending support.

Contents

Chapter 1

Introduction

Modeling constitutes an important instrument in science and engineering. Being a representation of some thing – on a smaller scale or in a simplified way – is common to several kinds of models.

We usually create models in one of two ways. The first way is by reduction, the second is by construction. Whereas reduction usually aims at the understanding of certain properties of a thing that is already in existence, construction aims at the understanding of properties of something typically prior to its existence. A model can be material, such as a mechanical model of a machine and a wodden architectural model of a building, or it can be immaterial, such as a mathematical model, e. g., a formula to calculate the turbulences that occur on an aeroplane wing.

Modeling has several applications in all fields of computer science. Regarding models of algorithms, one of the first and still a very important model in computer science is the Turing machine. It provides a simple theoretical device that manipulates symbols contained on a strip of virtual tape [Tur36]. Despite its simplicity, a Turing machine can be adapted to simulate the computation of any algorithm. It plays an important role in studying and comparing properties of algorithms, e. g., whether an algorithm terminates.

Whereas models such as the Turing machine are commonly used as abstractions to study properties of algorithms that have been expressed in more complex languages already (i. e., in a programming language), other behavioral models exist that can be used for the construction of algorithms. Two very prominent behavioral models typically employed in this manner are flow charts, such as Nassi-Shneiderman diagrams [NS73], and state chart diagrams [Har87]. Such models can be constructed prior to implementing software systems in order to study and communicate properties of the future system.

As for algorithms, models have also been used for decades in the development of data or information structures. The relational database model [Cod70] provides a sound mathematical foundation for dealing with structured data that still constitutes the basis of most database systems in the world. The Entity-Relationship (ER) model [Che76] has been used widely, too, in the field of database engineering. In contrast to the relational database model, it makes a clear distinction between logical information entities and relationships, supporting a higher level of abstraction. In a typical database development process, system requirements are first captured as ER models and then translated into relational models prior to implementation.

The concept of information entities also emerged in the field of computer programming. The idea of object-orientation (OO) evolved first as a programming paradigm that uses 'objects' – encapsulated data structures and methods to access the behavior of an object – to design applications and computer programs. The earliest identifiable object-oriented programming language is Simula [DN66], later followed by several other prominent languages such as Smalltalk (e.g., in [Kay93]), C++ [Str93], and Eiffel [Mey97].

There has been a large number of approaches to adopt the object-oriented paradigm for the analysis and modeling of computer systems and software. Three very successful ones were the Object-Oriented Analysis and Design (OOAD) method by Booch [Boo94], the Object Modeling Technique (OMT) by Rumbaugh [JRE91], and the use case driven Object-oriented Software Engineering approach of Jacobson [Jac95].

These three authors, commonly referred to as the 'three amigos', joined their methods in 1996 to establish a unified approach to the modeling of computer systems and software [Rum96] – the Unified Modeling Language was born [Rat97] . Being under the roof of Rational Software in the beginning, the UML was put under the aegis of the Object Management Group (OMG) standardization process later. Today, the current version of UML is 2.3 [OMG10]. It comprises several structural and behavioral modeling instruments such as use case modeling, class modeling, and statechart modeling, that can be used to describe different facets of an information system.

The UML can be regarded as a very rich modeling language, providing a broad assortment of modeling paradigms. Most of them having a visual notation. The major exception of this rule is the Object Constraint Language (OCL, [WK03]) which has been added to UML in version 1.3 [OMG99a]. OCL is a textual language in the spirit of first order predicate logic. It allows to formulate logical propositions for a model that typically cannot be expressed in the visual modeling paradigms of UML. For example, class invariants can express structural properties for objects that have to be fulfilled for a valid state. Pre- and postconditions for operations can be used to describe characteristics of operations, that is, the 'before' and 'after' of an operation invocation. Further applications of OCL for transitions in state charts and for other model artifacts exist. OCL is called 'side-effect free', the evaluation of an OCL expression never changes the state of a system.

While there are several visual paradigms for behavioral models in UML, especially state machines and activity diagrams, there is no pendant in the standard which allows us to express algorithms in a textual syntax. Although this is not a principle problem, as the visual paradigms of UML can express every algorithm (they are computationally complete), it constitutes a practical problem when a larger number of smaller algorithms is involved. There are (at least) two important approaches that require such a complementary textual modeling paradigm, because they involve considerable numbers of small algorithms: Executable UML and the Model-Driven Architecture (MDA). The Executable UML approach [Mel02] combines the Shlaer-Mellor method [SM92] and the UML standard to achieve software models that can be actually executed. Executable UML provides a 'profile' for UML requiring that the dynamic behavior of all objects (classes) is precisely defined by finite state machines with Moore models (in such state machines, output is specific to states, not to transitions). The state machines are described visually using UML state chart diagrams. A textual Object Action Language (OAL) is then used to describe the effects of the states in the state machines using UML Actions, which was first proposed in [MTAL98] and later adopted in UML to formalize the semantics of primitive standard operations such as object creation, link manipulation etc. However, OAL is not based on OCL as its expression language. Instead an SQL like query language is included. Furthermore we need to note that the larger behavioral specification is done using state machines and only the primitives are specified using OAL. Thus, OAL is not meant to be a general purpose imperative language.

The second approach requiring a precise textual representation of behavior for the manipulation of UML models is the Model-Driven Architecture (MDA) [OMG03, MSUW04], more specifically stated in the OMG Query, Views, Transformation (QVT) specification [OMG08a]. MDA aims at the development of models from other models. Typically, more abstract models are transformed into more concrete models. In MDA, most or all of this transformation is performed automatically. Therefore, MDA deals with algorithms that process a model as input, producing another model as their output. The QVT specification provides several languages and layers that are employed to specify model transformations. At its core, it comprises a textual imperative language based on OCL. This language is called ImperativeOCL. It is defined as a general purpose imperative language that can be used in several places in MDA tools. Therefore, ImperativeOCL is targeted as a widely applied standard for an imperative programming language in the context of UML modeling and transformation.

However, a major problem with ImperativeOCL is that it does not really fit with OCL. The way ImperativeOCL embeds OCL leads to unexpected changes in the meaning of OCL expressions and introduces redundancies in the language. In consequence, existing formal work for OCL such as transformation rules for expressions, proofs for formal properties of expressions, and model checking algorithms cannot be applied to expressions in ImperativeOCL anymore. Furthermore, the QVT specification prohibits a modular separation of OCL evaluators and model transformation tools, which in turn prohibits the employment of reusable OCL libraries.

In this work, we explain how a simple OCL-based imperative language (SOIL) can be constructed on top of OCL without introducing the flaws of ImperativeOCL. We provide informal and formal semantics for the language SOIL and prove its soundness with respect to syntax and semantics. The language can be implemented 'out of the box' in UML tools. This has be done for the tool USE (UML-based Specification Environment) and for the MDA tool XGenerator2 which is employed in the context of eGgovernment standardization. However, SOIL is not meant to be only the '701th Programming Language' (referring to Landin's article 'The Next 700 Programming Languages' [Lan66]). We believe it can also serve as a general guideline for how to safely embed OCL into other languages, in a modular way.

Further Related Work

A denotational set-theoretic semantics for OCL has been defined by Richters in [Ric02]. This formalization has been adopted by the OMG as an appendix to the OCL standard. Richters furthermore implemented the first OCL evaluator as part of the UML-based Specification Environment (USE) [RG00, GBR07a]. There is already research based on this formalization, e. g., by Flake on temporal state-oriented OCL [F03]. We ground on Richters' formalization of OCL in our work.

Jiang et al. define a language 'OCL for Execution (OCL4X)' to be used in the context of Executable UML [JZM08]. We will show in Chap. 2 that this language suffers from the same problems as ImperativeOCL. Siikarla et al. discuss how to combine OCL and existing programming languages to achieve effective model processing [MSS04].

The ATLAS Transformation Language (ATL) [JABK08] is a hybrid language which provides a mix of declarative and imperative constructs for the specification of model-to-model transformation. ATL is in accordance with the OMG QVT requirements. It includes OCL to formulate queries, value expressions, and helpers for transformations. The ATL transformations itself are, however, graph transformation-like objects, ATL is not meant to be a general purpose imperative programming language for UML models.

Süß et al. develop a language framework 'Prime' for the creation of QVT languages [SLB04]. OCL is employed as the reference language for query expressions in Prime.

Unlike more common model-to-model transformation approaches, the OMG Model-to-Text specification [OMG08b] aims at the need to produce various text artifacts such as code, deployment specifications, reports, documents, etc. from MOF and UML models. Model-to-Text addresses this requirement by using a text template-based approach which builds on OCL for data extraction from the model.

Ziemann embeds OCL into extended graph transformation rules to achieve integrated operational semantics for UML models in [Zie06].

Warmer et al. provided an extension of OCL by an 'action' clause to specify the interchange of messages in the context of pre- and postconditions [War00]. This extension was proposed for OCL 2.0 but was not adopted by the OMG. The scope of the action clauses is the description of collaborating objects, e.g., in business process modeling. Warmer et al. did not propose a general imperative extension for OCL.

In [MFJ05], Muller et al. researched the weaving of operational descriptions in MOF metamodels, following a similar compositional approach as we do in our work.

The Epsilon Object Language (EOL) [KPP06] is the core language in the Epsilon tool set [EPS]. Within Epsilon, EOL embeds OCL for the evaluation of expressions. EOL incorporates major elements from OCL for queries and navigation and furthermore provides mechanisms such as statement sequencing, simple programming idioms and model modification capabilities.

Brucker and Wolff embedded OCL into the Isabelle/HOL theorem prover. Their solution HOL-OCL allows to reason over UML class models annotated with OCL specifications. Although we did not use this environment in our work, it might be a candidate for future extensions of our language SOIL.

Approaches related to OCL expression rewriting, transformation, and analysis include the work of Markovic and Baar [MB08], Cabot [CT07, Cab07], Cuadrado et al [CJMB08], and our own work [BBG05, BB06, GKB08].

Hudak investigated the composition of domain-specific languages around a functional core (λ-calculus) in [Hud98] as modular algebraic semantics. Our definition of SOIL follows a similar modular structure. Akehurst, Zschaler and Howells address the topic of modularizing OCL and OCL extensions such as temporal logic in [AZH08]. Kran, Rumpe, and Völkel address modularity and composition of domain-specific languages in [KRV08].

Today, we have a number of tools with OCL support. A non exhaustive list includes the Dresden OCL toolkit [HDF02], the UML-based Specification Environment (USE) [GBR07b], the OCL Environment (OCLE) [CPC+04], the ATL tool [JABK08], the Eclipse Model Development Tools (MDT) Eclipse MDT OCL [MDT], KMF [AP08], the Octopus tool [Kla05], and RoclET [RT].

An evaluation of OCL for large scale applications has been performed by Aydal et at. in [APW08].

Research Contributions

We provided several contributions regarding the validation of UML models and OCL in general as well as regarding model transformations in particular in several journals, conferences, and workshops.

- We presented the USE approach for the validation of UML models and OCL constraints based on animation and certification in [GBR07b] and [GRB+04].

- We addressed several aspects of the formal semantics of UML and OCL, in specifically the semantics of collections [BGH+10] and the semantics of generalization [BG04a].

- In [KHGB11] and [GKB08] we introduced a benchmark to measure the accuracy, determinateness, and efficiency of OCL engines.

- An approach to amalgamate UML, OCL, and graph transformation has been developed in [BG06, GBD08, BB06, BG04b, Büt05, BBG05].

- We studied the relationship between models, metamodels, and transformation models in [BBG+06] and [GFB05].

- In [BK09] we discussed the shortcomings of the embedding of OCL into QVT ImperativeOCL. A corresponding request for improvement has been submitted to OMG for MOV QVT ImperativeOCL as an official issue [Büt08].

- We presented the XGenerator2 tool, as part of a model-driven eGovernment strategy, in [BKG+08]. The tool has been developed as part of a joint project of the Technologie-Zentrum Informatik und Informationstechnik (TZI), init AG, Bundesministerium des Innern, and the Senatorin für Finanzen (Bremen) [SF].

- Finally, in [BRLG04], we introduced an approach to embed multi-method semantics in programming languages such as Java.

Thesis Structure

This thesis is structured as follows.

Chapter 2 illustrates how OCL is embedded in current imperative languages and discusses the problems that arise from a non-modular embedding, with ImperativeOCL constituting the most prominent example. We postulate requirements for a modular embedding at the end of this chapter.

In Chap. 3 we provide the set theoretic formalizations for UML and OCL as introduced by Richters. This chapter further contributes addenda to the original formalization to adopt it to the current version of UML and OCL and to provide missing definitions regarding the construction of collection literals and their typing. We also introduce our running example 'Project World' in this chapter.

Chapter 4 is about our imperative language SOIL which is based on OCL in a modular way. We first informally introduce the language. Then we provide formal definitions for the language, including examples for the formalization. In the remaining chapter, we investigate the type-soundness of SOIL and discuss how to extend the language by a more sophisticated error handling. We conclude the chapter with a comparison of SOIL to other existing OCL-based imperative languages.

Chapter 5 shows two real world applications of our approach – the first is the implementation of SOIL into the case tool USE, the second is an application of OCL and SOIL in the eGovernment MDA tool XGenerator2.

We conclude our thesis with a summary and identify future work in Chapter 6.

Appendix A contains proofs for the type-soundness theorems. Appendix B provides the complete USE specification for the 'Project World' example used throughout this work.

Chapter 2

Motivation

OCL has proven to be a valuable ingredient in a lot of areas and in many object-oriented model-based approaches. First of all, OCL has been used to specify properties of models. These properties include constraints (class invariants, state chart guard conditions, and operation pre- and postconditions) as well as the definition of side-effect free operations (query operations).

Beside being a part of the modeling language, OCL has also been successfully employed in several other fields as a simple and general purpose query language that provides the full expressiveness of first order predicate logic in an object-oriented manner.

In model transformation approaches, OCL queries are widely used to specify source objects for transformations. This can be done using OCL solely, or in conjunction with other specification mechanisms such as graph patterns (c.f. [Ehr92, Roz97] for an introduction on graph grammars, c.f. [Baa05, WTEK08, Zie06, BG04b] for graph transformation based UML/OCL approaches). For the actual transformation step, several other paradigms are employed, such as graph transformation, relational approaches, and (textual) imperative approaches. The OMG provides the OCL-based language MOF ImperativeOCL as such a textual language.

In Executable UML, an imperative language with query support is required as well. However, the Object Action Language (OAL) employed in [Mel02] uses a proprietary expression language instead of OCL. Thus, the use of an OCL-based language such as ImperativeOCL seems to be very appropriate for Executable UML with regard to the further standardization of MDA.

Unfortunately, several OCL-based imperative languages, including ImperativeOCL, suffer from semantic problems due to a non-modular embedding of OCL. In this section we discuss these problems for ImperativeOCL, OCL

for Execution (OCL4X), the OMG MOF Model-to-Text standard, and the
Epsilon Object Language (EOL). As a résumé we formulate requirements
for a safe, modular embedding of OCL into an imperative language. In the
remaining chapters of this thesis, we will follow this requirements in our own
definitions.

2.1   The Goal: Reusing OCL in a Modular Way

Having a lot of approaches that employ OCL, a proper notion of reusing OCL
is needed. A weak notion of reuse would be to take the syntax and semantics
of OCL as a starting point in the definition of a new language, modifying
and extending them where necessary. A strong notion of reuse could be a
non-intrusive one. In this sense of reuse, we want to keep the syntax and
semantics of OCL unchanged, and therefore clearly separated. In software
engineering, we find this kind of reuse in modules or components. Speaking
in terms of software systems that provide languages that are based on OCL,
this means that the OCL evaluation could be (and should be) encapsulated
in a module or component that has been created without knowledge of the
way OCL is going to be applied in the system. Under this premise, one
implementation of OCL can be reused in several places, such as several kinds
of MDA transformation processors.

This very practical consideration of modularity has its pendant in the metamodel and in the formal definition of OCL. Here, we want to have *one* OCL
metamodel and *one* formal definition of OCL's semantics. There are lots
of approaches already that deal with OCL expressions and OCL-annotated
UML models. Existing work such as expression transformations (e.g., in
[MB08, CT07, Büt05]), expression analysis (e.g., in [CJMB08]), reasoning
(e.g., in [BW08]), and model checking (e.g., [DKR00, KK08]) could not be
applied if there is no agreement on the semantics of OCL as soon as it is
embedded in some other language.

In the remaining chapter, we first look on the reuse of OCL in the definition
of MOF QVT ImperativeOCL. This is a very prominent and also an 'official' example for the embedding of OCL into another language (the QVT
imperative transformation language) as MOF QVT is a standard for model
transformation published by the OMG. Unfortunately, this is also an example of 'weak reuse'. ImperativeOCL modifies the syntax and semantics of
OCL itself, it could not be realized using an OCL library. Furthermore, ImperativeOCL introduces several OCL (or better: OCL-like) expressions that
do not longer have a well-defined meaning w.r.t. to the OCL standard. This
leads to a couple of semantic and practical problems as we will point out
in the following. We have already presented these issue in[BK09]. An official
issue has been submitted to the OMG issue process in [Büt08].

2.2 MOF QVT ImperativeOCL

The MOF 'Query, Views, Transformations' (QVT) specification [OMG08a] standardizes transformations of MOF and UML models. It is part of the Model-Driven Architecture (MDA) efforts of the OMG.

QVT provides a hybrid declarative/operational architecture for model transformation. The specification defines a declarative and an operational kind of transformation description. In the declarative approach, the 'Relations' language, transformations are specified by sets of relations over the source and target model. In the operational approach, the language 'ImperativeOCL' is used to specify the effect of a model transformation by means of imperative programming. The language provides facilities for model resp.[1] state manipulation, and constructs known from other programming languages, like loops and conditional execution. Both approaches can be combined, such that some transformations (or sub-transformations) are given by relations, and others are specified imperatively. In the following, we focus on ImperativeOCL only, and do not go into further details of the Relations language or the QVT approach in general.

While the usefulness of a combination of OCL and imperative language elements is unquestioned, we criticize the way OCL is extended to ImperativeOCL. The language design leads to several semantic problems, which we point out in this section.

2.2.1 Language Overview

The core element of ImperativeOCL is the notion of an 'imperative expression'. It is introduced in [OMG08a, Sect. 8.8.2] as follows: "The imperative expression is an abstract concept serving as the base for the definition of all side-effect oriented expressions defined in this specification. Note: In contrast with pure OCL side-effect free expressions, imperative expressions do not behave as functions. For instance, executing interrupt constructs like break, continue, raise, and return have an effect in the control flow of the imperative expressions that contain them.".

We will demonstrate later, actually *all* expressions (imperative or not) become side-effected and do not longer behave as functions in the QVT approach.

As usual in OMG specifications, the language is defined by means of an abstract syntax model (language metamodel). Figures 2.1 and 2.2 depict the

---

[1]Usually, QVT transformations operate on models, that are instances (i. e., states) of a metamodel

structures of this abstract syntax. Only a subset of the metaclasses and their relationships are depicted for clarity. We will regard the individual elements displayed in the diagrams later in this section.

The first language element we need to describe is the concept of *blocks* (*Block-Exp*). In ImperativeOCL, expressions $e_1, \ldots, e_n$ can be combined to a block

$$e_1; \ldots; e_n.$$

Such a block expression is, again, an expression. Regarding the semantics of this (and all other imperative expressions) we need to regard the effect and the value of the expression. The effect of an imperative expression describes the changes it applies to its context (the objects, their attribute values, the links between objects, values of variables, etc.). As all imperative expressions are defined as subclasses of OclExpression (indicated by the star symbol at the top of Fig. 2.1), they also have a value, in the sense as the expression $1 + 2$ has the value 3. The effect of $e_1; \ldots; e_n$ is determined by successively executing the expressions e_1 to e_n. The value of a block is the Undefined value ('null', or formally $\bot$).

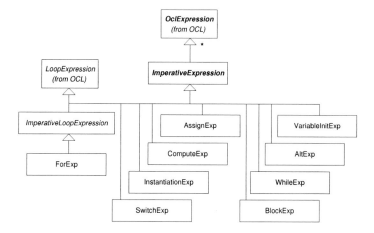

Figure 2.1: ImperativeOCL abstract syntax – selected metaclasses

Basic Expressions

Having the concatenation of expressions into block, we now explain the basic state manipulation commands. The language provides a general assignment expression (*AssignExp*). Assignment can be made to variables as well as to

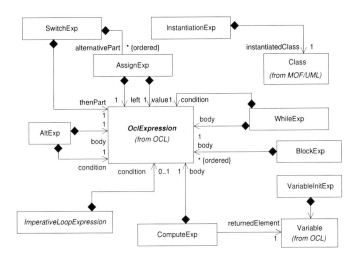

Figure 2.2: ImperativeOCL abstract syntax – selected aggregations

properties of objects. For multi-valued variables and properties, an alternative kind of assignment is defined as well which adds a new element to the collection. The general syntax is as follows.

```
v := e          // variable assignment
v :+ e          // adding a value to a multi-valued variable
e₁.p := e       // property assignment
e₁.p += e       // adding a value to a multi-valued property
```

Assume a class c which declares an Integer typed attribute x and a Set(Integer) typed attribute y. Assume furthermore an instance o of c, an Integer typed variable v, and a Set(Integer) typed variable w. Concrete examples for assignments are:

```
v := 1 + 2
w := Set{1,2,3}
w += 4
o.x := 1 + 2
o.y := Set{1,2,3}
o.y += 4
```

The value of an assignment expression is always the assigned value. Notice that ImperativeOCL does not provide explicit expressions to manipulate

links (instances of associations) between objects. They have to be modified
by assignments to the properties which are induced by the association ends.

Notice that variables need be to be declared before they can be assigned. This
is achieved by a variable declaration expression (*VariableInitExp*). Given a
variable name v, a type t, and an optional initialization expression e, there
are three different flavors of declarations:

```
var v : t
var v : t := e
var v : t ::= e
```

The first line simply declares v to be of type t in the following. The second line
additionally assigns an initial value to v. The first and the second version
have a value of 'null'. The third version behaves like the second, but this
variable declaration expression has the value of e.

New objects can be created by the instantiation expression (*Instantiation-
Exp*). Given a class c, the syntax is

```
new c
```

The value of this expression is the newly created object. Often, this expression occurs as the right-hand side of an assignment expression, e. g.,
`v := new C`. Notice, that no corresponding 'destroy' expression exists in ImperativeOCL (in a model transformation, metaobjects that are no longer
used, are detached from the model using a special library operation).

The last basic expression we explain is the compute expression (*Compute-
Exp*). A compute expression contains a block expression and a variable declaration. The effect of this expression is the effect after executing the block
expression. The value of the compute expression is the value of the declared
variable after executing the block. Given a variable name v, a type t and a
body expression e, the general syntax is:

```
compute(v : t) { e }
```

Although *ComputeExp* is connected to exactly one *OclExpression* in Fig. 2.2
on the previous page, the body can consist of a sequence of expressions as
a block expression. We give an example of an application of the compute
expression.

```
var x : Integer;
x := compute(y : Integer) { y := 1 + 2 }
      + compute(y : Integer) { y := 3 }
```

The effect of this expression (spanning all three lines) is an assignment of 6 to the variable x. Its value is null. The value of the second statement (lines 2–3), regarded in isolation, is 6.

Flow Control Expressions

ImperativeOCL provides several flow control constructs. These include variants of loops, conditional execution, exception handling, and operation invocation.

The while loop (*WhileExp*) is the most fundamental loop, as all other loops can be expressed by it. Given a Boolean typed expression e_1 and a body expression e_2, the syntax for a while loop is

```
while (e₁) { e₂ }
```

For a practical application, the body expression e_2 should modify the environment in some way that is recognized by e_1 (e. g., change a variable, or modify the properties of an object). The value of a while expression is null. The following example calculates the sum $1 + \cdots + n$ using a while loop. We assume n to be defined previously.

```
var r : Integer := 1;
var i : Integer := 1;
while (i <= n) { r := r + i; i := i + 1 }
```

This example also illustrates that the body of the while expression (as enclosed by '' and '') may modify variables declared outside of the body.

A more specialized loop is the for loop (*ForExp*). It comes in several flavors which are distinguished by the name attribute of the metaclass. We only present the 'forEach' loop. Given a collection typed range expression e_1, a variable name x, and a body expression e_2, the syntax is

```
e₁->forEach(x) { e₂ }
```

The effect is as follows. The body e_2 is executed once for each element in e_1, with the current element being assigned to x. The value of the forEach expression is null. The previous example can expressed as

```
var r : Integer := 1;
Sequence{1..n}->forEach (i) { r := r + i }
```

Finally, the last flow control expression we explain is the conditional execution of expressions. Given a Boolean typed expression c, the conditional execution of a body expression e (*AltExp*) has the following syntax.

```
if (c)
  e
endif
```

Conditional executions with more than one branch are constructed by a *SwitchExp* and one or more *AltExp* metaobjects. Given Boolean expressions $c_1, \ldots c_{n-1}$ and expressions $e_1, \ldots, n$, the syntax is

```
if (c₁)
  e₁
elif (c₂)
  e₂
...
else
   eₙ
endif
```

The value of both forms is the value of the expression e_i that was executed, or null, if none was executed. In contrast to the previous expressions, the syntax does not include curly braces to delimit the body expressions e_i.

2.2.2   Amalgamation of OCL Expressions and Imperative Expressions

The most important aspect of the abstract syntax we refer to in this paper, is the fact that all imperative expression classes inherit from OclExpression (indicated by the star at the top of Fig. 2.1 on page 12). OclExpression is the base class for all expressions in conventional OCL (c. f. [OMG06]). Consequently, imperative expressions can be used at all locations where OCL expressions may occur. This has been used intensively in all language elements explained above. For example, when calculating the sum $1 + \cdots + n$ using a while loop. Figure 2.3 on the next page depicts this example on the metamodel level. The body of a *WhileExp* is an *OclExpression* in Fig. 2.2. Here, we actually use a *BlockExp* containing two *AssignExp*. These are all subclasses of *ImperativeExpression*. The expressions used as the condition for *WhileExp* and as the right-hand sides of the two *AssignExp* are conventional OCL expressions. Thus, we have a directed structure, where imperative expressions contain imperative and OCL (sub-)expressions. Most of the examples above follow this structure. However, the amalgamation of imperative

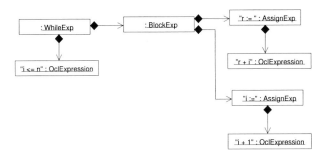

Figure 2.3: ImperativeOCL abstract syntax – calculating $1 + \cdots + n$

expressions and OCL expressions works in both ways. There are imperative expressions consisting of OCL expressions that again consist of imperative ones. For example,

```
var z : Set(Integer) := Set1,2,3->select(y |
  compute(x:Integer) { x := y * 2 } < 5
)
```

The right-hand side of this imperative variable declaration expression is an OCL select expression. This OCL select expression requires a boolean body expression, which is given by a relational OCL expression whose left-hand side is an imperative compute expression. The body of this compute expression is an assignment expression whose right-hand side is again a conventional OCL expression (y * 2). While this is a rather simple example, trickier mixtures of imperative expressions and OCL expressions can be constructed, that lead into several semantic problems.

2.2.3 Semantic Problems

We now explain semantic problems that arise from the embedding-by-inheritance of OCL into ImperativeOCL. First, we elaborate on the fact, that ImperativeOCL redefines the interpretation of OCL expressions, and that this redefined interpretation leads to undefined semantics of several OCL expressions which had a perfectly well-defined semantics in conventional OCL. Second, we show that several important equivalence rules for OCL do not longer hold in ImperativeOCL, even for the OCL part in ImperativeOCL. We furthermore show that some of the new imperative expressions are redundant w.r.t. conventional OCL expressions. Finally, we generalize this critique and discuss that the abstract syntax of ImperativeOCL violates the subtype substitution principle in UML.

Undefined Semantics for OCL Expressions

In conventional OCL, the semantics of an OCL expression e can be formally expressed by an interpretation function

$$I[\![\, e \,]\!] : \text{Env} \to \text{Value}$$

where $\text{Env} = (\sigma, \beta)$ is the environment in which the expression is evaluated (σ is a system state – objects, links, and attribute values –, and β maps bound variables to their values). Cf. Chap. 3, [OMG06, Annex A] and [Ric02] for the formal semantics of OCL.

However, for ImperativeOCL expressions, the interpretation function described above is not sufficient. The evaluation (or execution) of an ImperativeOCL expression does not only return a value, it also results in a (possibly) modified state and a (possibly) modified variable binding. To take this into account, the interpretation of an ImperativeOCL expression must be defined as follows:

$$I_{\text{IMP}}[\![\, e \,]\!] : \text{Env} \to \text{Value} \times \text{Env}$$

While this is not done formally in [OMG08a], the effect of all imperative expressions are described in natural language, and one could define $I_{\text{IMP}}[\![\, e \,]\!]$ for all imperative expressions from this descriptions.

But, since ImperativeExpression is modeled as a subclass of OclExpression, the imperative semantics must be defined for all "ordinary" OCL expression, too, as ImperativeOCL expression can occur everywhere an OCL expression is expected. Figure 2.4 depicts this structural problem using the OCL metamodel – the redefinition of eval() in ImperativeExpression is inconsistent to the definition of eval() in OclExpression.

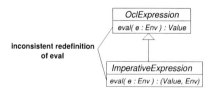

Figure 2.4: Problem illustrated using the OCL metamodel

The following imperative expression illustrates this problem:

```
compute(z:Boolean) {
```

```
   var x : Boolean := true
   var y : Boolean := true
   if ((x:=false) and (y:=false)) { ... }
   z := x
}
```

The value of this compute expression is obviously false (it returns the value of z at the end of the block). But what happens if we change the last line as follows:

```
compute(z:Boolean) {
   var x : Boolean := true
   var y : Boolean := true
   if ((x:=false) and (y:=false)) { ... }
   z := y
}
```

Is the value of this expression true or false? It depends on how we define the imperative semantics of the logical connectives. Given boolean expressions e_1 and e_2, we have at least two choices to define $I_{\mathrm{IMP}}[\![\, e_1 \text{ and } e_2\,]\!](\tau)$:

1. Lazy evaluation semantics like in Java or C (returns true for the above example):

$$I_{\mathrm{IMP}}[\![\, e_1 \text{ and } e_2\,]\!](\tau) = \begin{cases} I_{\mathrm{IMP}}[\![\, e_2\,]\!](\tau_1) & \text{if } v_1 = \text{true} \\ (v_1, \tau_1) & \text{otherwise} \end{cases}$$

where $(v_1, \tau_1) = I_{\mathrm{IMP}}[\![\, e_1\,]\!](\tau)$. Under this semantics (also called short-circuit evaluation) the right-hand side of the *and* operator is not evaluated if the left-hand side already evaluates to *false*. Therefore, y stays *true*.

2. Strict evaluation semantics (returns false for the above example):

$$I_{\mathrm{IMP}}[\![\, e_1 \text{ and } e_2\,]\!](\tau) = \begin{cases} (\text{true}, \tau_2) & \text{if } v_1 = \text{true} \wedge v_2 = \text{true} \\ (\text{false}, \tau_2) & \text{otherwise} \end{cases}$$

where $(v_1, \tau_1) = I_{\mathrm{IMP}}[\![\, e_1\,]\!](\tau)$ and $(v_2, \tau_2) = I_{\mathrm{IMP}}[\![\, e_2\,]\!](\tau_1)$. Under this semantics, both sides of the *and* operator are always evaluated. Therefore, *false* is assigned to y.

The QVT specification does not say which semantics should hold. But since imperative expressions may occur everywhere where OCL expressions can occur, this semantics has to be defined. One can find further similar locations where the imperative semantics of OCL expression is not obvious, e. g., for the collection operation iterate (what happens if the body of the expressions modifies the range variable?) or the treatment of undefined values in arithmetic expressions (similar to the logical connectives – lazy or not?).

Breaking Equivalence Rules

In conventional OCL, several equivalence rules hold, most of them well-known from predicate logic. If we include imperative expressions into the set of OCL expressions, they all do not longer hold. This is not necessarily a problem but at least contrary to the logical character of conventional OCL.

1. Substituting variables by let expressions. In conventional OCL, the following equivalence holds (we use $e\{x/y\}$ to denote 'e with all occurrences of x replaced by y)':

$$\text{let } x : T = e_1 \text{ in } e_2 \Leftrightarrow e_2\{x/e_1\}$$

   In ImperativeOCL, this equivalence does not hold. The left-hand and right-hand term are only equivalent if x occurs exactly once in e2.

2. Commutativity laws.

$$e_1 \text{ and } e_2 \Leftrightarrow e_2 \text{ and } e_1$$

   In ImperativeOCL, the commutativity laws for conjunction (and also disjunction) do not longer hold. Notice that this is a different problem than the one discussed in subsection 2.2.3. The following example illustrates it (the first expression evaluates to false, the second evaluates to true):

```
compute(z:Boolean) {
  y := (z:=true) and (z:=false) }

compute(z:Boolean) {
  y := (z:=false) and (z:=true) }
```

Redundancy of Existing OCL Language Features

Some of the new language features in ImperativeOCL, such as forEach and the imperative conditional, are not really necessary (as long as ImperativeExpression is a subclass of OclExpression). Their effects can be achieved using conventional OCL expressions:

```
company.employees->forEach(c) {
  c.salary := c.salary * 1.1
}
```

has the same effect and the same value as

```
company.employees->iterate(c; r:Real=Undefined |
  r = c.salary := c.salary * 1.1
)
```

and

```
if ( x < 0 )  x := 0 else x := 1 endif // imperative version
```

is the same as

```
if x < 0 then x := 0 else x := 1 endif
```

Of course, the forEach version is more concise than the iterate version. Thus, one can argue for its existence. The major problem we see, is rather the fact that each of these loops is described without any regard to the other. This may lead to irritations for the user of ImperativeOCL.

Further Problems

Apart from the problems illustrated above, we can find several other locations where allowing imperative expressions does not make sense. Especially, as ImperativeOCL allows us to modify the system state from within an invariant or a precondition. The evaluation of the invariant or the precondition could evaluate to true and invalidate the state at the same time. While this seems to be a problem that could be easily solved by adding an according well-formedness rule, the situation is more complex if we regard query operations that are defined by ImperativeOCL. An undesired, maybe overlooked, state manipulation may hide deep inside an innocent looking query operation. Therefore, sophisticated propagation rules would be required for the fact, that an expression might change the system state, in order to prevent situations as described above. Similar problems will probably arise, when such 'query' operations are used in the pattern matching parts of model transformations, if these are applied to the living model. However, this matter is not addressed in ImperativeOCL.

Apart from the structural problems discussed above, we think that the subtype relation between ImperativeExpression and OclExpression violates the substitutability of subtypes for supertypes (e.g., [LW94]) very clearly. This is a bad object-oriented design in our opinion (c.f. [Mar96a]). An imperative expression cannot be used everywhere where an OCL expression is expected. On the contrary, there are only very few locations where imperative expressions can be safely used where an OCL expression is expected.

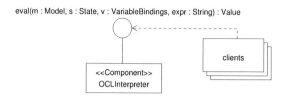

Figure 2.5: Hypothetical OCL interpreter component and interface

2.2.4   Practical Issues

Beside the aforementioned semantical problems that result from the definition of ImperativeOCL, further problems arise on the level of technical realization, i. e., compilers and interpreters for languages such as ImperativeOCL.

As there are several applications of OCL as part of larger systems, it is desirable to have an OCL implementation (interpreter or compiler) as a component or module, in order to enable the reuse of existing OCL implementations in several places. As such, an OCL component or module needs to expose an interface of functions or methods.

Depicted as a UML class diagram, an OCL compiler module looks as in Fig. 2.5. This diagram illustrates an (probably simplified) interface to an OCL interpreter. In its most simple form, the interface will comprise just one operation *eval*, with the following in-parameters: some data structure to represent the underlying model (i. e., which classes, attributes, and associations exist), a system state (i. e., objects and links), some variable bindings (for the free variables that might occur in OCL expressions), and of course a character string representation of an OCL expression. Ignoring things like error handling for simplicity, the only out-parameter of the *eval* operation will be the value of the expression (given the variable bindings).

Such a component could be used in several applications to realize the process of OCL evaluation. For example, the OCL evaluator of the Eclipse Modeling Framework [MDT] and the UML-based Speficiation Environment (USE) [GBR07c] provide such interfaces and can be used as a component (EMF OCL) or library (USE).

However, existing OCL implementations like these cannot be used to realize the OCL part of ImperativeOCL: Even if we assume, the OCL component foresees such future extensions and provides a way to 'plug in' new expression types (i. e., add syntax rules and evaluation routines) (c. f. [Mar96b]), the component interface itself will not be sufficient. There is no out-parameter to capture the modified system state.

Therefore, to implement ImperativeOCL, one cannot reuse existing OCL interpreters or compilers as components. One needs to rebuild ImperativeOCL as a monolithic component.

2.3 Other Imperative Languages Based on OCL in a Non-Modular Way

In the following we will discuss two more approaches to embed OCL into an imperative language in a non-modular way.

2.3.1 OCL for Execution (OCL4X)

Jiang et al. present 'OCL for Execution' (OCL4X) in [JZM08] as an Action Semantics Language (ASL) for Executable UML. OCL4X follows the same approach as ImperativeOCL by extending the OCL metamodel. The classes and inheritance relationships of OCL4X are depicted in Fig. 2.6 on the following page. OCL4X defines a couple of basic expressions. These are variable assignment and property assignment, object creation and object destruction. There seem to be no metaclasses for link creation and link deletion. It is unclear in [JZM08] how link manipulation shall be handled. Apart from these basic expressions, OCL4X comprises a while loop for flow control. Several expressions can be combined as blocks.

All language elements in OCL4X are subclasses of OclExpression from the OCL specification [OMG06]. The semantic issues we discussed in Sect. 2.2.3 exist in OCL4X as well. However, even more consequently than ImperativeOCL, OCL4X does not define other loop constructs than a while loop, and does not define a new language element for conditional execution. Thus, there is no redundancy between the new language elements and the OCL elements, whereas ImperativeOCL had two iterate loops and two kinds of conditional executions.

2.3.2 MOF Model-to-Text

Unlike more common model-to-model transformation approaches, the OMG Model-to-Text specification [OMG08b] aims at the need to produce various text artifacts such as code, deployment specifications, reports, documents, etc. from MOF and UML models. Model-to-Text addresses this requirement by using a template-based approach wherein the text to be generated from models is specified as a set of text templates that are parameterized with placeholders for data that is to be extracted from the model. These placeholders are essentially expressed using OCL. The values are then converted

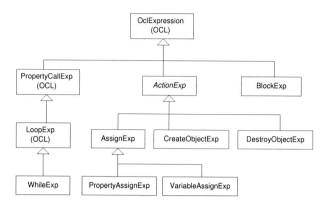

Figure 2.6: OCL4X metamodel (classes and inheritance relationships)

into text fragments using an expression language augmented with a string manipulation library. Templates can be composed to address complex transformation requirements.

Unlike the other approaches presented in this section, MOF Model-to-Text does not manipulate a system state. Nevertheless MOF Model-to-Text comprises an imperative language.

The following listing gives an example of a Model-to-Text template.

```
1   @text-explicit
2   [template public classToJava(c : Class)]
3   class [c.name/]
4   {
5       // Constructor
6       [c.name/]() {}
7
8       [for(a : Attribute | c.attribute)]
9       // here follows the attribute [a.name]
10      [/for]
11  }
12  [/template]
```

The listing defines a template named 'classToJava' which is to be parameterized by an instance of the UML metaclass Class. The purpose of the (abbreviated) template is to output a Java file for the UML class. Model-to-Text knows two modes for templates, text-explicit and code-explicit. The example is text-explicit, meaning that everything not included in braces produces textual output, whereas everything included in braces is an expression. Thus, in the output file, the first line will be something like 'class MyClass'

where 'class ' is the constant text from the template and 'MyClass' is the
evaluation of [c.name].

Model-to-Text employs OCL as its expression language but extends it by
several new elements. In the previous template, the 'for' loop expression
is employed which outputs the line '//here follows the attribute ' several
times, once for each attribute in the class c. Thus, the complete output of
this template could be as follows.

```
1  class MyClass
2  {
3     // Constructor
4     MyClass() {}
5
6     // here follows the attribute name
7     // here follows the attribute age
8     // here follows the attribute gender
9  }
```

Figure 2.7 depicts the relevant elements of the Model-to-Text metamodel.
Again, we find the same pattern as for ImperativeOCL and OCL4X. All
elements of the imperative language are derived from OclExpression. We
have the notion of a block of expressions, which can occur in for loops, if
blocks, or as the body of a whole template.

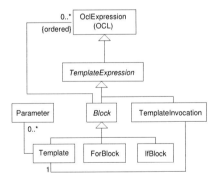

Figure 2.7: Model-to-Text metamodel (only relevant classes, associations, and
inheritance relationships)

However, unlike ImperativeOCL and OCL4X, Model-to-Text does not suffer
from semantic problems. The reason is that there is neither any state manipulation commands nor any variable assignment statements in Model-to-Text.
Actually, Model-to-Text templates can be translated into a functional form
straightforward. The metaclass TemplateExpression is a String typed OCL
expression, and the sequential execution of template expressions through
blocks is simply a concatenation of string.

The previous Model-to-Text template example can be rewritten as pure
OCL:

```
1   'class '.concat(c.name).concat('{')
2     .concat('  //Constructor')
3     .concat(c.name).concat('() {}').concat(
4       c.attribute->iterate( a ; res : String = '' |
5         res.concat('// here follows the attribute ')
6             .concat(a.name) )
7             .concat('}')
```

Thus, Model-to-Text is essentially a 'syntactic sugar' for text production using OCL. The imperative OCL-based language cannot be applied universally
as it lacks essential elements for state and variable manipulation.

2.4   The Epsilon Object Language (EOL)

The Epsilon Object Language (EOL) [KPP06, KRP10] is an imperative language for model management. It is part of the rich Epsilon tool set [EPS]
where Epsilon stands for Extensible Platform for Specification of Integrated
Languages for mOdel maNagement.

EOL is used in one of two ways: first, as a generic language to manage (query
and modify) models, and second, as a basis for a family of task-specific languages such as for model-to-model and model-to-text transformations. EOL
is technology agnostic and can be used to manage models from several tech-
nologies, such MOF, EMF, and XML. It is not bound to a specific metamodel.

The core operations of EOL can be classified as follows:

- *create* new models and model elements

- *read* or *query* models and model elements

- *update* models and model elements

- *delete* models and model elements

Thus, we can compare the general scope of EOL to ImperativeOCL.

The language incorporates several elements of OCL for queries to models but
it does not include or import OCL in a formal sense. Instead, EOL provides
a self-contained monolithic language design which is 'inspired' by OCL. For
example, most of the type system and the built-in operations of OCL have
been adopted in EOL.

An important difference between EOL and ImperativeOCL can be seen comparing the metamodels of both languages. Whereas imperative expressions (statements) are modeled as a specific kind of expressions in ImperativeOCL (c. f. Fig. 2.1 on page 12), expressions are modeled as a special kind of statements in EOL which not only have an operational meaning w. r. t. the system state but also functional semantics. This is shown in Fig. 2.8 which depicts an excerpt of the EOL metamodel. Therefore, the problems of ImperativeOCL regarding undefined functional semantics for statements do not occur in EOL, because expressions have been designed in the context of statement semantics from the beginning. We want to point out, however,

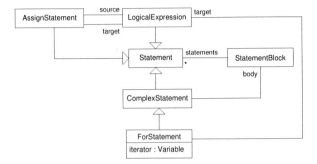

Figure 2.8: EOL metamodel (excerpt)

that existing OCL engines (implementing the OCL metamodel) can not be used out of the box to implement the expression language of EOL, as the language is only 'inspired' (quoting [KRP10]) by OCL.

2.5   Requirements for a Modular Embedding

Basing on the observations we made in the previous sections, we now formulate requirements for a modular reuse of OCL in other imperative programming languages. A modular reuse will not lead the aforementioned semantic problems, and it will enable a practical reuse of existing implementations of OCL interpreters and compilers. The requirements effectively regard the formal syntax and semantics of such a programming language. This is reflected on the level of the language metamodel.

Assuming an imperative programming language l has to be defined, we distinguish between the top level entities *expression* and *statement* in l. An expression can be evaluated in a functional sense. Let the set of expressions of l be Expr_l. A statement is interpreted as a change to the environment. It has no value in a functional sense. Let the set of the statements of l be

Stat$_l$. A statement $s \in$ Stat$_l$ may contain sub-statements $s_i \in$ Stat$_i$ and sub-expressions $e_i \in$ Expr$_l$. An expression $e \in$ Expr$_l$. may contain sub-expressions $e_i \in$ Expr$_l$.

Let E_l be the set of environments. Depending on l, an environment will contain everything that is necessary for the interpretation of statements: the objects and links that exist, local and global variables, a call stack, exception handling information, and so on. Let V_l be the set of all values (e. g., numbers, strings, collections, tuples, and object values) that exist in l. The semantics of an expression $e \in$ Expr$_l$ is determined by an interpretation function $I[\![\, e\,]\!]_l : E \rightarrow V_l$. The semantics of a statement $s \in$ Stat$_l$ is determined by an interpretation function $I[\![\, s\,]\!]_l : E_l \rightarrow E_l$.

Let Expr$_{\mathrm{OCL}}$ denote the set of OCL expressions as defined in the OCL specification [OMG06, Appendix A, Def. A.29]. Let $I[\![\, e\,]\!]_{\mathrm{OCL}} :$ Expr$_{\mathrm{OCL}} \rightarrow V_{\mathrm{OCL}}$ denote the semantics of OCL. We define the modular embedding of OCL into l as follows.

Definition 2.1 (Modular embedding of OCL into an imperative programming language l)**.** We say OCL is modular embedded into l if the following conditions are true:

1. Expr$_{\mathrm{OCL}} \subseteq$ Expr$_l$,

2. Expr$_{\mathrm{OCL}}$ is disjoint from Stat$_l$, and

3. For sub-expressions e_i of s, the interpretation $I[\![\, e\,]\!]_{\mathrm{OCL}}$ is used to achieve the value of e_i within the definition of $I[\![\, s\,]\!]_l$ if $e \in$ Expr$_{\mathrm{OCL}}$.

$\square$

The first requirement allows us to use OCL for the expressions in l. It does not require that no other expressions may exist. Notice that our definition refers to the set of OCL expressions defined in the Appendix of the OCL specification. While the metamodel part of the specification does not explicitly forbid the addition of further language elements (by inheritance from the metaclass *OclExpression*), the definition of expressions by Expr$_{\mathrm{OCL}}$ is final. Thus, there cannot be any non-OCL sub-expression e_i of an OCL expression e.

As EOL is only loosely based on OCL, it violates the first requirement in the above definition. For ImperativeOCL, OCL4X, and Model-to-Text, imperative expressions / statements are both, statements and expressions. Therefore, these languages all violate the second requirement of the above definition.

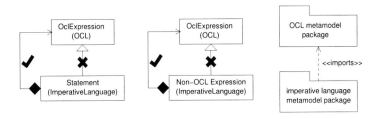

Figure 2.9: Modular embedding (metaclass level)

The requirements can be depicted on the metamodel level as in Fig. 2.9. A modular embedding of OCL will always connect the metaclasses of an imperative langage l using directed compositions to the OCL metaclasses. This regards the statements of l as well as any non-OCL expressions: the instance set of OCL expressions will not be extended by introducing new subclasses of OclExpression. Furthermore, the OCL metamodel package will be embedded in the metamodel package of an OCL-based language unchanged, by means of an package import. This understanding of metamodel composition is in accordance with several related research, such as the work of Akehurst et al. on modularizing OCL and OCL extensions such as temporal logic [AZH08].

A similar argumentation for composition and modularity of domain specific languages can be found in [KRV08] and [Hud98]. Siikarla et al. mentioned some of the issues stated in Sect. 2.2.3 [MSS04]. They conclude that side-effected non-modular extensions of OCL should be avoided. They shortly address some of the problems we criticize in Chap. 2. They suggest to combine OCL for side-effect free querying purposes with existing languages such as Python for those aspects that require imperative programming.

The phenomena observed regarding the non-modular embedding of OCL are similar to those discussed by Renggli et al. in [RGN10], but in the reverse direction. In the case of ImperativeOCL, it is the embedded language (OCL) which is broken, not the host language.

2.6 Summary

In this chapter we discussed how OCL has been embedded into the imperative languages MOF QVT ImperativeOCL, OCL4X, Model-to-Text, and EOL, and we formalized requirements for a sound modular embedding of OCL into (general purpose) imperative programming languages.

The first three languages define their language as an extension of OCL by adding further (imperative) expressions. According to our definition, these languages do not embed OCL in a modular way. We have shown that the non-modular embedding of OCL in these languages leads to several semantic problems as soon as a true imperative paradigm is involved, with state manipulation or variable assignments. The non-modular embedding is manifested in the identification of statements and expressions, visible as a subclass relationship between the statement metaclasses and OclExpression on the metamodel level.

There are no such semantic problems in EOL. However, EOL only incorporates some aspects of OCL and provides its own, monolithic language design and metamodel. Therefore, existing OCL tools and instruments cannot be reused out of the box for EOL. For this reason, we did not regard its reuse of OCL as a modular embedding according to our (strict) definition.

In the Chapters 4 and 5 of this thesis we will follow this requirements in the definition of an imperative language SOIL which embeds OCL as its expression sub-language in a modular way.

Chapter 3

Formal Foundations

In this chapter, we provide necessary foundations for our thesis. We first give a short historical overview of the development of UML and OCL. Then we introduce the formal definitions for the syntax and the semantics of UML static structure modeling and OCL expressions.

3.1 On Syntax and Semantics of UML and OCL

UML is a modeling language that differs from many of its predecessors in that a structured and semi-formal approach has been applied for its definition. The UML specification comprises a metamodel to precisely describe the notions and elements of UML and OCL in terms of metaclasses. In the OMG terminology, this is called the abstract syntax, as opposed to the concrete syntax. The concrete syntax provides all visual and textual representations of a model, the abstract syntax just captures the meaning. Therefore, several different concrete representations may represent the same model, as aspects like organization of diagrams etc. do not matter w. r. t. the meaning of a model. The correct assembly of metaobjects to a well-formed model is ensured by a large number of well-formedness rules. Most of them are expressed by OCL invariants, i. e., by logical expressions over the metaclasses. However, the actual interpretation (the meaning) of a model is mostly described in natural language only in [OMG10] and [OMG06].

In [Ric02], Richters addressed this issue and provided formal (denotational) semantics for a subset of static structure models and OCL expressions. These definitions have been included as an appendix in the OMG OCL specification since version 2.0.

For OCL expressions, an alternative, axiomatic semantics has been included in OMG OCL 2.0 as well. This description uses UML classes, invariants, and pre- and postconditions to describe the evaluation process. It is based on the work of Kleppe [Kle09] and describes the evaluation of OCL expression by means of evaluation classes, operation, and postconditions. In our work, we build on Richters denotational semantics, because it is widely accepted in the research community and it suits our purpose of a soundness proof better than an axiomatic definition. There is already research based on Richters' formalization, such as the work of Flake and Mueller on temporal state-oriented constraints [F03]. Furthermore, there is a one-to-one implementation of Richters definition in the tool USE.

The following sections provide the formal definitions for UML static structure modeling and OCL expressions. These sections closely reflect the definitions in [Ric02] and [OMG06]. However, as the focus of our work is not to introduce formal semantics for UML and OCL, our presentation is shorter and more compressed. Elements that are not required for our work have been omitted. More examples and a more in-depth motivation can be found in [Ric02].

At some points, we modified or extended the original definitions, either to overcome semantic problems or because these extensions are required for our definition of SOIL in Chapter 4. These modifications are clearly displayed by remarks. The first major modification we made is the inclusion of the type OclVoid in the type system and the unification of the undefined value $\bot$ (p. 46). The second major modification is the definition of the least common supertype resolution rule and its application to collection constructor literals (Definitions 3.30 on page 58 and 3.31 on page 61).

3.2 Formal Semantics of UML Static Structure Modeling

In this section we provide the necessary definitions for the formal treatment of static structure modeling as given by Richters. Only a small core of UML structure is formalized here. This core is called Basic Modeling Language (BML).

3.2.1 Syntax of Object Models

We formally define the syntax of object models. An object model has the following components:

- a set of classes,

- a set of attributes for each class,

- a set of operations for each class,

- a set of associations with role names and multiplicities,

- a generalization hierarchy over classes.

Additionally, types such as *Integer* and *String* are available for describing the types of attributes and operation parameters. In the following, formal descriptions are provided for each of the above components, and illustrating examples are given.

The following definitions are combined later to a complete definition of the syntax of object models on page 41. For the naming of model components, we assume in this work an alphabet $\mathcal{A}$ and a set of finite, non-empty names $\mathcal{N} \subseteq \mathcal{A}^+$ over alphabet $\mathcal{A}$ to be given.

3.2.1.1 Running Example

The examples in this and the following chapter frequently refer to the 'Project World' model, as depicted in Fig. 3.1 on the next page. The main actors in this examples are companies, projects, and workers: A company employs workers and carries out projects with them, by making employees members of projects. Projects require certain qualifications, like computer programming, documentation, and medicine. Workers can have such qualifications. Projects are further categorized by their status (planned, active, suspended, or finished) and size (small, medium, or big). These categorizations are provided as enumerations. A project can have prerequisites, in the sense that certain predecessor projects have to be finished before a successor project can be started. There is a special kind of training projects that are performed to teach new qualifications to employees.

The model declares three side-effect free query operations. The class Project provides an operation to obtain the missing qualifications for a project, and to check, if a certain worker would be helpful for a project. The class Worker provides an operation to check, if a worker is overloaded with work (has too many, or too big, projects). The class Company furthermore declares four non-query operations. Unlike for query operations, the implementations for these operations can be state changing. Companies can hire and fire workers, and they can start and finish projects.

We will also add several constraints to this project later in Chap. 5, e. g., to ensure that active projects have the members that provide all required qualifications, and that no employee is overloaded with work. For this chapter, we will stick to model elements visible in Fig. 3.1.

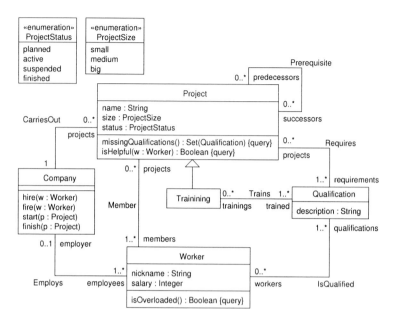

Figure 3.1: Example class diagram 'Project World'

3.2.1.2 Types

A few primitive types including numbers and strings are predefined in UML and OCL. For example, Project World uses the primitive type *String* for the attributes *name, nickname* and *description*, and the primitive type *Integer* for the attribute *salary.*

We consider types in-depth later. For now, we assume that there is a signature $\Sigma = (T, \Omega)$ where T is a set of type names, and Ω is a set of operations over types in T. The set T includes basic types such as *Integer*, *Boolean*, and *String*. All type domains include the value $\bot$ that allows to operate with undefined values. Operations in Ω include, for example, the usual arithmetic operations for integers.

3.2.1.3 Classes

"The central concept of UML for modeling entities of the problem domain is the class. A class provides a common description for a set of objects sharing the same properties.

Definition 3.1 (Classes, from [Ric02]). The set of classes is a finite set of names $\mathrm{CLASS} \subseteq \mathcal{N}$. □

Each class $c \in \mathrm{CLASS}$ induces an *object type* $t_c \in T$ having the same name as the class. A value of an object type refers to an object of the corresponding class. The main difference between classes and object types is that the interpretation of the latter includes the special undefined value $\bot$." [Ric02]

Example. The Project World class diagram in Fig 3.1 on the facing page defines the following set of classes.

$$\mathrm{CLASS} = \{\, Company, Project, Training, Qualification, Worker\,\}$$

□

3.2.1.4 Attributes

"Attributes are part of a class declaration in UML. Objects are associated with attribute values describing properties of the object. An attribute has a name and a type specifying the domain of attribute values." [Ric02]

Definition 3.2 (Attributes, from [Ric02]). Let $t \in T$ be a type. The attributes of a class $c \in \mathrm{CLASS}$ are defined as a set ATT_c of signatures $a : t_c \to t$ where the attribute name a is an element of $\mathcal{N}$, and $t_c \in T$ is the type of class c. □

Example. The attributes of the class *Project* are defined by the following set.

$$\mathrm{ATT}_{Project} = \{\, \text{name} : Project \to String,$$
$$\text{size} : Project \to ProjectSize$$
$$\text{status} : Project \to ProjectStatus\}$$

□

3.2.1.5 Operations

Operations, as part of a class definition, describe behavioral properties of objects. The effect of an operation may be specified in various ways. It can be given in a declarative way with OCL pre- and postconditions, or it might be defined using an operational description (e. g., in an imperative programming language such as the one we will introduce in Chap. 4). An operation performing computations without side effects is called a query operation. Such operations can be specified by an explicit OCL expression.

For now we just focus on the syntax of operation signatures declaring the
interface of user-defined operations (queries and operations with side-effects).
Other kinds of (side-effect free) operations which are not explicitly defined by
a modeler are, for example, navigation operations derived from associations.
These derived operations are described later in this section.

Definition 3.3 (Operations, changed w. r. t. [Ric02]). Let t and $t_1, \ldots, t_n$
be types in T. Operations of a class $c \in \mathrm{CLASS}$ with type $t_c \in T$ are defined
by a set OP_c of signatures $\omega : t_c \times t_1 \times \cdots \times t_n \to t$ (operation with result
type) and $\omega : t_c \times t_1 \times \cdots \times t_n$ (operation without result type) with operation
symbols ω being elements of $\mathcal{N}$.   □

Remark. In general, UML allows multiple return values, whereas the work
of Richters [Ric02] only allows a single return types. In our definition, we
extend Richters definition and allow operations with one as well as operations
without any result type, as we need the latter ones in our definition of SOIL
in Chap. 4.

Example. The operations in the Project World example are defined by the
following sets:

$$\mathrm{OP}_{Project} = \{\text{missingQualifications} : Project \to Set(Qualficiation)$$
$$\text{isHelpful} : Project \times Worker \to Boolean\}$$
$$\mathrm{OP}_{Worker} = \{\text{isOverloaded} : Worker \to Boolean\}$$
$$\mathrm{OP}_{Company} = \{\text{hire} : Company \times Worker$$
$$\text{fire} : Company \times Worker$$
$$\text{start} : Company \times Project$$
$$\text{finish} : Company \times Project\}$$

□

3.2.1.6   Associations

"Associations describe structural relationships between classes. Generally,
classes may participate in any number of associations, and associations may
connect two or more classes.

Definition 3.4 (Associations, from [Ric02]). The set of associations is given
by

    i. a finite set of names $\mathrm{ASSOC} \subseteq \mathcal{N}$,

    ii. a function associates : $\begin{cases} \mathrm{ASSOC} \to \mathrm{CLASS}^+ \\ as \mapsto \langle c_1, \ldots, c_n \rangle \text{ with } (n \geq 2) \end{cases}$.

□

The function associates maps each association name $as \in \text{ASSOC}$ to a finite list $\langle c_1, \ldots, c_n \rangle$ of classes participating in the association. The number n of participating classes is also called the *degree* of an association; associations with degree n are called n-ary associations. For many problems the use of binary associations is often sufficient. A *self-association* (or reflexive association) sa is a binary association where both ends of the association are attached to the same class c such that associates$(sa) = \langle c, c \rangle$. The function associates does not have to be injective. Multiple associations over the same set of classes are possible. " [Ric02]

Example. The Project World class diagram in Fig 3.1 on page 34 has seven binary associations, one of them self-associative.

$$\text{ASSOC} = \{ \text{CarriesOut}, \text{Employs}, \text{IsQualified},$$
$$\text{Member}, \text{Prerequisite}, \text{Requires}, \text{Trains}, \}$$

$$
\begin{aligned}
\text{CarriesOut} &= \langle \textit{Company}, \textit{Project} \rangle \\
\text{Employs} &= \langle \textit{Company}, \textit{Worker} \rangle \\
\text{IsQualified} &= \langle \textit{Worker}, \textit{Qualification} \rangle \\
\text{Member} &= \langle \textit{Project}, \textit{Worker} \rangle \\
\text{Prerequisite} &= \langle \textit{Project}, \textit{Project} \rangle \\
\text{Requires} &= \langle \textit{Project}, \textit{Qualification} \rangle \\
\text{Trains} &= \langle \textit{Training}, \textit{Qualification} \rangle \}
\end{aligned}
$$

□

3.2.1.7   Role names

Classes may appear more than once in an association each time playing a different role. For example, in the self-association Prerequisite on class *Project*, we need to distinguish between the project having the role of a successor and another project being the predecessor. Therefore, a unique role name is assigned to each class participating in an association. Role names are also important for OCL navigation expressions. A role name of a class is used to determine the navigation path in this kind of expressions.

Definition 3.5 (Role names, from [Ric02]). Let $as \in \text{ASSOC}$ be an association with associates$(as) = \langle c_1, \ldots, c_n \rangle$. Role names for an association are defined by a function

$$\text{roles} : \begin{cases} \text{ASSOC} \to \mathcal{N}^+ \\ as \mapsto \langle r_1, \ldots, r_n \rangle \text{ with } (n \geq 2) \end{cases}$$

where all role names must be distinct, i. e.,

$$\forall i, j \in \{1, \ldots, n\} : i \neq j \implies r_i \neq r_j \ .$$

□

The function $\mathrm{roles}(as) = \langle r_1, \ldots, r_n \rangle$ assigns each class c_i for $1 \leq i \leq n$ participating in the association a unique role name r_i. If role names are omitted in a class diagram, implicit names are constructed in UML by using the name of the class at the target end and changing its first letter to lower case. For example, the role name of the association CarriesOut at the association end targeting the class *Company* is 'company'. As mentioned above, explicit role names are mandatory for self-associations.

Example. These are the role names of classes participating in associations in our example.

$$
\begin{aligned}
\mathrm{roles(CarriesOut)} &= \langle \mathrm{company}, \mathrm{projects} \rangle \\
\mathrm{roles(Employs)} &= \langle \mathrm{employer}, \mathrm{employees} \rangle \\
\mathrm{roles(IsQualified)} &= \langle \mathrm{workers}, \mathrm{qualifications} \rangle \\
\mathrm{roles(Member)} &= \langle \mathrm{projects}, \mathrm{members} \rangle \\
\mathrm{roles(Prerequisite)} &= \langle \mathrm{predecessors}, \mathrm{successors} \rangle \\
\mathrm{roles(Requires)} &= \langle \mathrm{projects}, \mathrm{requirements} \rangle \\
\mathrm{roles(Trains)} &= \langle \mathrm{trainings}, \mathrm{trained} \rangle \}
\end{aligned}
$$

□

"Additional syntactical constraints are required for ensuring the uniqueness of role names when a class is part of many associations. We first define a function participating that gives the set of associations a class participates in." [Ric02]

$$
\mathrm{participating} : \begin{cases} \mathrm{CLASS} \to \mathcal{P}(\mathrm{ASSOC}) \\ c \mapsto \{as \mid as \in \mathrm{ASSOC} \wedge \mathrm{associates}(as) = \langle c_1, \ldots, c_n \rangle \\ \qquad\qquad \wedge \exists i \in \{1, \ldots, n\} : c_i = c\} \end{cases}
$$

Example. The class *Project* participates in four associations.

$$\mathrm{participating}(\mathit{Project}) = \{\mathrm{CarriesOut}, \mathrm{Member}, \mathrm{Prerequisite}, \mathrm{Requires}\}$$

□

"The following function navends gives the set of all role names reachable (or *navigable*) from a class over a given association." [Ric02]

$$
\mathrm{navends} : \begin{cases} \mathrm{CLASS} \times \mathrm{ASSOC} \to \mathcal{P}(\mathcal{N}) \\ (c, as) \mapsto \{r \mid \mathrm{associates}(as) = \langle c_1, \ldots, c_n \rangle \\ \qquad\qquad \wedge \mathrm{roles}(as) = \langle r_1, \ldots, r_n \rangle \\ \qquad\qquad \wedge \exists i, j \in \{1, \ldots, n\} : (i \neq j \wedge c_i = c \wedge r_j = r)\} \end{cases}
$$

Example. The role names reachable from class *Project* are given. Note that for the self-association Prerequisite both role names are reachable from *Project*.

$$\text{navends}(\textit{Project}, \text{CarriesOut}) = \{\text{company}\}$$
$$\text{navends}(\textit{Project}, \text{Member}) = \{\text{members}\}$$
$$\text{navends}(\textit{Project}, \text{Prerequisite}) = \{\text{predecessors}, \text{successors}\}$$
$$\text{navends}(\textit{Project}, \text{Requires}) = \{\text{requirements}\}$$

□

"The set of role names that are reachable from a class along all associations the class participates in can then be determined by the following function." [Ric02]

$$\text{navends}(c) : \begin{cases} \text{CLASS} \to \mathcal{P}(\mathcal{N}) \\ c \mapsto \bigcup_{as \in \text{participating}(c)} \text{navends}(c, as) \end{cases}$$

Example. These are all role names reachable from class *Project* over all associations the class participates in (CarriesOut, Member, Prerequisite, and Requires).

$$\text{navends}(\textit{Project}) = \{\text{company}, \text{members}, \text{predecessors},$$
$$\text{successors}, \text{requirements}\}$$

□

3.2.1.8 Multiplicities

"An association specifies the possible existence of links between objects of associated classes. The number of links that an object can be part of is specified with *multiplicities*. This concept is also known as cardinality ratio in Entity-Relationship modeling. A multiplicity specification in UML can be represented by a set of natural numbers." [Ric02]

Definition 3.6 (Multiplicities, from [Ric02]). Let $as \in \text{ASSOC}$ be an association with associates$(as) = \langle c_1, \ldots, c_n \rangle$. The function multiplicities$(as) = \langle M_1, \ldots, M_n \rangle$ assigns each class c_i participating in the association a non-empty set $M_i \subseteq \mathbb{N}_0$ with $M_i \neq \{0\}$ for all $1 \leq i \leq n$. □

For example, the multiplicities of the Employs association are defined as

$$\text{multiplicities}(\text{Employs}) = \langle \{0, 1\}, \mathbb{N} \rangle.$$

The precise meaning of multiplicities is given as part of the interpretation of object models (Def. 3.12).

3.2.1.9 Generalization

"A generalization is a taxonomic relationship between two classes. This relationship specializes a general class into a more specific class. Specialization and generalization are different views of the same concept. Generalization relationships form a hierarchy over the set of classes.

Definition 3.7 (Generalization hierarchy, from [Ric02]). A generalization hierarchy $\prec$ is a partial order on the set of classes CLASS. $\square$

Pairs in $\prec$ describe generalization relationships between two classes. For classes $c_1, c_2 \in$ CLASS with $c_1 \prec c_2$, the class c_1 is called a *child class* of c_2, and c_2 is called a *parent class* of c_1." [Ric02]

Example. The class diagram shown in Fig. 3.1 contains one generalization. *Project* is the parent class of *Training*.

$$\prec = \{(\mathit{Training}, \mathit{Project})\}$$

$\square$

3.2.1.10 Full descriptor of a class

"A child class implicitly inherits attributes, operations and associations of its parent classes. The set of properties defined in a class together with its inherited properties is called the *full descriptor* [...]" [Ric02]

The formal definition of the full descriptor a convenience functions parents, that yields all superclasses of a class

$$\text{parents} : \begin{cases} \text{CLASS} \to \mathcal{P}(\text{CLASS}) \\ c \mapsto \{c' \mid c' \in \text{CLASS} \land c \prec c'\}. \end{cases}$$

Using parents, we can define the sets ATT_c^*, OP_c^*, and $\text{navends}^*(c)$ of all (own and inherited) attributes, operations and navigable role of a class:

$$\text{ATT}_c^* = \text{ATT}_c \cup \bigcup_{c' \in \text{parents}(c)} \text{ATT}_{c'}$$

$$\text{OP}_c^* = \text{OP}_c \cup \bigcup_{c' \in \text{parents}(c)} \text{OP}_{c'}$$

$$\text{navends}^*(c) = \text{navends}(c) \cup \bigcup_{c' \in \text{parents}(c)} \text{navends}(c')$$

Definition 3.8 (Full descriptor of a class, from [Ric02]). The full descriptor of a class $c \in$ CLASS is a structure $\text{FD}_c = (\text{ATT}_c^*, \text{OP}_c^*, \text{navends}^*(c))$ containing all attributes, user-defined operations, and navigable role names defined for the class and all of its parents. $\square$

3.2.1.11   Formal Syntax

The components introduced in the previous section are now combined to formally define the syntax of object models.

Definition 3.9 (Syntax of object models, from [Ric02]). The syntax of an object model is a structure

$$\mathcal{M} = (\text{CLASS}, \text{ATT}_c, \text{OP}_c, \text{ASSOC}, \text{associates}, \text{roles}, \text{multiplicities}, \prec)$$

where

    i. CLASS is a set of classes (Definition 3.1).

    ii. ATT_c is a set of operation signatures for functions mapping an object of class c to an associated attribute value (Definition 3.2).

    iii. OP_c is a set of signatures for user-defined operations of a class c (Definition 3.3).

    iv. ASSOC is a set of association names (Definition 3.4).

        (a) associates is a function mapping each association name to a list of participating classes (Definition 3.4).

        (b) roles is a function assigning each end of an association a role name (Definition 3.5).

        (c) multiplicities is a function assigning each end of an association a multiplicity specification (Definition 3.6).

    v. $\prec$ is a partial order on CLASS reflecting the generalization hierarchy of classes (Definitions 3.7 and 3.8).

$\square$

3.2.2   Interpretation of Object Models

In the previous section we provided definitions for the syntax of object models. Now we define the interpretation of object models.

3.2.2.1   Objects

"The domain of a class $c \in$ CLASS is the set of objects that can be created by this class and all of its child classes. Objects are referred to by unique object identifiers. In the following, we will make no conceptual distinction between objects and their identifiers. Each object is uniquely determined by its identifier and vice versa. Therefore, the actual representation of an object is not important for our purposes." [Ric02]

Definition 3.10 (Object identifiers, from [Ric02]).   i. The set of object identifiers of a class $c \in$ CLASS is defined by an infinite set
$$\mathrm{oid}(c) = \{\underline{c}_1, \underline{c}_2, \dots\}.$$

ii. The domain of a class $c \in$ CLASS is defined as
$$I_{\mathrm{CLASS}}(c) = \bigcup\{\mathrm{oid}(c') \mid c' \in \mathrm{CLASS} \wedge c' \preceq c\}.$$

$\square$

In this thesis, we will omit the index for a mapping I when the context is obvious.

Example. Semantic domains for some classes of our example model are given. Note that the domain of class *Project* includes the domain of its child class *Training*.

$$I(Company) = \{\underline{com}_1, \underline{com}_2, \dots\}$$
$$I(Project) = \{\underline{prj}_1, \underline{prj}_2, \dots\}$$
$$I(Training) = \{\underline{trn}_1, \underline{trn}_2, \dots\} \cup I(Project)$$

$\square$

3.2.2.2   Generalization

"The above definition implies that a generalization hierarchy induces a subset relation on the semantic domain of classes. The set of object identifiers of a child class is a subset of the set of object identifiers of its parent classes. With other words, we have

$$\forall c_1, c_2 \in \mathrm{CLASS} : c_1 \prec c_2 \implies I(c_1) \subseteq I(c_2) \ ." \ [\mathrm{Ric02}]$$

"In general, the interpretation of classes is pairwise disjoint if two classifiers are not related by generalization and do not have a common child." [Ric02]

3.2.2.3 Links

"An association describes possible connections between objects of the classes participating in the association. A connection is also called a link in UML terminology.

Definition 3.11 (Links, from [Ric02]). Each association $as \in$ ASSOC with associates(as) $= \langle c_1, \ldots, c_n \rangle$ is interpreted as the Cartesian product of the sets of object identifiers of the participating classes: $I_{\text{ASSOC}}(as) = I_{\text{CLASS}}(c_1) \times \cdots \times I_{\text{CLASS}}(c_n)$. A *link* denoting a connection between objects is an element $l_{as} \in I_{\text{ASSOC}}(as)$. □

The interpretation of an association is a relation describing the set of all possible links between objects of the associated classes and their children." [Ric02]

Example. The interpretation of the seven associations in our Project World example are binary relations.

$$I(\text{CarriesOut}) = I(Company) \times I(Project)$$
$$I(\text{Employs}) = I(Company) \times I(Worker)$$
$$I(\text{IsQualified}) = I(Worker) \times I(Qualification)$$
$$I(\text{Member}) = I(Project) \times I(Worker)$$
$$I(\text{Prerequisite}) = I(Project) \times I(Project)$$
$$I(\text{Requires}) = I(Project) \times I(Qualification)$$
$$I(\text{Trains}) = I(Training) \times I(Qualification)$$

□

3.2.2.4 System State

"Objects, links and attribute values constitute the state of a system at a particular moment in time. A system is in different states as it changes over time. Therefore, a system state is also called a snapshot of a running system. With respect to OCL, we can in many cases concentrate on a single system state given at a discrete point in time. For example, a system state provides the complete context for the evaluation of OCL invariants. For pre- and postconditions, however, it is necessary to consider two consecutive states." [Ric02]

Definition 3.12 (System state, from [Ric02]). A system state for a model $\mathcal{M}$ is a structure $\sigma(\mathcal{M}) = (\sigma_{\text{CLASS}}, \sigma_{\text{ATT}}, \sigma_{\text{ASSOC}})$.

i. The finite sets $\sigma_{\text{CLASS}}(c)$ contain all objects of a class $c \in \text{CLASS}$ existing in the system state: $\sigma_{\text{CLASS}}(c) \subset \text{oid}(c)$.

ii. Functions σ_{ATT} assign attribute values to each object:
$\sigma_{\text{ATT}}(a) : \sigma_{\text{CLASS}}(c) \to I(t)$ for each $a : t_c \to t \in \text{ATT}_c^*$.

iii. The finite sets σ_{Assoc} contain links connecting objects. For each $as \in \text{ASSOC}: \sigma_{\text{Assoc}}(as) \subset I_{\text{Assoc}}(as)$. A link set must satisfy all multiplicity specifications defined for an association (the function $\pi_i(l)$ projects the ith component of a tuple or list l, whereas the function $\bar{\pi}_i(l)$ projects *all but* the ith component):

$$\forall i \in \{1, \ldots, n\}, \forall l \in \sigma_{\text{Assoc}}(as) :$$
$$|\{l' \mid l' \in \sigma_{\text{Assoc}}(as) \wedge (\bar{\pi}_i(l') = \bar{\pi}_i(l))\}| \in \pi_i(\text{multiplicities}(as))$$

$\square$

Example. Figure 3.2 shows a minimal, but complete, system state of the Project World model as a UML object diagram. The system state includes one *Qualification* object and two *Worker* objects. Both *Worker* objects are connected to the *Qualification* object by links of the IsQualified association.

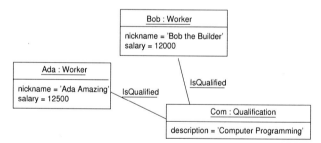

Figure 3.2: Object diagram showing a system state of the Project World model

The information in the object diagram can be formally described as a state $\sigma = (\sigma_{\text{CLASS}}, \sigma_{\text{ATT}}, \sigma_{\text{Assoc}})$ as follows.

$\sigma_{\text{CLASS}}(\textit{Worker}) = \{\underline{Ada}, \underline{Bob}\}$
$\sigma_{\text{CLASS}}(\textit{Qualification}) = \{\underline{Com}\}$

$\sigma_{\text{ATT}}(\text{nickname})(\underline{Ada}) = \text{'Ada Amazing'}$
$\sigma_{\text{ATT}}(\text{nickname})(\underline{Bob}) = \text{'Bob the Builder'}$
$\sigma_{\text{ATT}}(\text{salary})(\underline{Ada}) = 12500$
$\sigma_{\text{ATT}}(\text{salary})(\underline{Bob}) = 12000$

$$\sigma_{\text{ATT}}(\text{description})(\underline{Com}) = \text{'Computer Programming'}$$
$$\sigma_{\text{Assoc}}(\text{IsQualified}) = \{(\underline{Ada}, \underline{Com}), (\underline{Bob}, \underline{Com})\}$$

All other sets being part of σ that are not mentioned above are empty in this example, e.g., $\sigma_{\text{Assoc}}(\text{Prerequisite}) = \emptyset$. $\square$

3.2.2.5   Formal Interpretation of Object Models

"The semantics of an object model is the set of all possible system states." [Ric02]

Definition 3.13 (Interpretation of object models, from [Ric02]). The interpretation of an object model $\mathcal{M}$ is the set of all possible system states $\sigma(\mathcal{M})$. $\square$

3.3   Formal Semantics of OCL Expressions

OCL Expressions can be used in various contexts, for example, to define constraints such as class invariants and pre- and postconditions on operations. In this section, we provide the formal definition for type system of OCL (Sect. 3.3.1) and for the syntax and semantics of OCL expressions.

3.3.1   Types and Operations

"OCL is a strongly typed language. A type is assigned to every OCL expression and typing rules determine in which ways well-formed expressions can be constructed. In addition to those types introduced by UML models, there is a number of predefined OCL types and operations available for use with any UML model. This section formally defines the type system of OCL. Types and their domains are fixed, and the abstract syntax and semantics of operations is defined." [Ric02]

3.3.1.1   Concepts

Figure 3.3 gives an overview of the types of OCL. The diagram shows the names of types and their subtype relationships. An arrow from one type to another indicates that the former is a subtype of the latter. The subtype relation is transitive, for example, *Integer* is a subtype of *Real*, and both are subtypes of *OclAny*. The type *OclVoid* is a subtype of all other types. For

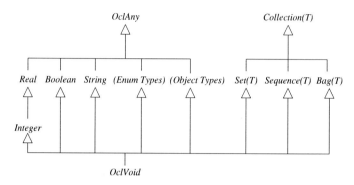

Figure 3.3: Overview of OCL types

non-collection types, the subtype relationship creates a lattice with *OclAny* on the top and *OclVoid* at the bottom.

The Types in OCL can be classified as follows: The group of (predefined) basic types includes *Integer*, *Real*, *Boolean*, and *String*. Each object type corresponds to a classifier in an object model. Collections of values are described by the collection types *Set(T)*, *Sequence(T)*, and *Bag(T)*, where the parameter T denotes the type of the elements. A common supertype of the collection types is *Collection(T)*.

Richters approach to define the type system is as follows. Types are associated with a set of operations. These operations describe functions combining or operating on values of the type domains. A data signature $\Sigma = (T, \Omega)$ is used to describe the syntax of types and operations. The semantics of types in T and operations in Ω is defined by a mapping that assigns each type a domain and each operation a function. The definition of the syntax and semantics of types and operations will be developed and extended in several steps. At the end of this section, the complete set of types is defined in a single data signature.

Remark. We have extended Richters definition of the type system and included the type OclVoid. The OclVoid type has been added by the OMG in OCL 2 [OMG06].

We decided to include OclVoid in Richters type system, as it overcomes a semantic problem with respect to the undefined value $\bot$.

In [Ric02], Richters is not clear whether there is just one undefined value $\bot$ that belongs to $I(t)$ for every type t, or if there is one distinct value $\bot_t$ per type t.

If there is a distinct value $\perp_t$ for each type t, problems arise with subtyping. As $t_1 \leq t_2$ implies $\perp_{t_1} \in I(t_2)$, we have $\perp_{t_1}, \perp_{t_1} \in I(t_2)$. Therefore, we have more than one distinct undefined value in $I(t)$ for each type t that is subtype of another. This is undesirable for practical reasons.

As in OCL 2, we define only on undefined value $\perp$, with $\perp \in I(t)$ for any type t and $I(\text{OclVoid}) = \{\perp\}$.

This lattice-like definition of a type hierarchy is typical in type theory, c.f. [AC96]. It has been first proposed for OCL 2 by Schürr in [Sch02].

3.3.1.2 Operations

The signature of an operations without side-effects describes the name, the parameter types, and the result type of an operation.

Definition 3.14 (Syntax of query operations, from [Ric02])**.** The syntax of a query operation is defined by a signature $\omega : t_1 \times \cdots \times t_n \rightarrow t$. The signature contains the operation symbol ω, a list of parameter types $t_1, \ldots, t_n \in T$, and a result type $t \in T$. $\qquad\square$

Definition 3.15 (Semantics of query operations, from [Ric02])**.** The semantics of a query operation with signature $\omega : t_1 \times \cdots \times t_n \rightarrow t$ is a total function $I(\omega : t_1 \times \cdots \times t_n \rightarrow t) : I(t_1) \times \cdots \times I(t_n) \rightarrow I(t)$. $\qquad\square$

When we refer to an operation, we usually omit the specification of the parameter and result types and only use the operation symbol if the full signature can be derived from the context.

Remark. In his formalization of OCL expressions, Richters refers to operations without side-effects (query operations) as 'operations'. We need to distinguish between both operation kinds. Query operations will be used in this section for the formalization of OCL expressions. Operations with side-effects will be introduced for our definition of SOIL in Chap. 4.

3.3.1.3 Common Operations on all Types

"For each type $t \in T$, the constant operation undefined$_t :\rightarrow t$ generates the undefined value $\perp$. The semantics is given by $I(\text{undefined}_t) = \perp$. The equality of values of the same type can be checked with the operation $=_t:$ $t \times t \rightarrow Boolean$. Furthermore, the semantics of $=_t$ defines undefined values to be equal. For two values $v_1, v_2 \in I(t)$, we have

$$I(=_t)(v_1, v_2) = \begin{cases} \text{true} & \text{if } v_1 = v_2, \text{ or } v_1 = \perp \text{ and } v_2 = \perp, \\ \text{false} & \text{otherwise.} \end{cases}$$

A test for inequality $\neq_t$: $t \times t \to$ *Boolean* can be defined analogously. It is
also useful to have an operation that allows to check whether an arbitrary
value is well-defined or undefined. This can be done with the operations
isDefined$_t$: $t \to$ *Boolean* and isUndefined$_t$: $t \to$ *Boolean*.

$$I(\text{isDefined}_t)(v) = I(\neq)(v, \bot)$$
$$I(\text{isUndefined}_t)(v) = I(=)(v, \bot) \text{ " [Ric02]}$$

3.3.1.4   Basic Types

"Basic types are *Integer*, *Real*, *Boolean* and *String*. The syntax of basic types
and their operations is defined by a signature $\Sigma_B = (T_B, \Omega_B)$. T_B is the set
of basic types, Ω_B is the set of signatures describing operations over basic
types." [Ric02]

Definition 3.16 (Syntax of basic types, from [Ric02]). The set of basic
types T_B is defined as $T_B = \{Integer, Real, Boolean, String\}$.   □

The semantics of basic types is given by a mapping from each type to a
domain.

Definition 3.17 (Semantics of basic types, from [Ric02]). Let $\mathcal{A}^*$ be the set
of finite sequences of characters from a finite alphabet $\mathcal{A}$. The semantics of
a basic type $t \in T_B$ is a function I mapping each type to a set:

- $I(Integer) = \mathbb{Z} \cup \{\bot\}$

- $I(Real) = \mathbb{R} \cup \{\bot\}$

- $I(Boolean) = \{\text{true}, \text{false}\} \cup \{\bot\}$

- $I(String) = \mathcal{A}^* \cup \{\bot\}$.

□

"The basic type *Integer* represents the set of integers, *Real* the set of real
numbers, *Boolean* the truth values true and false, and *String* all finite strings
over a given alphabet." [Ric02]

Each domain of a basic type t contains the special value $\bot$. This value represents an undefined value (c. f. p. 46).

There are a several predefined operations on basic types. The set Ω_B contains the signatures of these operations. Ω_B includes the usual arithmetic
operations $+, -, *, /$, etc. for integers and real numbers, and comparison operations $(<, >, \leq, \geq)$. For example, $+Integer \times Integer \to Integer \in \Omega_B$.

The set of predefined operations also includes operations for equality and inequality.

There are further parameter-less operations in Ω_B that produce constant values of basic types. For example, the integer value 42 is constructed by the operation $42 :\to$ *Integer*. Similar operations exist for the other basic types. For each value, there is an operation with no parameters and an operation symbol that corresponds to the common notational representation of this value. The semantics of all individual operations for basic types can be found in [Ric02].

3.3.1.5 Collection Types

"OCL provides the complex types $Set(t)$, $Sequence(t)$, and $Bag(t)$ for describing collections of values of type t. There is also an abstract supertype $Collection(t)$ which describes common properties of these types. The OCL collection types are homogeneous in the sense that all elements of a collection must be of the same type t. This restriction is slightly relaxed by the substitution rule for subtypes in OCL [...]. The rule says that the actual elements of a collection must have a type which is a subtype of the declared element type. For example, a $Set(Project)$ may contain elements of type *Project* or *Training*." [Ric02]

The syntax of collection types is defined recursively by means of type expressions.

Definition 3.18. Type expressions (from [Ric02] Let $\hat{T}$ be a set of types. The set of type expressions $T_{\text{Expr}}(\hat{T})$ over $\hat{T}$ is defined as follows.

  i. If $t \in \hat{T}$ then $t \in T_{\text{Expr}}(\hat{T})$.

  ii. If $t \in T_{\text{Expr}}(\hat{T})$ then $Set(t), Sequence(t), Bag(t) \in T_{\text{Expr}}(\hat{T})$.

  iii. If $t \in T_{\text{Expr}}(\hat{T})$ then $Collection(t) \in T_{\text{Expr}}(\hat{T})$.

$\square$

"The definition says that every type $t \in \hat{T}$ can be used as an element type for constructing a set, sequence, bag, or collection type. Furthermore, these complex types may again be used as element types for constructing other complex types. The recursive definition allows unlimited nesting of type expressions.

For the definition of the semantics of type expressions we make the following conventions. Let $\mathcal{F}(S)$ denote the set of all finite subsets of a given set S, S^* is the set of all finite sequences over S, and $\mathcal{B}(S)$ is the set of all finite multisets (bags) over S." [Ric02]

Definition 3.19. Semantics of type expressions (from [Ric02] Let $\hat{T}$ be a set of types where the domain of each $t \in \hat{T}$ is $I(t)$. The semantics of type expressions $T_{\text{Expr}}(\hat{T})$ over $\hat{T}$ is defined for all $t \in \hat{T}$ as follows.

    i. $I(t)$ is defined as given.

    ii. $I(Set(t)) = \mathcal{F}(I(t)) \cup \{\bot\}$,
       $I(Sequence(t)) = (I(t))^* \cup \{\bot\}$,
       $I(Bag(t)) = \mathcal{B}(I(t)) \cup \{\bot\}$.

    iii. $I(Collection(t)) = I(Set(t)) \cup I(Sequence(t)) \cup I(Bag(t))$.

□

There are several operations defined for collection types. Most of them can be regarded as shorthand forms of the 'iterate' operation, which is defined later. Apart from iterate, collection constructors are defined to provided to construct values such as $\texttt{Set\{1,2,5\}}$ for the collection types. For $t \in T_{\text{Expr}}(\hat{T})$ constructors in $\Omega_{T_{\text{Expr}}(\hat{T})}$ are defined as follows. A parameter list $t \times \cdots \times t$ denotes n $(n \geq 0)$ parameters of the same type t.

Richters defines constructors mkSet_t, mkSequence_t, and mkBag_t are defined for any type t and for any finite number n of parameters as follows:

$$\text{mkSet}_t : t \times \cdots \times t \rightarrow Set(t)$$
$$\text{mkSequence}_t : t \times \cdots \times t \rightarrow Sequence(t)$$
$$\text{mkBag}_t : t \times \cdots \times t \rightarrow Bag(t)$$

$$I(\text{mkSet}_t)(v_1, \ldots, v_n) = \{v_1, \ldots, v_n\}$$
$$I(\text{mkSequence}_t)(v_1, \ldots, v_n) = \langle v_1, \ldots, v_n \rangle$$
$$I(\text{mkBag}_t)(v_1, \ldots, v_n) = \{\!\!\{ v_1, \ldots, v_n \}\!\!\}$$

Notice that for collection literals with heterogeneous values, such as $\texttt{1}$, $\texttt{'One'}$, several collection constructor operations are applicable, due to the principle of substitution. This problem is not fully addressed by [Ric02]. We give a definition for the resolution of collection constructor applications later on page 61.

3.3.1.6 Enumeration Types

"The syntax of enumeration types and their operations is defined by a signature $\Sigma_E = (T_E, \Omega_E)$. T_E is the set of enumeration types and Ω_E the set of signatures describing the operations on enumeration types. " [Ric02]

Definition 3.20 (Syntax of enumeration types (from [Ric02])). An enumeration type $t \in T_E$ is associated with a finite non-empty set of enumeration literals by a function literals$(t) = \{e_{1_t}, \ldots, e_{n_t}\}$. $\square$

An enumeration type is interpreted by the set of literals used for its declaration.

Definition 3.21 (Semantics of enumeration types (from [Ric02])). The semantics of an enumeration type $t \in T_E$ is a function $I(t) = $ literals$(t) \cup \{\bot\}$. $\square$

The semantics of the enumeration types from the example in Fig. 3.1 is defined as follows.

$$I(ProjectStatus) = \{\text{planned}_{\text{ProjectStatus}}, \text{active}_{\text{ProjectStatus}},$$
$$\text{suspended}_{\text{ProjectStatus}}, \text{finished}_{\text{ProjectStatus}}\}$$
$$I(ProjectSize) = \{\text{small}_{\text{ProjectSize}}, \text{medium}_{\text{ProjectSize}}, \text{big}_{\text{ProjectSize}}\}$$

3.3.1.7 Object Types

"A central part of a UML model are classes that describe the structure of objects in a system. For each class, we define a corresponding object type describing the set of possible object instances. The syntax of object types and their operations is defined by a signature $\Sigma_C = (T_C, \Omega_C)$. T_C is the set of object types, and Ω_C is the set of signatures describing operations on object types." [Ric02]

Definition 3.22 (Syntax of object types, from [Ric02]). Let $\mathcal{M}$ be a model with a set CLASS of class names. The set T_C of object types is defined such that for each class $c \in$ CLASS there is a type $t \in T_C$ having the same name as the class c. $\square$

Richters defines the following two functions for mapping a class to its type and vice versa:

$$\text{typeOf} : \text{CLASS} \rightarrow T_C$$
$$\text{classOf} : T_C \rightarrow \text{CLASS}$$

The interpretation of classes is used for defining the semantics of object types. The set of object identifiers $I_{\text{CLASS}}(c)$ was introduced in Def. 3.10 on page 42.

Definition 3.23 (Semantics of object types, from [Ric02]). The semantics of an object type $t \in T_C$ with classOf$(t) = c$ is defined as $I(t) = I_{\text{CLASS}}(c) \cup \{\bot\}$. $\square$

3.3.1.8 Operations on Object Types

"There are four different kinds of operations that are specific to object types.

- *Predefined operations*: These are operations which are implicitly defined in OCL for all object types.

- *Attribute operations*: An attribute operation allows access to the attribute value of an object in a given system state.

- *Object operations*: A class may have operations that do not have side effects. These operations are marked in the UML model with the tag *isQuery* [OMG99b, p. 2-25]. In general, OCL expressions could be used to define object operations. The semantics of an object operation is therefore given by the semantics of the associated OCL expression.

- *Navigation operations*: An object may be connected to other objects via association links. A navigation expression allows to follow these links and to retrieve connected objects." [Ric02]

3.3.1.9 Predefined operations

"For all classes $c \in \text{CLASS}$ with object type $t_c = \text{typeOf}(c)$ the operations

$$\text{allInstances}_{t_c} : \to Set(t_c)$$

are in Ω_C. The semantics is defined as

$$I(\text{allInstances}_{t_c} : \to Set(t_c)) = \sigma_{\text{CLASS}}(c) \ ."[\text{Ric02}]$$

3.3.1.10 Attribute operations, from [Ric02]

"Attribute operations are declared in a model specification by the set ATT_c for each class c. The set contains signatures $a : t_c \to t$ with a being the name of an attribute defined in the class c. The type of the attribute is t. All attribute operations in ATT_c are elements of Ω_C. The semantics of an attribute operation is a function mapping an object identifier to a value of the attribute domain. An attribute value depends on the current system state." [Ric02]

Definition 3.24 (Semantics of attribute operations, from [Ric02]). An attribute signature $a : t_c \to t$ in Ω_C is interpreted by an attribute value function $I_{\text{ATT}}(a : t_c \to t) : I(t_c) \to I(t)$ mapping objects of class c to a value of type t.

$$I_{\text{ATT}}(a : t_c \to t)(\underline{c}) = \begin{cases} \sigma_{\text{ATT}}(a)(\underline{c}) & \text{if } \underline{c} \in \sigma_{\text{CLASS}}(c), \\ \bot & \text{otherwise.} \end{cases}$$

$\square$

3.3.1.11 Object query operations

"Object operations are declared in a model specification. For side effect-free [query] operations the computation can often be described with an OCL expression. The semantics of a side effect-free object operation can then be given by the semantics of the OCL expression associated with the operation." [Ric02]

Example. We have defined an operation isOverloaded in class *Worker* that determines if the worker is not assigned to too many, or too big projects. The computation required for this operation is given as an OCL expression.

```
isOverloaded() : Boolean =
  let active = projects->select(p|p.status = #active) in
  active->select(p|p.size=#big)->size * 2 +
  active->select(p|p.size=#medium)->size > 3
```

$\square$

3.3.1.12 Navigation operations

"A fundamental concept of OCL is navigation along associations. Navigation operations start from an object of a source class and retrieve all connected objects of a target class. In general, every n-ary association induces a total of $n \cdot (n-1)$ directed navigation operations, because OCL navigation operations only consider two classes of an association at a time. For defining the set of navigation operations of a given class, we have to consider all associations the class is participating in. A corresponding function named participating was defined on page 38." [Ric02]

Definition 3.25 (Syntax of navigation operations, from [Ric02]). Let $\mathcal{M}$ be a model

$$\mathcal{M} = (\text{CLASS}, \text{ATT}_c, \text{OP}_c, \text{ASSOC}, \text{associates}, \text{roles}, \text{multiplicities}, \prec) \ .$$

The set $\Omega_{\text{nav}}(c)$ of navigation operations for a class $c \in \text{CLASS}$ is defined such that for each association $as \in \text{participating}(c)$ with $\text{associates}(as) = \langle c_1, \ldots, c_n \rangle$, $\text{roles}(as) = \langle r_1, \ldots, r_n \rangle$, and $\text{multiplicities}(as) = \langle M_1, \ldots, M_n \rangle$ the following signatures are in $\Omega_{\text{nav}}(c)$.

For all $i, j \in \{1, \ldots, n\}$ with $i \neq j$, $c_i = c$, $t_{c_i} = \text{typeOf}(c_i)$, and $t_{c_j} = \text{typeOf}(c_j)$

    i. if $n = 2$ and $M_j - \{0, 1\} = \emptyset$ then $r_{j(as, r_i)} : t_{c_i} \to t_{c_j} \in \Omega_{\text{nav}}(c)$,

ii. if $n > 2$ or $M_j - \{0,1\} \neq \emptyset$ then $r_{j_{(as,r_i)}} : t_{c_i} \to Set(t_{c_j}) \in \Omega_{\text{nav}}(c)$.

All navigation operations are elements of Ω_C.   □

Example. Below we give the navigation operations of the class *Project* (see Fig. 3.1 on page 34).

$\Omega_{\text{nav}}(Project) = \{$

company$_{(\text{CarriesOut,projects})}$: $Project \to Company$,

members$_{(\text{Member,projects})}$: $Project \to Set(Worker)$,

successors$_{(\text{Prerequisite,predecessors})}$: $Project \to Set(Project)$,

predecessors$_{(\text{Prerequisite,successors})}$: $Project \to Set(Project)$,

requirements$_{(\text{Requires,projects})}$: $Project \to Set(Qualification)\}$

□

"Navigation operations are interpreted by navigation functions. Such a function has the effect of first selecting all those links of an association where the source object occurs in the link component corresponding to the role of the source class. The resulting links are then projected onto those objects that correspond to the role of the target class." [Ric02]

Definition 3.26 (Semantics of navigation operations, from [Ric02]). The set of objects of class c_j linked to an object $\underline{c_i}$ via association as is defined as

$$L(as)(\underline{c_i}) = \{\underline{c_j} \mid (\underline{c_1}, \ldots, \underline{c_i}, \ldots, \underline{c_j}, \ldots, \underline{c_n}) \in \sigma_{\text{Assoc}}(as)\}$$

The semantics of operations in $\Omega_{\text{nav}}(c)$ is then defined as

i. $I(r_{j_{(as,r_i)}} : t_{c_i} \to t_{c_j})(\underline{c_i}) = \begin{cases} \underline{c_j} & \text{if } \underline{c_j} \in L(as)(\underline{c_i}), \\ \bot & \text{otherwise.} \end{cases}$

ii. $I(r_{j_{(as,r_i)}} : t_{c_i} \to Set(t_{c_j}))(\underline{c_i}) = L(as)(\underline{c_i})$.

□

Example. The following functions show possible navigations between objects and the results. The interpretation is based on the system state presented in Fig. 3.2 on page 44.

$$I(\text{qualifications}_{(\text{IsQualified,workers})})(\underline{Ada}) = \{\underline{Com}\}$$

$$I(\text{qualifications}_{(\text{IsQualified,workers})})(\underline{Bob}) = \{\underline{Com}\}$$

$$I(\text{workers}_{(\text{IsQualified,qualifications})})(\underline{Com}) = \{\underline{Ada}, \underline{Bob}\}$$

□

3.3.1.13 Type Hierarchy

The type hierarchy reflects the subtype/supertype relationship between types. The following relationships are defined in OCL.

1. *Integer* is a subtype of *Real*.

2. All types, except for the collection types, are subtypes of *OclAny*.

3. All types are supertypes of *OclVoid*.

4. *Set(t)*, *Sequence(t)*, and *Bag(t)* are subtypes of *Collection(t)*.

5. The hierarchy of types introduced by UML model elements mirrors the generalization hierarchy in the UML model.

Definition 3.27 (Type hierarchy, from [Ric02]). Let T be a set of types and T_C a set of object types with $T_C \subset T$. The relation $\leq$ is a partial order on T and is called the *type hierarchy* over T. The type hierarchy is defined for all $t, t', t'' \in T$ and all $t_c, t'_c \in T_C$ as follows.

 i. $\leq$ is (a) reflexive, (b) transitive, and (c) antisymmetric:

   (a) $t \leq t$
   (b) $t'' \leq t' \wedge t' \leq t \implies t'' \leq t$
   (c) $t' \leq t \wedge t \leq t' \implies t = t'$.

 ii. *Integer* $\leq$ *Real*.

iii. $t \leq OclAny$ for all $t \in (T_B \cup T_E \cup T_C)$.

iv. $Set(t) \leq Collection(t)$,
    $Sequence(t) \leq Collection(t)$, and
    $Bag(t) \leq Collection(t)$.

 v. If $t' \leq t$ then $Set(t') \leq Set(t)$, $Sequence(t') \leq Sequence(t)$,
    $Bag(t') \leq Bag(t)$, and $Collection(t') \leq Collection(t)$.

vi. If $\text{classOf}(t'_c) \prec \text{classOf}(t_c)$ then $t'_c \leq t_c$.

$\square$

"If a type t' is a subtype of another type t (i. e., $t' \leq t$), we say that t' *conforms* to t. Type conformance is associated with the principle of substitutability. A value of type t' may be used wherever a value of type t is expected. This rule is defined more formally in Sect. 3.3.2 which defines the syntax and semantics of expressions.

The principle of substitutability and the interpretation of types as sets suggest that the type hierarchy should be defined as a subset relation on the type domains. Hence, for a type t' being a subtype of t, we postulate that the interpretation of t' is a subset of the interpretation of t. It follows that every operation ω accepting values of type t has the same semantics for values of type t', since $I(\omega)$ is already well-defined for values in $I(t')$." [Ric02]

3.3.1.14   Data Signature for Expressions

The elements defined to so far can now be combined to define the final data signature!expressions for OCL expressions. "The signature provides the basic set of syntactic elements for building expressions. It defines the syntax and semantics of types, the type hierarchy, and the set of operations defined on types." [Ric02]

Definition 3.28 (Data signature for expressions, changed from [Ric02]). Let $\hat{T}$ be the set of non-collection types: $\hat{T} = T_B \cup T_E \cup T_C \cup T_S$. The syntax of a data signature over an object model $\mathcal{M}$ is a structure $\Sigma_{\mathcal{M}} = (T_{\mathcal{M}}, \leq, \Omega_{\mathcal{M}})$ where

i. $T_{\mathcal{M}} = T_{\text{Expr}}(\hat{T})$,

ii. $\leq$ is a type hierarchy over $T_{\mathcal{M}}$,

iii. $\Omega_{\mathcal{M}} = \Omega_{T_{\text{Expr}}(\hat{T})} \cup \Omega_B \cup \Omega_E \cup \Omega_C \cup \Omega_S$.

The semantics of $\Sigma_{\mathcal{M}}$ is a structure $I(\Sigma_{\mathcal{M}}) = (I(T_{\mathcal{M}}), I(\leq), I(\Omega_{\mathcal{M}}))$ where

i. $I(T_{\mathcal{M}})$ assigns each $t \in T_{\mathcal{M}}$ an interpretation $I(t)$.

ii. $I(\leq)$ implies for all types $t', t \in T_{\mathcal{M}}$ that $I(t') \subseteq I(t)$ if $t' \leq t$.

iii. $I(\Omega_{\mathcal{M}})$ assigns each operation $\omega : t_1 \times \cdots \times t_n \to t \in \Omega_{\mathcal{M}}$ a total function $I(\omega) : I(t_1) \times \cdots \times I(t_n) \to I(t)$.

$\square$

Remark. The above definition was named 'data signature' in [Ric02]. We have qualified the name to distinguish the data signatures for expressions and statements in Chap. 4.

3.3.2 Expressions

In this section, we provide the definitions of the syntax and semantics of expressions. The definition of expressions is based upon the data signature for expressions introduced earlier. A data signature [for expressions] $\Sigma_{\mathcal{M}} = (T_{\mathcal{M}}, \leq, \Omega_{\mathcal{M}})$ provides a set of types $T_{\mathcal{M}}$, a relation $\leq$ on types reflecting the type hierarchy, and a set of operations $\Omega_{\mathcal{M}}$. The signature contains the initial set of syntactic elements upon which the expression syntax is constructed.

3.3.2.1 Syntax of Expressions

Richters defines the syntax of expressions inductively, so that more complex expressions are recursively built from simple structures. For each expression the set of free occurrences of variables is also defined.

Definition 3.29 (Syntax of expressions, from [Ric02]). Let $\Sigma_{\mathcal{M}} = (T_{\mathcal{M}}, \leq, \Omega_{\mathcal{M}})$ be a data signature for expressions over an object model $\mathcal{M}$. Let $\mathrm{Var} = \{\mathrm{Var}_t\}_{t \in T_{\mathcal{M}}}$ be a family of variable sets where each variable set is indexed by a type t. The syntax of expressions over the signature $\Sigma_{\mathcal{M}}$ is given by a set $\mathrm{Expr} = \{\mathrm{Expr}_t\}_{t \in T_{\mathcal{M}}}$ and a function free : $\mathrm{Expr} \to \mathcal{F}(\mathrm{Var})$ that are defined as follows.

  i. If $v \in \mathrm{Var}_t$ then $\boldsymbol{v} \in \mathrm{Expr}_t$ and free$(v) := \{v\}$.

  ii. If $v \in \mathrm{Var}_{t_1}, e_1 \in \mathrm{Expr}_{t_1}, e_2 \in \mathrm{Expr}_{t_2}$ then **let** $\boldsymbol{v = e_1}$ **in** $\boldsymbol{e_2} \in \mathrm{Expr}_{t_2}$ and free(let $v = e_1$ in e_2) := free$(e_2) - \{v\}$.

  iii. If $\omega : t_1 \times \cdots \times t_n \to t \in \Omega_{\mathcal{M}}$ and $e_i \in \mathrm{Expr}_{t_i}$ for all $i = 1, \ldots, n$ then $\boldsymbol{\omega(e_1, \ldots, e_n)} \in \mathrm{Expr}_t$ and free$(\omega(e_1, \ldots, e_n)) := \mathrm{free}(e_1) \cup \cdots \cup \mathrm{free}(e_n)$.

  iv. If $e_1 \in \mathrm{Expr}_{\mathrm{Boolean}}$ and $e_2, e_3 \in \mathrm{Expr}_t$ then **if** $\boldsymbol{e_1}$ **then** $\boldsymbol{e_2}$ **else** $\boldsymbol{e_3}$ **endif** $\in \mathrm{Expr}_t$ and free(if e_1 then e_2 else e_3 endif) := free$(e_1) \cup \mathrm{free}(e_2) \cup \mathrm{free}(e_3)$.

  v. If $e \in \mathrm{Expr}_t$ and $t' \leq t$ or $t \leq t'$ then $(\boldsymbol{e}$ **asType** $\boldsymbol{t'}) \in \mathrm{Expr}_{t'}$, $(\boldsymbol{e}$ **isTypeOf** $\boldsymbol{t'}) \in \mathrm{Expr}_{\mathrm{Boolean}}$, $(\boldsymbol{e}$ **isKindOf** $\boldsymbol{t'}) \in \mathrm{Expr}_{\mathrm{Boolean}}$ and free$((e$ asType $t')) := \mathrm{free}(e)$, free$((e$ isTypeOf $t')) := \mathrm{free}(e)$, free$((e$ isKindOf $t')) := \mathrm{free}(e)$.

  vi. If $e_1 \in \mathrm{Expr}_{Collection(t_1)}$, $v_1 \in \mathrm{Var}_{t_1}, v_2 \in \mathrm{Var}_{t_2}$, and $e_2, e_3 \in \mathrm{Expr}_{t_2}$ then $\boldsymbol{e_1 \to \mathbf{iterate}(v_1; v_2 = e_2 \mid e_3)} \in \mathrm{Expr}_{t_2}$ and free$(e_1 \to \mathrm{iterate}(v_1; v_2 = e_2 \mid e_3)) := (\mathrm{free}(e_1) \cup \mathrm{free}(e_2) \cup \mathrm{free}(e_3)) - \{v_1, v_2\}$.

An expression of type t' is also an expression of a more general type t. For all $t' \leq t$: if $e \in \mathrm{Expr}_{t'}$ then $e \in \mathrm{Expr}_t$. $\qquad\square$

"Following the principle of substitutability, the syntax of expressions is defined such that wherever an expression $e \in \text{Expr}_t$ is expected as part of another expression, an expression with a more special type $t', (t' \leq t)$ may be used. In particular, operation arguments and variable assignments in let and iterate expressions may be given by expressions of more special types." [Ric02]

3.3.2.2   Collection constructor resolution

There are collection value constructor operations

$$
\begin{aligned}
\text{mkSet} &\quad : t \times \cdots \times t \to \text{Set}(t), \\
\text{mkBag} &\quad : t \times \cdots \times t \to \text{Bag}(t), \text{and} \\
\text{mkSequence} &\quad : t \times \cdots \times t \to \text{Sequence}(t)
\end{aligned}
$$

for each type t.

OCL allows the construction of collection values of heterogeneous types, as long as the types of all element value have the same level nesting. For example, Set{1,'abc'} is a valid collection value (the type of this value is Set(OclAny), whereas Set{Set{1},'abc'} is no collection value. This follows directly from the homogeneous signature of $\text{mkSet}_t : t \times \cdots \times t \to \text{Set}(t)$ (mkSequence and mkBag analogously). Heterogeneous collection values can be constructed only by subtype substitution.

For a collection construction expression $\text{mkSet}(e_1, \ldots, e_n)$ with different argument types, there may be more than one applicable operation mkSet_t with $e_i \in I(t)$ for $i \in 1 \ldots n$, due to subtyping. Therefore, it is not clear which operation (which signature) mkSet_t to chose.

According to [OMG06], the type of the collection literal expression is derived by the *least common supertype* rule: The type of a collection literal is the collection type of the most specific type that is a common supertype of all element types.

First, we formally define the notion of the least common supertype of a set of types.

Definition 3.30 (Least common supertype). Given a set of types $T_{\mathcal{M}}$ and a partially ordered subtype relation $\leq$ over an object model $\mathcal{M}$. The least common supertype of types $t_1, \ldots, t_n \in T_{\mathcal{M}}$ is a function $\text{lcs} : T_{\mathcal{M}} \times \cdots \times T_{\mathcal{M}} \to T_{\mathcal{M}}$.

$$
\text{lcs}(t_1, \ldots, t_n) := \min(\text{lcs}'(t_1, \ldots, t_n))
$$

where $\text{lcs}' : T_{\mathcal{M}} \times \cdots \times T_{\mathcal{M}} \to \mathcal{P}(T_{\mathcal{M}})$

$$
\text{lcs}'(t_1, \ldots, t_n) := \Big\{ t \ \Big| \ t \in T_{\mathcal{M}} \wedge \ \forall i \in 1..n : t_i \leq t
$$
$$
\wedge \Big[\big(\forall t' \in T_{\mathcal{M}} : \forall j \in 1..n : t_j \leq t' \big) \to (t \leq t' \vee t' \leq t) \Big] \Big\}
$$

and

$$\mathrm{min}(\{t\}) := t$$

$$\mathrm{min}(\{t_1,\ldots,t_n\}) := \begin{cases} t_1 & \text{if } t_1 \leq \mathrm{min}(\{t_2,\ldots,t_n\}) \\ \mathrm{min}(\{t_2,\ldots,t_n\}) & \text{otherwise} \end{cases}$$

$\square$

The set $\mathrm{lcs}'(t_1,\ldots,t_n)$ comprises all types that are supertypes of all of $t_1,\ldots,t_n$ and that are further *comparable* (in the subtyping sense) with all other common supertypes of $t_1,\ldots,t_n$. Therefore, min is well-defined in the above definition because the subtyping relation – which is a partial order over $T_{\mathcal{M}}$ in general – forms a total order over $\mathrm{lcs}'(t_1,\ldots,t_n)$.

Example. Figure 3.4 provides two class hierarchies for models $\mathcal{M}_1$ and $\mathcal{M}_2$. The types and the subtype relation $\leq$ follow straightforward by Def. 3.3.1.13: we get an object type for each class, and the subtype relation is derived from the subclass relations. Additionally, OclAny is the supertype of all other types. Table 3.1 on the following page shows the least common supertypes for some sets of types, as well as the intermediate result lcs'. For the sake of brevity, we refer to the object types as $A, B, C, \ldots$ instead as $\mathrm{typeOf}(A), \mathrm{typeOf}(B), \mathrm{typeOf}(C), \ldots$.

The first model $\mathcal{M}_1$ does not contain multiple inheritance. Therefore, the least common supertype of $t_1,\ldots,t_n$ can be easily found by looking for the most specific common ancestor. The second model $\mathcal{M}_2$ does contain multiple inheritance. Therefore, the examples for this model show, that the our definition disregards some common supertypes because they are not mutually comparable. In the first row for $\mathcal{M}_2$, B and C are disregarded in $\mathrm{lcs}'(D, E)$ when evaluating $\mathrm{lcs}(D, E)$. In the second row for $\mathcal{M}_2$, we can see that adding a B to $\mathrm{lcs}(B, D, E)$ type dissolves this problem, and B occurs in $\mathrm{lcs}'(B, D, E)$. The third and the fourth row for $\mathcal{M}_2$ again show simple situations that are not affected by the multiple inheritance relationship: in both rows, one of the two types is a supertype of the other. $\square$

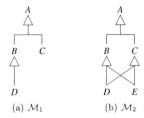

(a) $\mathcal{M}_1$ (b) $\mathcal{M}_2$

Figure 3.4: Examples models for the least common supertype

Model	$t_1, \ldots, t_n$	$\mathbf{lcs'(t_1, \ldots, t_n)}$	$\mathbf{lcs(t_1, \ldots, t_n)}$
$\mathcal{M}_1$	C, D	$\{A, OclAny\}$	A
$\mathcal{M}_1$	B, D	$\{A, B, OclAny\}$	B
$\mathcal{M}_2$	D, E	$\{A, OclAny\}$	A
$\mathcal{M}_2$	B, D, E	$\{A, B, OclAny\}$	B
$\mathcal{M}_2$	B, D	$\{A, B, OclAny\}$	B
$\mathcal{M}_2$	C, E	$\{A, C, OclAny\}$	C

Table 3.1: Examples for the least common supertypes

In contrast to the indeterministic algorithm for determing the least common supertype in [OMG06], our definition of the least common supertype is deterministic. The original definition of the additional operation *commonSuperType* in [OMG06, p56] is as follows:

```
context Classifier
def: commonSuperType (c : Classifier) : Classifier =
  Classifier.allInstances()->select (cst |
    c.conformsTo (cst) and self.conformsTo (cst) and
    not Classifier.allInstances()->exists (clst |
      c.conformsTo (clst) and self.conformsTo (clst)
      and clst.conformsTo (cst) and clst <> cst)
  )->any (true)
```

For the first row in Tab. 3.1, the OMG definition indeterministicly evaluates to either B or C, depending on the implementation of the collection operation any. Cf. [GKB08] for a comparison of the determinateness of OCL tools under such circumstances. Our definition yields $lcs(C, D) = A$ for the supertype relation $\leq$ given above.

Proof for total ordering of $\leq$ over $lcs'(t_1, \ldots, t_n)$. The relation $\leq$ is a partial order over $T_{\mathcal{M}}$ by definition. Therefore we have to show that $t \leq t' \vee t' \leq t$ holds for each pair $t, t' \in lcs'(t_1, \ldots, t_n)$.

Proof by contradiction: Assume there is a pair of unrelated types $t, t' \in lcs(t_1, t_2)$. Then, by instantiating t in the predicate of the above definition, we have

$$\forall i \in 1..n \ : \ t_i \leq t \wedge \forall t' \in T_{\mathcal{M}} \ : \ \Big[\big(\forall j \in 1..n \ : \ t_j \leq t'\big) \rightarrow (t \leq t' \vee t' \leq t)\Big]$$

and

$$\forall t' \in T_{\mathcal{M}} \ : \ \Big[\big(\forall j \in 1..n \ : \ t_j \leq t'\big) \rightarrow (t \leq t' \vee t' \leq t)\Big].$$

Then, by instantiating the quantification for t', we have

$$\Big[\big(\forall j \in 1..n \; : \; t_j \leq t' \big) \to \big(t \leq t' \vee t' \leq t \big) \Big].$$

The conclusion of in the inner implication is false by assumption. Then, by transposition, we have

$$\neg \big(\forall j \in 1..n \; : \; t_j \leq t' \big)$$

resp.

$$\exists j \in 1..n \; : \; t_j \not\leq t'.$$

This contradicts $t' \in \mathrm{lcs}'(t_1, \ldots, t_n)$. Therefore, there is no unrelated pair $t, t' \in \mathrm{lcs}'(t_1, \ldots, t_n)$. $\qquad\square$

Schürr proposed an extended type system of OCL 2.0 in [Sch02] under which expression such as the one given above can be typed by intersection types such as $C \cap D$, but this proposal has not been incorporated into OCL. Since it required several modifications to the OCL semantics, it will not be further regarded in this work.

Having the above definition for the least common supertype, we can define which collection constructor operation to apply:

Definition 3.31 (Collection constructor operation resolution). The expressions

$$\begin{aligned}
\mathrm{mkSet} & \quad (e_1, \ldots, e_n) \\
\mathrm{mkBag} & \quad (e_1, \ldots, e_n) \\
\mathrm{mkSequence} & \quad (e_1, \ldots, e_n)
\end{aligned}$$

are shorthand forms for

$$\begin{aligned}
\mathrm{mkSet}_{\mathrm{lcs}(t_1, \ldots t_n)} & \quad (e_1, \ldots, e_n) \\
\mathrm{mkBag}_{\mathrm{lcs}(t_1, \ldots t_n)} & \quad (e_1, \ldots, e_n) \\
\mathrm{mkSequence}_{\mathrm{lcs}(t_1, \ldots t_n)} & \quad (e_1, \ldots, e_n)
\end{aligned}$$

where $t_i = \mathrm{typeOf}(e_i)$. $\qquad\square$

Remark. This resolution of the correct overloaded mkSet, mkBag, and mkSequence operations is missing in [Ric02].

3.3.2.3 Semantics of Expressions

The semantics of expressions is made precise in the following definition. A context for evaluation is given by an environment $\tau = (\sigma, \beta)$ consisting of a system state σ and a variable assignment $\beta : \mathrm{Var}_t \to I(t)$. A system state σ provides access to the set of currently existing objects, their attribute values, and association links between objects. A variable assignment β maps variable names to values.

Definition 3.32 (Semantics of expressions, from [Ric02]). Let Env be the set of environments $\tau = (\sigma, \beta)$. The semantics of an expression $e \in \text{Expr}_t$ is a function $I[\![\, e \,]\!] : \text{Env} \to I(t)$ that is defined as follows.

   i. $I[\![\, v \,]\!](\tau) = \beta(v)$.

  ii. $I[\![\, \text{let } v = e_1 \text{ in } e_2 \,]\!](\tau) = I[\![\, e_2 \,]\!](\sigma, \beta\{v / I[\![\, e_1 \,]\!](\tau)\})$.

 iii. $I[\![\, \omega(e_1, \dots, e_n) \,]\!](\tau) = I(\omega)(\tau)(I[\![\, e_1 \,]\!](\tau), \dots, I[\![\, e_n \,]\!](\tau))$.

 iv. $I[\![\, \text{if } e_1 \text{ then } e_2 \text{ else } e_3 \text{ endif} \,]\!](\tau) = \begin{cases} I[\![\, e_2 \,]\!](\tau) & \text{if } I[\![\, e_1 \,]\!](\tau) = \text{true}, \\ I[\![\, e_3 \,]\!](\tau) & \text{if } I[\![\, e_1 \,]\!](\tau) = \text{false}, \\ \bot & \text{otherwise}. \end{cases}$

  v. $I[\![\, (e \text{ asType } t') \,]\!](\tau) = \begin{cases} I[\![\, e \,]\!](\tau) & \text{if } I[\![\, e \,]\!](\tau) \in I(t'), \\ \bot & \text{otherwise}. \end{cases}$

     $I[\![\, (e \text{ isTypeOf } t') \,]\!](\tau) = \begin{cases} \text{true} & \text{if } I[\![\, e \,]\!](\tau) \in I(t') - \bigcup_{t'' < t'} I(t''), \\ \text{false} & \text{otherwise}. \end{cases}$

     $I[\![\, (e \text{ isKindOf } t') \,]\!](\tau) = \begin{cases} \text{true} & \text{if } I[\![\, e \,]\!](\tau) \in I(t'), \\ \text{false} & \text{otherwise}. \end{cases}$

 vi. $I[\![\, e_1 \to \text{iterate}(v_1; v_2 = e_2 \mid e_3) \,]\!](\tau) = I[\![\, e_1 \to \text{iterate}'(v_1 \mid e_3) \,]\!](\tau')$
where $\tau' = (\sigma, \beta')$ and $\tau'' = (\sigma, \beta'')$ are environments with modified variable assignments

$$\beta' := \beta\{v_2 / I[\![\, e_2 \,]\!](\tau)\}$$
$$\beta'' := \beta'\{v_2 / I[\![\, e_3 \,]\!](\sigma, \beta'\{v_1/x_1\})\}$$

and iterate$'$ is defined as:

  (a) If $e_1 \in \text{Expr}_{Sequence(t_1)}$ then $I[\![\, e_1 \to \text{iterate}'(v_1 \mid e_3) \,]\!](\tau') =$
$\begin{cases} I[\![\, v_2 \,]\!](\tau') \\ \quad \text{if } I[\![\, e_1 \,]\!](\tau') = \langle\,\rangle, \\ I[\![\, \text{mkSequence}_{t_1}(x_2, \dots, x_n) \to \text{iterate}'(v_1 \mid e_3) \,]\!](\tau'') \\ \quad \text{if } I[\![\, e_1 \,]\!](\tau') = \langle x_1, \dots, x_n \rangle. \end{cases}$

  (b) If $e_1 \in \text{Expr}_{Set(t_1)}$ then $I[\![\, e_1 \to \text{iterate}'(v_1 \mid e_3) \,]\!](\tau') =$
$\begin{cases} I[\![\, v_2 \,]\!](\tau') \\ \quad \text{if } I[\![\, e_1 \,]\!](\tau') = \emptyset, \\ I[\![\, \text{mkSet}_{t_1}(x_2, \dots, x_n) \to \text{iterate}'(v_1 \mid e_3) \,]\!](\tau'') \\ \quad \text{if } I[\![\, e_1 \,]\!](\tau') = \{x_1, \dots, x_n\}. \end{cases}$

(c) If $e_1 \in \text{Expr}_{Bag(t_1)}$ then $I[\![e_1 \rightarrow \text{iterate}'(v_1 \mid e_3)]\!](\tau') =$

$$
\begin{cases}
I[\![v_2]\!](\tau') \\
\quad \text{if } I[\![e_1]\!](\tau') = \emptyset, \\
I[\![\text{mkBag}_{t_1}(x_2, \ldots, x_n) \rightarrow \text{iterate}'(v_1 \mid e_3)]\!](\tau'') \\
\quad \text{if } I[\![e_1]\!](\tau') = \{\!\{ x_1, \ldots, x_n \}\!\}.
\end{cases}
$$

$\square$

The computation of a side effect-free operation $\omega \in \Omega_{\mathcal{M}}$ can often be described with OCL expressions. Richters extends the above definition to allow object operations whose effects are defined in terms of OCL expressions. The semantics of a side effect-free operation can then be given by the semantics of the OCL expression which is associated with the operation: "Recall that object operations in Op_c are declared in a model specification. Let oclexp : $\text{Op}_c \rightarrow \text{Expr}$ be a partial function mapping object operations to OCL expressions. We define the semantics of an operation with an associated OCL expression as

$$
I[\![\omega(p_1 : e_1, \ldots, p_n : e_n)]\!](\tau) = I[\![\text{oclexp}(\omega)]\!](\tau')
$$

where $p_1, \ldots, p_n$ are parameter names, and $\tau' = (\sigma, \beta')$ denotes an environment with a modified variable assignment defined as

$$
\beta' := \beta\{p_1/I[\![e_1]\!](\tau), \ldots, p_n/I[\![e_n]\!](\tau)\} \ .
$$

Argument expressions are evaluated and assigned to parameters that bind free occurrences of $p_1, \ldots, p_n$ in the expression oclexp(ω). For a well-defined semantics, we need to make sure that there is no infinite recursion resulting from an expansion of the operation call. A strict solution that can be statically checked is to forbid any occurrences of ω in oclexp(ω). However, allowing recursive operation calls considerably adds to the expressiveness of OCL [...]. We therefore allow recursive invocations as long as the recursion is finite. Unfortunately, this property is generally undecidable." [Ric02]

Chapter 4

SOIL

In this chapter we introduce a simple OCL-based imperative language (SOIL) which is based on UML object models and OCL expressions as defined in [OMG06] and [Ric02] and rendered in Chap. 3. SOIL embeds OCL in a modular way as given by Def. 2.1 in Sect. 2.5.

The language is not meant to be a particular rich programming language. It is meant as a simple but still practically useful example of how to define a language that embeds OCL, providing a sound denotational semantics. Although it is a simple language, it has been successfully employed as a general purpose scripting and programming language in the UML-based Specification Environment, as described later in Sect. 5.1. The spirit of SOIL has also been successfully transferred into an industrial project in the construction of the eGovernment MDA tool XGenerator2, as described in Sect. 5.2.

This chapter is structured as follows: We first informally introduce the language SOIL in Sect. 4.1. Then, we formally define the language in Sections 4.2–4.4. In Sect. 4.5, we revisit the type-safety of the language. In Sect. 4.6, we discuss an approach to an extended handling of error conditions. Finally, in Sect. 4.7, we compare SOIL to other OCL-based imperative programming languages.

4.1 Introduction

The language SOIL provides a way to define imperative programs based on UML information structures (class and object diagrams) and OCL expressions, enabling the construction of executable UML models. The language comprises manipulation of objects and their properties, scoped variables, and flow control such as conditional execution, loops, and operation invocation. SOIL can be used to provide definitions for operations with side-effects, i.e., to provide method bodies for UML operations. The language is statically typed and provides implicit definition of local variables.

Unlike non-modular OCL-based languages such as ImperativeOCL that we described in Sect. 2.2, SOIL does not change the semantics of OCL itself. It is constructed as an additional layer on top of OCL.

Given the Project World class diagram from Fig. 3.1 on page 34 in the last chapter, a simple SOIL program that increases the incomes of all underpaid employees looks as follows:

```
1  minimum := 12100;
2  totalIncrease := 0;
3  for emp in Worker.allInstances->select(w| w.employer.isDefined and
       w.salary < minimum)->asSequence do
4    emp.salary := emp.salary + 200;
5    totalIncrease := totalIncrease + 200
6  end
```

Listing 4.1: A first SOIL program

On the top level, this program consists of three statements, two assignment statements (lines 1 and 2) and one iteration statement (lines 3–6). The iteration statement contains two sub-statements (lines 4 and 5). Consecutive statements have to be separated by ';'.

The first two statements assign constant values to the variables *minimum* and *totalIncrease*. It is not necessary (and not possible) to declare variables in order to assign values to them. Instead, variables declarations are implicitly inferred in SOIL. In this example, the inferred type of the variables *minimum* and *totalIncrease* is Integer. Subsequently to line 2, both variables can occur in OCL expressions as free Integer variables. The right-hand side of a variable assignment is always an OCL expression. Thus, instead of the constant values 12100 and 0, any closed OCL expressions (without free variables) could have been used in lines 1 and 2.

The third statement iterates over all Worker instances which are connected to a company and whose salary is less than the value of *minimum*. The body (lines 4 and 5) is executed for each element of this range expression. For each iteration the current element (i. e., a Worker value) is bound to the variable *emp*. This variable is assigned before each iteration of the body statement (between do and end). The range of an iteration statement is the second place in this example where OCL expressions occur. Any sequence typed expression is allowed, the range variable is bound within the body and typed with the element type of the sequence. Notice that the range expression contains a free variable *minimum* when viewed in isolation – this variable is bound by the surrounding SOIL program. The same situation follows within the iteration body, where new values are assigned to the *salary* attribute of the current *emp*, and to the variable *totalIncrease*. The OCL expressions on both right-hand sides contain free variables, the range variable *emp* and *totalIncrease*.

The previous example used three language elements of SOIL (iteration, variable assignment and attribute assignment). It already shows how OCL is embedded into SOIL. All of the above statements contain OCL expressions, but, statements and expressions are disjoint entities. In a technical sense, the connection between statements and expressions is as follows: Statements evaluate expressions, which may contain free variables. The interpretation of these expressions depends on the values that are provided for the free variables, and, of course, the system state (i. e., the objects, links, and attribute values). Both, system state and variables can be modified by statements. Figure 4.1 illustrates this dependency in an evaluation chain.

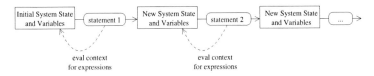

Figure 4.1: Evaluation Chain for Statements and Expressions

Apart from attribute assignments, SOIL comprises further basic statements to manipulate the system state. These are object creation, object destruction, link insertion, and link destruction. The following example illustrates these statements, as well as conditional execution.

```
1  prg := new Qualification;
2  c := new Company;
3  w1 := new Worker;
4  w2 := new Worker;
5  insert (w2,prg) into IsQualified;
6  insert (c,w1) into Employs;
7  insert (c,w2) into Employs;
8  p1 := new Project;
9  p2 := new Project;
10 insert (c,p1) into CarriesOut;
11 insert (p1, c.employees->any(e | e.qualifications->includes(prg)))
       into Member;
12 delete (c,w2) from Employs;
13 if (p2.members->isEmpty) then
14   destroy p2
15 end
```

Listing 4.2: Example for state manipulation commands in SOIL

Lines 1–4 and 8-9 contain object creation statements. These statements also
assign a new (object) value to a variable, but 'new Qualification' is not
an OCL expression. This form can only occur on the right-hand side of
an object creation statement. Thus, x := if happy then new Project else
Undefined endif is not a statement (neither object creation nor variable
assignment), as if happy then new Project else Undefined endif is not an
OCL expression.

Lines 5-7 and 10-12 contain link manipulation statements (insertion and
deletion). For both statements, the tuple that is to be inserted into, respec-
tively, deleted from the association extend, is given by OCL expressions.
These OCL expressions must conform to the types required by the association ends. Finally, line 13–15 show conditional execution. The condition is
given by a Boolean typed OCL expression. The body of this statement contains other statements. Line 14 shows the object destruction statement. The
object to be destroyed is determined by an OCL expression, which has to be
of an object type.

4.1.1   Execution Context

SOIL statements can be used to specify operations in UML models. They can
also be executed stand-alone, e. g., to create or animate system states.

If a SOIL statement is used to specify an implementation for an operation,
the formal parameters of the operation are available as if the variables were
bound in the statements.

As a second example, let us now consider the (non-query) operation *fire(w :
Worker)* in class Company from the 'Project World' class diagram in Fig. 3.1
on page 34. The operation has a single parameter *w* of type *Worker*.

We can use SOIL to define the semantics of *fire*, as shown in Listing 4.3.

```
1   def Company::fire(w : Worker)
2     delete (self, w) from Employs;
3     for p in w.projects do
4       delete (p,w) from Member
5     end
```

Listing 4.3: Operation definition for Company::fire

Within the body of *fire*, the variables *self* (the object on which *fire* is invoked)
and *w* (the parameter) are available as bound variables. If the operation has
a return type, the value of the variable *result* refers to the return value of
the operation. Such an operation is illustrated in the next subsection.

4.1.2   Operation Invocations

All operations defined in a class can be applied to an object. We need to distinguish between (side-effect free) query operations and operations with side-effects.

Query operations can be applied (only) in expressions. This is already part of OCL and independent from SOIL. Given there is a bound variable IBM referring to a Company object, the statement in the following example stores the number of employees that are overloaded with work in the variable *numOverloaded*. This is achieved by using the operation isOverloaded(), which we defined by an OCL expression on page 53.

```
1  numOverloaded := IBM.employees->select(w|w.isOverloaded())->size
```

Non-query operations are invoked by one of two explicit statements, one for operations without result values, and one for operations with result values. We can use *fire()* to illustrate the first one.

```
1  IBM := new Company;
2  Bob := new Worker;
3  insert (IBM, Bob) into Employs;
4  IBM.fire(Bob)
```

The statement in line 4 is the operation invocation. After executing the last statements, the objects IBM and Bob will not longer be connected by the Employs association.

To illustrate the second kind of invocation of operations, those with result values, we assume a class *Calculator* with a single *Integer* typed attribute *myState* and an operation *fac(n : Integer)* → *Integer*, defined as follows:

```
1  def Calculator::fac(n : Integer) : Integer
2    self.myState := 1;
3    if (n >= 1) then
4      self.myState := self.fac(n -  1);
5      self.myState := n * self.myState
6    end;
7    result := self.myState
```

We can invoke this operation as follows:

```
1  c := new Calculator;
2  n := c.fac(4)
```

After executing the above statements, the variable n will contain the value 24. In the recursive evaluation the *myState* attribute of the Calculator object referenced by c will bet set to $1, 2, 6$, and finally 24. Notice that line 2 is an explicit invocation statement for operations with result value, and not a variable assignment statement. Thus, analogously to the object creation command, n := c.fac(3) * c.fac(3) is not a statement, because c.fac(3) * c.fac(3) is not an OCL expression. The operation *fac()* is not a query operation. We defined it, by purpose, as an operation with side-effects (although it can be expressed in a functional manner very easily). The last example also shows that operation invocations can be nested. Of course, this introduces potentially non-terminating statements. However, for practical reasons, recursion is allowed in SOIL. We will discuss recursion in more depth later.

4.1.3   Type-Safety and Variable Scopes

A well-typed statement will never produce type errors at evaluation time (i. e., at runtime). Therefore, a statement such as the compound statement x := 1; y := '2'; z := x + y is not valid in SOIL, assuming there is no operation $+$: Integer $\times$ String $\rightarrow t$ defined for any type t. The meaning of this statement would be undefined. Therefore, it is rejected statically by the type-checker.

We also exclude statements that *may* have an undefined meaning, depending on actual variable values. Consider the following compound statement which is not a valid in SOIL:

```
1  x := 1;
2  b := <any boolean expression>
3  if b then
4    x := '1'
5  end;
6  x := x + 1
```

The above statement would have a well-defined interpretation if the Boolean expression evaluates to false. However, if the expression evaluates to true, the meaning of the statement would be undefined, for the same reason as described above (we assume there is no way to add strings and numbers). We formally discuss type-soundness for SOIL later in Sect. 4.5.

We already mentioned that variables are implicitly declared (we say 'bound') in SOIL. There are no explicit variable declarations. In general, a variable can be regarded as declared, as soon as a value is assigned to it. The language automatically infers the type for us. There are, however, restrictions w. r. t. iteration and conditional execution. As variables can be assigned several times, the declaration of a variable does not necessarily remain constant for all subsequent statements. Fig. 4.2 on the facing page illustrates the binding by examining a sequence of statements (i. e., a compound statement).

In statement (1), an *Integer* typed value is assigned to x. Thus, x is implicitly declared as type *Integer* until there is a further (non-*Integer*) assignment to x

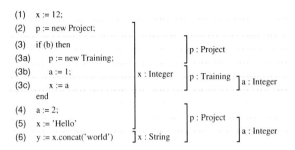

Figure 4.2: Implicit Variable Declarations in SOIL

(until after statement (5)). Thus, within statements (2) – (5), an *Integer* value can be assumed for x in OCL expressions.

Similarly, after statement (2), the variable p is implicitly declared as type *Project*. In statement (3a), within the conditional execution (3), a new value of type *Training* is assigned to p (we assume b to be a Boolean-typed expression). Thus, from now on, p can be assumed to be of type *Training*, which is a subtype of *Project* (c. f. Fig. 3.1 on page 34). For example, the term p.trained may occur in expressions after the assignment in (3a). However, variables bound within conditional executions and iteration statements are not propagated by these statements. Thus, after statement (3), we have to assume p to be of type *Project*, again. The reason for this typing scheme is, that the sub-statements within these compound statements are not guaranteed to be executed. For the same reasons, only type-conforming assignments are allowed within conditional executions and iterations: We could not say p := 42 as a replacement for statement (3a). The syntax of SOIL does not allow such an assignment.

In addition to the restrictions on variable assignments that are imposed by the type system, an additional restriction regards the iterator variable of a *for* loop. Within the body statement of a loop, the iterator variable must not be changed (no matter which type). Therefore, the following statement is not valid:

```
1  for x in Sequence{1,2,3} do x := 1 end
```

On Explicit and Implicit Variable Declaration

As we explained in the previous section, no explicit variable declarations are required in SOIL. Types for variables are automatically inferred. There are, however, certain situations where an upfront variable *initialization* is required. These initializations are ordinary assignments. They are needed, whenever a variable would have been assigned otherwise within a conditional execution or an iteration for the first time. As these constructs do not propagate their bound variables, we need to put an explicit initialization in front of them. Thus, we cannot write

```
1  for i in Sequence{1,2,3} do
2    x := i;
3  end;
4  y := x;
```

The type-checker of SOIL rejects the previous statement as, in general, the sequence expression which determines the range of a *for* loop might evaluate to the empty sequence. We have to add an initialization for x to the beginning of this example.

```
1  x := 0;
2  for i in Sequence{1,2,3} do
3    x := i;
4  end;
5  y := x;
```

We find a similar pattern for variables being initialized (assigned for the first time) within blocks in several scripting languages with implicit variable declaration, for example in Ruby [FM08].

4.1.4   Error Handling

For the sake of simplicity, there is no sophisticated exception or error handling mechanism in SOIL. This does, however, not mean that SOIL programs may just abort in an undefined way. In fact, there is no statement in SOIL that could lead to program abortion. Therefore, the following situations are treated specifically:

Inserting tuples into an association extent more than once: If a tuple is already present in an association extent, a second insert operation has no further effect, as in the following example.

```
1    x := new C;
2    y := new D;
3    insert (x,y) into A;
4    insert (x,y) into A
```

Deleting non-existing tuples from an association extent: If a tuple is not present in an association extent, a delete operation has no effect.

```
1    x := new C;
2    y := new D;
3    delete (x,y) from A
```

Inserting tuples with undefined components: If a tuple contains an undefined value, the insert operation has no effect.

```
1    x := new C;
2    insert (x,Undefined) into A
```

Assigning attribute values for an undefined object: The assignment of an attribute value to Undefined has no effect.

```
1    x := new C;
2    destroy x;
3    x.a := 42
```

Operation invocation on Undefined: An operation invocation on the undefined value has no effect. In the following example, line 3 does nothing.

```
1    x := new C;
2    x := Undefined;
3    x.f()
```

Destroying an undefined object: The destruction of Undefined has no effect.

```
1    destroy Undefined
```

Remark. Although a different treatment for multiple inserts of the same tuple and for the removal of non-existing links seems reasonable, the above treatment for the first two items is in accordance with the common understanding of association extents as relations.

However, the latter items clearly lead to unexpected behavior. An error could be expected. Nevertheless, for reasons of simplicity, we have decided not to include a more sophisticated error handling mechanism in this version of SOIL. After our presentation of the formal semantics for SOIL, we sketch how more sophisticated error handling could be added to SOIL in Sect. 4.6.

4.1.5   Garbage Collection

There is no implicit garbage collection for objects. Objects are destroyed explicitly only by the *destroy* command. Therefore, objects can exist without any reference from variables, links or attribute values to them.

Example. This following program creates an instance of class C, storing the instance reference in the variable x, and then assigns the undefined value to x in the next step.

```
1    x := new C;
2    x := Undefined
```

After executing these two statements, no reference to the new instance of C exists. However, the object itself still exists in the system state. It can be referenced by the *allInstances* property of class C (assuming there is no other instance of C):

```
1    x := C.allInstances->any(true)
```

$\square$

However, objects generally need to be distinguishable by some proposition φ about their properties (i. e., their attribute values and the links they participate in) in order to be uniquely identified by C.allInstances $\rightarrow$ any(φ). This is not possible in general, as there is no way to guarantee the identity uniqueness of an object by an OCL expression.

While there is no garbage collection for objects, there is implicit garbage collection for links. If an object is destroyed, all links, in which this object is participating in, are deleted as well.

Example. The following program creates a company and a project, establishes a link between them, and then destroys one of the objects.

```
1    c : = new Company;
2    p : = new Project;
3    insert (c,p) into CarriesOut;
4    destroy c
```

After executing these statements, the tuple (c, p) is not longer present in the extent of the CarriesOut association, and the expressions c and p.company will evaluate to Undefined. $\square$

Notice that all variables that reference an object are set to Undefined when the object is destroyed. Thus, after

```
1    x := new Project;
2    y := x;
3    destroy y
```

Both variables x and y contain the undefined value.

4.1.6 Modularity of SOIL and OCL

We already described that only query operations can be used within OCL expressions, even if these expressions occur embedded in statements. For the same reason we did not allow, for example, *new Qualification* to occur in expressions. We motivated this restriction in Sect. 2.2.

Consequently, SOIL does not support a *compute* expression, as ImperativeOCL does. We shortly recapitulate *compute*. The following 'expression' is valid in ImperativeOCL (but not in OCL).

```
1  y := 1 + compute(x)(<statements calculating x>) + 2
```

Since SOIL embeds OCL unchanged, such constructions are not possible in SOIL and have to be rewritten using pure OCL.

```
1  <statements calculating x>;
2  y := 1 + x + 2
```

Of course, more complex, nested compute expressions require more than two statements. The following imperative expression

```
1  s : = Set{1,2,3}
2  z := 1 + s.collect(y|compute(x)(<calculate x based on y>)->sum + 2)
```

could be rewritten as

```
1  s : = Set{1,2,3};
2  sx := oclEmpty(Bag(Integer));
3  for y in s do
4    <calculate x based on y>;
5    sx := sx->including(x)
6  end;
7  z := 1 + sx->sum + 2
```

Remark: We use the predefined constructor oclEmpty(Bag(Integer)) in the above example to get an empty Bag of type *Bag(Integer)*.

4.1.7 Summary

Table 4.1 on the following page summarizes the informal introduction of SOIL.

Operation invocation
<ul><li>Query operations can be only used in OCL expressions.</li><li>Operations with side-effects be only invoked by a special kind of invocation statements. They cannot be used as part of expressions such as $z := f(x) + g(y)$ or $z := f(g(x), h(y))$ (given f, g, h being operations with side-effects). Such nested constructions have to be split up into several statements using intermediate variables.</li></ul>
Variable declaration and type-safety
<ul><li>There is no explicit variable declaration. The general rule is: If a statement assigns a value to a variable, this variable is allowed to occur as a free variable in subsequent statements (assuming consistent types). The type of the variable is inferred.</li><li>A variable may be assigned more than once in a compound statement. This overrides previously inferred variable types.</li><li>Special rules hold for *if* and *for* statements:<ul><li>If a variable is assigned within the body of such a statement, the inferred type is not propagated.</li><li>In the body, only type-conforming assignments must be made to variables which are bound by a previous statement.</li><li>No assignments are allowed to an iterator variable.</li></ul></li></ul>
Garbage collection
<ul><li>Objects are destroyed explicitly. An object's lifetime is not related to variables referencing it.</li><li>If an object is destroyed, all references to it (variables, attributes, links) are removed implicitly.</li></ul>
Error handling
<ul><li>There is no sophisticated error handling (this is future work, as explained later in Sect. 4.6).</li><li>The occurrence of the undefined value where it is not expected results in a statement that has no effect.</li></ul>

Table 4.1: Summary of important aspects of SOIL

4.2 Variable Stacks and Data Signatures for Statements

In the previous section, we introduced SOIL informally. In this and the following sections we now provide a formal definition for SOIL. We follow the denotational, set-theoretic approach that is applied for UML and OCL in Chap. 3. We first introduce some preliminaries regarding the environment for statements. Then, we define the syntax and semantics of statements in Sect. 4.3. Section 4.4 provides several examples to illustrate these definitions.

This section provides two important definitions: (1) the notion of a variable stack over a system state, and (2) the notion of a data signature for statements, which builds on the notion of an operation with side-effects, that we also define in this section.

4.2.1 Variable Stack

The evaluation of OCL expressions, as defined in Sect. 3.3.2.3, requires a 'flat' mapping $\beta : \mathrm{Var}_t \rightarrow I(t)$ which assigns values to typed variables. For the evaluation of statements, we require a stack-like structure. The elements ('frames') of this structure correspond to invocations of operations with side-effects. When it comes to the evaluation of expressions (as part of statements), the most recent frame of the stack contains those variables that are visible for the evaluation of expressions in the current context. Such a stack architecture is very common in the implementation of computer language (c.f. [ALSU07]).

Definition 4.1 (Variable Stack). Given a data signature for expressions $\Sigma_{\mathcal{M}} = (T_{\mathcal{M}}, \leq, \Omega_{\mathcal{M}})$ over $\mathcal{M}$. Let B be the set of all assignments of typed variables to their domains $\beta : \mathrm{Var}_t \rightarrow I(t)$. Let $\overline{B}$ be the set of all mappings from variable names to any domain $b : \mathrm{Varname} \rightarrow \bigcup_{t \in T_{\mathcal{M}}} I(t)$.

The set of variable stacks S over a system state σ is the set of all sequences of mappings $\zeta = \langle b_1, \ldots, b_n \rangle$, $b_i \in \overline{B}$ with the following property:

$$\forall i, v, c, x : (v \mapsto x) \in b_i \wedge c \in \mathrm{CLASS}_{\mathcal{M}} \wedge x \in I\big(\mathrm{typeOf}(c)\big)$$
$$\rightarrow x \in \sigma_{\mathrm{CLASS}}(c) \cup \{\bot\}$$

I. e., all object values in a variable stack ζ over σ have to be in σ (no dangling object references).

We define five functions to query and manipulate variable stacks. These functions $\downarrow : S \rightarrow S$ ('push'), $\uparrow : S \rightarrow S$ ('pop'), $/ : S \times \mathrm{Varname} \times \bigcup_{t \in T_{\mathcal{M}}} I(t) \rightarrow S$ ('assign'), $\mathrm{val} : S \times \mathrm{Varname} \rightarrow \bigcup_{t \in T_{\mathcal{M}}} I(t)$ ('current value') and $\mathrm{binding} : S \rightarrow B$ ('typed binding') are defined as follows.

i. $\downarrow\zeta = \zeta \circ \emptyset$

ii. $\uparrow\langle b_1, \ldots b_{n-1}, b_n\rangle = \langle b_1, \ldots, b_{n-1}\rangle$

iii. $\langle b_1, \ldots, b_n\rangle\{v/x\} := \langle b_1, \ldots, b_n\{v/x\}\rangle$

iv. $\mathrm{val}(\langle b_1, \ldots, b_n\rangle, v) := \begin{cases} x & \text{if } v \mapsto x \in b_n \\ \bot & \text{otherwise} \end{cases}$

v. $\mathrm{binding}(\zeta) := \{(v_t, x) \mid v \in \mathrm{Varname}, t \in T_{\mathcal{M}}, \mathrm{val}(\zeta, v) \in I(t)\}$

$\square$

Unlike β, which maps typed variables to the corresponding interpretations, ζ is untyped, it maps variable names to the union of the interpretations of all types. The functions 'push' and 'pop' achieve stack-like manipulation of variable stacks. The 'assign' function manipulates the most recent element. The function 'current value' retrieves the current value for a variable name, or $\bot$ if there is no binding for this variable name. The function 'typed binding' yields a mapping from typed variable to their domains. Notice that, for technical reasons, both of the last two functions are total functions.

Remark (On the usage of variable names and typed variables). Richters uses a family of typed variables $\mathrm{Var} = \{\mathrm{Var}_t\}_{t \in T_{\mathcal{M}}}$ in his formalization of OCL. Elements of Var are represented as v_t where v is the variable name and t is the variable type. In the formalization of SOIL, we stick to this concept but we define Var as the set of all variables.

Please note, that we treat a typed variable v_t as a tuple (v, t) where $v \in \mathrm{Varname}$ and $t \in T_{\mathcal{M}}$. At many locations we will quantify over the type independently from the variable name.

Especially, given $v_t, v_{t'} \in \mathrm{Var}$, v_t and $v_{t'}$ have the same variable name but (possibly) different types. Therefore, the two variables x_{Integer} and x_{String} have the same variable name (x). This is illustrated by the next definition below.

In subsequent formulas, we will use an upright type instead of an italic type to denote a concrete variable name. Thus, $\mathrm{v} := 1$ denotes an assignment to the variable named 'v', whereas $v := 1$ denotes an assignment to a variable whose name is given by v.

As we will explain later, the context for the evaluation of statements will be given by a pair of a system state σ and a variable stack ζ over σ. When we need to evaluate an expression $e \in \mathrm{Expr}$ in this context, we will use the binding function to get the context for expression evaluation

$I[\![e]\!](\sigma, \mathrm{binding}(\zeta))$. The following example illustrates the relationships of ζ, β, and σ.

Example. Assume a model $\mathcal{M}$ with $\mathrm{CLASS} = \{c_1, c_2\}$ and $c_2 \prec c_1$, and system states σ, σ' over $\mathcal{M}$ with $\sigma_{\mathrm{CLASS}}(c_1) = \{\underline{a}, \underline{b}\}$, $\sigma_{\mathrm{CLASS}}(c_2) = \{\underline{b}\}$ and $\sigma'_{\mathrm{CLASS}}(c_1) = \{\underline{b}\}$, $\sigma'_{\mathrm{CLASS}}(c_2) = \{\underline{b}\}$.

Let $x, y, z, w \in \mathrm{Varname}$ and

$$\zeta = \langle \{x \mapsto \underline{a}, y \mapsto 42\}, \{z \mapsto 12, w \mapsto \underline{b}\} \rangle$$

and

$$\zeta' = \langle \{x \mapsto \underline{b}\}, \{w \mapsto 42\} \rangle.$$

In this setting, ζ is a variable stack over σ, but not over σ' as $\underline{a} \notin \sigma'_{\mathrm{CLASS}}(c)$, whereas ζ' is a variable stack over both σ and σ'.

We have

$$\mathrm{binding}(\zeta) \supset \{w_{\mathrm{OclAny}} \mapsto \underline{b}, w_{\mathrm{typeOf}(c_1)} \mapsto \underline{b}, w_{\mathrm{typeOf}(c_2)} \mapsto \underline{b},$$
$$z_{\mathrm{OclAny}} \mapsto 12, z_{\mathrm{Integer}} \mapsto 12\}$$

and

$$\mathrm{binding}(\zeta') \supset \{w_{\mathrm{OclAny}} \mapsto 42, w_{\mathrm{Integer}} \mapsto 42\}.$$

$\square$

To simplify the following definition of the interpretation of Stat, we define shorthand notations for the previously defined functions for pairs (σ, ζ): $\downarrow(\sigma, \zeta) := (\sigma, \downarrow\zeta)$, $\uparrow(\sigma, \zeta) := (\sigma, \uparrow\zeta)$, $(\sigma, \zeta)\{v/x\} := (\sigma, \zeta\{v/x\})$, and $\mathrm{binding}(\sigma, \zeta) := \mathrm{binding}(\zeta)$.

Although a variable name will occur several times in $\mathrm{binding}(\zeta)$ due to polymorphism, all occurrences of this name will be mapped to the same value.

Theorem 4.2 (all equally named variables in $\mathrm{binding}(\zeta)$ have the same value).

$$\forall v, t, t', x, y \; : \; (v_t, x) \in \mathrm{binding}(\zeta) \wedge (v_{t'}, y) \in \mathrm{binding}(\zeta) \to x = y$$

$\square$

Remark. To compact and increase the readability of the following proofs we will silently apply Thm. 4.2 from here on. Therefore, from $(v_t, x) \in \mathrm{binding}(\zeta)$ and $(v_{t'}, y) \in \mathrm{binding}(\zeta)$ we will implicitly deduce $x = y$.

Theorem 4.3 (all supertype variables are included in $\mathrm{binding}(\zeta)$).

$$\forall v, t, t', x \; : \; (v_t, x) \in \mathrm{binding}(\zeta) \wedge t \leq t' \to (v_{t'}, x) \in \mathrm{binding}(\zeta)$$

$\square$

Proof for theorem 4.3. Assuming $(v_t, x) \in \text{binding}(\zeta)$ and $t \leq t'$. By definition of $I(t)$ we have $x \in I(t) \wedge t \leq t' \rightarrow x \in I(t')$. By definition of binding we
have $(v, x) \in I(t') \rightarrow (v_{t'}, x) \in \text{binding}(\zeta)$.   □

4.2.2   Operations with Side-Effects

So far, the notion of an operation already occurred twice in a formal sense:

1. within a model definition $\mathcal{M}$, as a part OP_c of a class definition (Def. 3.3
   on page 36).

2. within the formalization of OCL expressions, as side-effect free query
   operations $\omega \in \Omega$, as part of the data signature (Def. 3.28 on page 56).

In the following, we will introduce a third notion of operations with side-
effects, as part of the formalization of statements.

The interpretation of an operation with side-effects maps a system state, a
variable stack and zero or more parameters to a new system state and a new
variable stack. If the operation has a return value, the interpretation yields
a return value as well.

Definition 4.4 (Operation with side-effects). The syntax of an operation
with side-effects without return value is defined by a signature $\overline{\omega} : t_1 \times \cdots \times t_n$.
The signature contains the operation symbol $\overline{\omega}$ and a list of parameter types
$t_1, \ldots, t_n \in T$. The syntax of an operation with side-effects with return value
is defined by a signature $\overline{\omega} : t_1 \times \cdots \times t_n \rightarrow t$, additionally containing a return
type $t \in T$.

Let $\mu_{\mathcal{M}}$ be the set of all system states σ of $\mathcal{M}$. Let the statement environment
Env_{Stat} be the set of all pairs (σ, ζ) of a system state σ and variable stack ζ
over σ.

The semantics of an operation with side-effects without return value with a
signature $\overline{\omega} : t_1 \times \cdots \times t_n$ is a total function

$$I(\overline{\omega}) : \text{Env}_{\text{Stat}} \times I(t_1) \times \cdots \times I(t_n) \rightarrow \text{Env}_{\text{Stat}}$$

with the following property: Given

$$I(\overline{\omega})(\sigma, \langle b_1, \ldots, b_n \rangle, x_1, \ldots, x_n) = (\sigma', \langle b'_1, \ldots, b'_m \rangle)$$

then $n = m$ and

$$\forall v, i : 1 \leq i \leq n \rightarrow \left(b'_i(v) = b_i(v) \ \vee \ b'_i(v) = \bot \right).$$

The semantics of an operation with side-effects with return value with a signature $\overline{\omega} : t_1 \times \cdots \times t_n \to t$ is a total function

$$I(\overline{\omega}) : \text{Env}_{\text{Stat}} \times I(t_1) \times \cdots \times I(t_n) \to \text{Env}_{\text{Stat}} \times I(t)$$

with the following property: Given

$$I(\overline{\omega})(\sigma, \langle b_1, \ldots, b_n \rangle, x_1, \ldots, x_n) = (\sigma', \langle b'_1, \ldots, b'_m \rangle, y)$$

then $n = m$ and

$$\forall v, i : 1 \leq i \leq n \to \big(b'_i(v) = b_i(v) \ \vee \ b'_i(v) = \bot\big)$$

and – if t is an object type – $y \in \sigma'_{\text{CLASS}}\big(\text{classOf}(t)\big) \cup \{\bot\}$.

$\square$

Figure 4.3 illustrates the relationship between OP_c, $\Omega_\mathcal{M}$ and $\overline{\Omega}_\mathcal{M}$. For each operation op in OP_c that is a query operation (without side-effects), we have a correspondence ω in $\Omega_\mathcal{M}$ for the semantics of expressions. For each operation op in OP_c that is an operation with side-effects, we have, analogously, a correspondence $\overline{\omega}$ in $\overline{\Omega}_\mathcal{M}$ for the semantics of statements.

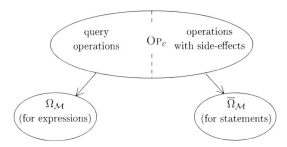

Figure 4.3: Operations

As said before, the interpretation of every operation invocation is evaluated in its own, initially empty frame. Thus, variable assignments are not visible in the caller's variable stack in general. However, object destruction can set variables to $\bot$ in any frame within the variable stack (c.f. 4.1.5 on page 73). Therefore, the interpretation of an operation with side-effects yields not only a new system state but also a new variable stack. Apart from setting variables to $\bot$, Def. 4.4 requires that the caller's variable stack is unchanged otherwise.

4.2.3   Data Signature for Statements

We combine the definition of a data signature for expressions and the definition of an operation with side-effects to a data signature that provides all elements which are required to formally define the syntax and semantics of statements.

Definition 4.5 (Data signature for statements). Given a model $\mathcal{M}$ and a data signature for expressions $\Sigma_{\mathcal{M}} = (T_{\mathcal{M}}, \leq, \Omega_{\mathcal{M}})$ over $\mathcal{M}$ with $I(\Sigma_{\mathcal{M}}) = \big(I(T_{\mathcal{M}}), I(\leq), I(\Omega_{\mathcal{M}})\big)$.

The syntax of a data signature for statements over $\mathcal{M}$ is a structure $\overline{\Sigma}_{\mathcal{M}} = (T_{\mathcal{M}}, \leq, \Omega_{\mathcal{M}}, \overline{\Omega}_{\mathcal{M}})$ where $\overline{\Omega}_{\mathcal{M}}$ is the set of operations with side-effects over $\mathcal{M}$.

The semantics of $\overline{\Sigma}_{\mathcal{M}}$ is a structure $I(\overline{\Sigma}_{\mathcal{M}}) = (I(T_{\mathcal{M}}), I(\leq), I(\Omega_{\mathcal{M}}), I(\overline{\Omega}_{\mathcal{M}}))$ where $I(\overline{\Omega}_{\mathcal{M}})$ assigns each operation $\overline{\omega} : t_1 \times \cdots \times t_n \in \overline{\Omega}_{\mathcal{M}}$ a total function $I(\omega) : \mathrm{Env}_{\mathrm{Stat}} \times I(t_1) \times \cdots \times I(t_n) \to \mathrm{Env}_{\mathrm{Stat}}$ and each operation $\overline{\omega} : t_1 \times \cdots \times t_n \to t \in \overline{\Omega}_{\mathcal{M}}$ a total function $I(\omega) : \mathrm{Env}_{\mathrm{Stat}} \times I(t_1) \times \cdots \times I(t_n) \to \mathrm{Env}_{\mathrm{Stat}} \times I(t)$. □

4.3   Statements

In the last section, we defined the notions of a variable stack and a data signature for statements. Now we have all preliminaries to define statements.

4.3.1   Syntax of Statements

Let $\overline{\Sigma}_{\mathcal{M}} = (T_{\mathcal{M}}, \leq, \Omega_{\mathcal{M}}, \overline{\Omega}_{\mathcal{M}})$ be a data signature for statements over a model $\mathcal{M} = (\mathrm{CLASS}, \mathrm{ATT}_c, \mathrm{OP}_c, \mathrm{ASSOC}, \mathrm{associates}, \mathrm{roles}, \mathrm{multiplicities}, \prec)$. Let $\mathrm{Var} = \bigcup_{t \in T_{\mathcal{M}}} \mathrm{Var}_t$ be the set of all typed variables with Var_t being the set of all variables of type t. The syntax of expressions over the signature $\Sigma_{\mathcal{M}}$ is given by a set $\mathrm{Expr} = \{\mathrm{Expr}_t\}_{t \in T_{\mathcal{M}}}$ and a function $\mathrm{free} : \mathrm{Expr} \to \mathcal{F}(\mathrm{Var})$ as defined in Sect. 3.3. The syntax of statements over $\overline{\Sigma}_{\mathcal{M}}$ is given by a set Stat and three functions $\mathrm{free} : \mathrm{Stat} \to \mathcal{F}(\mathrm{Var})$, $\mathrm{assigned} : \mathrm{Stat} \to \mathcal{F}(\mathrm{Var})$, and $\mathrm{bound} : \mathrm{Stat} \to \mathcal{F}(\mathrm{Var})$ defined in this section.

The set Stat contains the set of all SOIL statements. The three functions are the foundation to establish type-safety and to allow implicit variable declaration in SOIL.

- The set $\mathrm{free}(s)$ is the set of typed variables which must be present in a variable binding in order to execute the statement s. This function works analogously to the function free in the syntax of OCL expressions (Def. 3.3.2.1). It determines under which circumstances the interpretation of this statement is defined.

- The set assigned(s) contains all variables which might be modified by an execution of s. The emphasis is on 'might'. A variable which is in assigned(s) might as well stay unmodified. This set can be regarded as the maximum impact of a statement with respect to the variables in the variable stacks before and after executing this statement. Notice that the assignment of the undefined value $\perp$ will not be covered by this set. The reason is, that we use this set to determine which variable *types* are impacted by s. The actual change of the value is not important. As the value $\perp$ conforms to any type, it is 'harmless' w. r. t. type-safety and is not considered by this set.

- The set bound(s) contains all variables which definitely have a value of the corresponding type after executing this statement. This set can be regarded as the minimum impact of s. It determines which variables can be regarded as implicitly declared in a subsequent statement. Fig. 4.2 on page 71 in the first section of this chapter shows an example for the bound sets of several statements. For all types of statements in the following, the variable names in bound(s) are a subset of the variable names in assigned(s). The two sets differ, for example, for a conditional execution (if-statement). Variable modifications made within the then-clause are not guaranteed to be executed. Thus, a conditional execution always has an empty bound(s) set, whereas it can have a non-empty assigned set (if the then-clause contains variable modifications).

In order to concisely define Stat, free, assigned, and bound in the following, we first introduce the notion of the 'polymorphic difference' between two sets of variables:

Definition 4.6 (Polymorphic difference). We define the polymorphic difference of two sets of variables as $\ominus : \mathcal{F}(\text{Var}) \times \mathcal{F}(\text{Var}) \to \mathcal{F}(\text{Var})$ with

$$V_1 \ominus V_2 := \{v_t \mid v_t \in V_1 \wedge \not\exists t' : v_{t'} \in V_2\}$$

$\square$

This relation can be interpreted as: $\ominus$ removes all equally named variables, disregarding the type. For example: $\{v_{\text{Real}}, w_{\text{Real}}\} \ominus \{v_{\text{Integer}}\} = \{w_{\text{Real}}\}$.

We now define the syntax of SOIL statements. The definition consists of twelve different types of statements. Nine of them are atomic statements, and three of them construct statements from one or more other statements recursively. For the sake of clarity of this and the following definitions, we decided to present complete examples for the syntax and semantics of statements in Sect. 4.4 on page 96. We encourage the reader to consult the syntax part of the examples after reading this section for the first time.

Definition 4.7 (Syntax of Statements).

i. (empty statement)

$$\Diamond \in \text{Stat}$$

$$\text{free}(\Diamond) := \emptyset, \ \text{bound}(\Diamond) := \emptyset, \ \text{assigned}(\Diamond) := \emptyset.$$

ii. (sequence)

Given

(a) $s_1, s_2 \in$ Stat with

(b) $\forall v, t : v_t \in \text{bound}(s_1) \ominus \text{bound}(s_2) \rightarrow$
$\left[\forall t' : v_{t'} \in \text{assigned}(s_2) \rightarrow t' \leq t \right]$

(c) $\forall v, t : \exists t' : v_{t'} \in \text{assigned}(s_1) \land t' \not\leq t \rightarrow$
$v_t \notin \left[\text{free}(s_2) \ominus \text{bound}(s_1) \right]$

then $s_1; s_2 \in$ Stat and

$$
\begin{aligned}
\text{free}(s_1; s_2) &:= \text{free}(s_1) \cup \left(\text{free}(s_2) \ominus \text{bound}(s_1) \right) \\
\text{assigned}(s_1; s_2) &:= \text{assigned}(s_1) \cup \text{assigned}(s_2) \\
\text{bound}(s_1; s_2) &:= \text{bound}(s_2) \cup \left(\text{bound}(s_1) \ominus \text{bound}(s_2) \right).
\end{aligned}
$$

iii. (variable assignment)
If $v \in$ Varname, $e_t \in \text{Expr}_t$ then $\boldsymbol{v := e_t} \in$ Stat and
$\text{free}(v := e_t) := \text{free}(e_t)$, $\text{assigned}(v := e_t) := \{v_t\}$,
$\text{bound}(v := e_t) := \{v_t\}$.

iv. (attribute assignment)
If $e_1 \in \text{Expr}_{t_1}$, $e_2 \in \text{Expr}_{t_2}$, $c = \text{classOf}(t_1)$, and $a : t_1 \rightarrow t_2 \in \text{ATT}_c^*$
then $\boldsymbol{e_1.a := e_2} \in$ Stat, $\text{free}(e_1.a := e_2) = \text{free}(e_1) \cup \text{free}(e_2)$,
$\text{assigned}(e_1.a := e_2) = \emptyset$, $\text{bound}(e_1.a := e_2) := \emptyset$.

v. (object creation)
If $v \in$ Varname, $c \in$ CLASS, and $t = \text{typeOf}(c)$ then $\boldsymbol{v := \ \textbf{new} \ c}$
$\in$ Stat, $\text{assigned}(v := \ \text{new} \ c) = \{v_t\}$, $\text{bound}(v := \ \text{new} \ c) = \{v_t\}$, and
$\text{free}(v := \ \text{new} \ c) := \emptyset$.

vi. (object destruction)
If $e \in \text{Expr}_t$, $t = \text{typeOf}(c)$ and $c \in$ CLASS then $\boldsymbol{destroy \ e} \in$ Stat,
$\text{free}(\text{destroy} \ e) := \text{free}(e)$, $\text{assigned}(\text{destroy} \ e) := \emptyset$, and
$\text{bound}(\text{destroy} \ e) := \emptyset$.

vii. (link insertion)

If $e_i \in \text{Expr}_{t_i}$, $1 \le i \le n$, $a \in \text{ASSOC}$, associates$(a) = \langle c_1, \ldots, c_n \rangle$, $t_i \le \text{typeOf}(c_i)$ then **insert $(e_1, \ldots, e_n)$ into a** $\in$ Stat, free(insert $(e_1 \ldots, e_n)$ into a) := free$(e_1) \cup \cdots \cup$ free(e_n), assigned(insert $(e_1, \ldots, e_n)$ into a) := $\emptyset$, and bound(insert $(e_1, \ldots, e_n)$ into a) := $\emptyset$.

viii. (link deletion)

If $e_i \in \text{Expr}_{t_i}$, $i \in 1 \ldots n$, $a \in \text{ASSOC}$, associates$(a) = \langle c_1, \ldots, c_n \rangle$, $t_i \le \text{typeOf}(c_i)$ then **delete $(e_1, \ldots, e_n)$ from a** $\in$ Stat, free(delete $(e_1 \ldots, e_n)$ from a) := free$(e_1) \cup \cdots \cup$ free(e_n), assigned(delete $(e_1, \ldots, e_n)$ from a) := $\emptyset$, and bound(delete $(e_1, \ldots, e_n)$ from a) := $\emptyset$.

ix. (conditional execution)

If $e \in \text{Expr}_{\text{Boolean}}$ and $s_1 \in$ Stat then **if e then s_1 end** $\in$ Stat, free(if e then s_1 end) := free$(e) \cup$ free(s_1), assigned(if e then s_1 end) := assigned(s_1), and bound(if e then s_1 end) := $\emptyset$.

If further $s_2 \in$ Stat then **if e then s_1 else s_2 end** $\in$ Stat, free(if e then s_1 else s_2 end) := free$(e) \cup$ free$(s_1) \cup$ free(s_2), assigned(if e then s_1 else s_2 end) := assigned$(s_1) \cup$ assigned(s_2), and bound(if e then s_1 else s_2 end) := $\emptyset$.

x. (iteration)

If $e \in \text{Expr}_{\text{Sequence}(t)}$, $v \in$ Varname, $s \in$ Stat, $\nexists t' : v_{t'} \in$ assigned(s), and $\nexists t' : v_{t'} \in$ free$(s) \wedge t \not\le t'$ then **for v in e do s end** $\in$ Stat, free(for v in e do s end) := free$(e) \cup \big(\text{free}(s) \ominus \{v_t\}\big)$, assigned(for v in e do s end) := assigned$(s) \cup \{v_t\}$, and bound(for v in e do s end) := $\emptyset$.

xi. (operation call without result)

If $e_1 \in \text{Expr}_{t_1}, \ldots, e_n \in \text{Expr}_{t_n}$ and $\overline{\omega} : (v_1 : t_1, \ldots, v_n : t_n) \in \overline{\Omega}_\mathcal{M}$ then **$\overline{\omega}(e_1, \ldots, e_n)$** $\in$ Stat, free$\big(\overline{\omega}(e_1, \ldots, e_n)\big) = $ free$(e_1) \cup \cdots \cup$ free(e_n), assigned$\big(\overline{\omega}(e_1, \ldots, e_n)\big) = \emptyset$, and bound$\big((\overline{\omega}(e_1, \ldots, e_n)\big) = \emptyset$.

xii. (operation call with result)

If $e_1 \in \text{Expr}_{t_1}, \ldots, e_n \in \text{Expr}_{t_n}$, $v \in$ Varname, and $\overline{\omega} : (v_1 : t_1, \ldots, v_n : t_n \to t) \in \Omega_\mathcal{M}$ then **$v := \overline{\omega}(e_1, \ldots, e_n)$** $\in$ Stat, free$\big(v := \overline{\omega}(e_1, \ldots, e_n)\big) = $ free$(e_1) \cup \cdots \cup$ free(e_n), assigned$\big(v := \overline{\omega}(e_1, \ldots, e_n)\big) = \{v_t\}$, and bound$\big(v := \overline{\omega}(e_1, \ldots, e_n)\big) = \{v_t\}$.

$\square$

The above definition formalizes the properties of SOILthat we have introduced in Sect. 4.1.

The empty statement (i) is required to specify 'no effect' where a statement is required. Examples for empty statements are the body of an operation that does nothing, and the empty else-branch of a conditional execution (if-statement).

The sequence constructor for statements (ii) enables the construction of programs from sequences of statements. Given two statements, the concatenation of them is again a statement, as long as certain properties are fulfilled for the free, assigned, and bound sets of both statements. These properties ensure type-safety and are explained in the following subsection. While the sequence $s_1; s_2; s_3$ can be constructed as $(s_1; s_2); s_3$ and also as $s_1; (s_2; s_3)$, we assume left associativity when writing SOIL statements in the following. The (typed) free variables of a sequence $s_1; s_2$ are all variables that are free in the first statement plus those variables, that are free in the second statement and which are not bound by the first statement. For example, free$(x := 42; x := y_{\text{Integer}} + 1) = \{y_{\text{Integer}}\}$ and free$(x := 42; x := x_{\text{Integer}} + 1) = \emptyset$. The assigned set (i. e., the variables that *might* be modified) contains the assigned variables from both statements. The bound set contains all those variables that are bound by the first statement and which are not re-bound by the second one, plus all bound variables of the second statement. For example, bound$(x := 42; y := \text{'42'}) = \{x_{\text{Integer}}, y_{\text{String}}\}$ and bound$(x := 42; x := \text{'42'}) = \{x_{\text{String}}\}$. The second example shows how a previously bound variable type is changed ('re-bound') by a later statement.

The variable assignment (iii) contains a value expression of a certain type and a variable name. The free variables of the variable assignment are the free variables of the value expression. For example, free$(x := y_{\text{Integer}} + 1) = \{y_{\text{Integer}}\}$. The assigned and bound sets contain the variable name with the expression type. Thus, for $v := 12$, we have bound$(v := 12) = \{v_{\text{Integer}}\}$.

An attribute assignment (iv) requires two expressions that match the types required by the signature of the attribute. Thus, the type of the left-hand side expression has to be of an object type. The attribute mapping has to be in the full descriptor of the class identified by the left-hand side expression type. The free set contains the free variables from both expressions. An attribute assignment does not bind or assign any variables.

Object creation (v) requires a variable name and a class of $\mathcal{M}$. Obviously, it assigns and binds this variable. Object destruction (vi) requires an expression of an object type. The free variables are given by the free variables of this expression. While this statement actually modifies variables, as we will see shortly, the assigned as well as the bound sets are empty, as only the undefined value $\perp$ is assigned by this statement.

Link insertion (vii) and link deletion (viii) both require an association of $\mathcal{M}$ plus n expressions that match the types required by the classes participating in the association. Thus, the free variables of these statements are the free variables of all expressions. Link manipulation does neither assign nor bind any variables.

Iteration (x) requires a sequence typed range expression and a statement. The assigned and free set of this inner statement have to fulfill certain properties to ensure type-safety, as explained in the following section. An iteration can never bind any variables, as the statement is not guaranteed to be executed at least once. However, an iteration assigns all variables that the inner statement assigns, plus the iterator variable. The iterator variable cannot be changed within the body of an iteration, as explained in Sect. 4.1.3.

The operation call without a result value (xi) requires a corresponding imperative operation (without a result type) and n expressions that match the types of the operation signature. Therefore, the operation call has the free variables of all of its argument expressions. The operation call never binds or assigns any variables. Notice that, if we provide the definition for this operation by means of a statement, this statement might modify variables, but these variables are not visible w.r.t. the current context. The operation call with result (xii) is analogous to (xi), except that it requires an operation signature that has a return type, and that it binds and assigns its result variable (as for variable assignment).

4.3.1.1 Rules for Type-Safety

To achieve guaranteed variable assignments and type-safety, we distinguish between possible and guaranteed modifications of variables. A variable contained in the bound set of a statement is guaranteed to always contain a value of the corresponding type in the interpretation of the statement. This variable can be regarded as 'implicitly declared' for a subsequent statement. On the contrary, a variable contained in the assigned set might be modified by the statement, but this is not guaranteed to happen.

In the previous definition, the restrictions of the sequence constructor (ii) play a central role in enforcing type-safety. Restriction (iib) requires that a non-guaranteed modification of a variable in the second statement must be type-conformant with any guaranteed modification of this variable in the first statement. Therefore, x := 1; if 1 = 2 then x := 2 end is valid whereas x := 1; if 1 = 2 then x := '2' end is not (notice the different values in both example). The latter statement does not fulfill restriction (iib). The reason is, that we can neither guarantee that x is of type Integer nor that it is of type String after executing the above sequence (we can in this example, actually, but in general we have to assume a boolean expression of an unknown value for the condition).

Restriction (iic) ensures that no non-binding assignment must take place in the first statement that collides with the free variables of the second statement. Therefore, $x := 2 + y_{Integer}$ is a valid statement (having $y_{Integer}$ as a free variable), as well as $y := 1; x := 2 + y_{Integer}$ (having no free variables), but if b then $y := '1'$ end; $x := 2 + y_{Integer}$ is not (the last example violates restriction (iic). If it would be valid, it had a free variable $y_{Integer}$, because the conditional execution does never bind any variables. But even if we provided an Integer value in $y_{Integer}$ for the execution of the whole statement, we might have a String value for $y_{Integer}$ when it comes to the execution of $x := 2 + y_{Integer}$, yielding an undefined result.

For the same reason, the conditional execution (ix) does not bind any variables, even if the statements in the two bodies do. These sub-statements are not guaranteed to be executed. Thus, their assigned sets are propagated to the iteration statement, but the bound sets are not. A similar rule exists for iteration (iic). Assignments within the body of an iteration are not guaranteed to be executed, as the range expression could be the empty sequence.

Notice that in a sequence of statements, the type of the free variable of a statement may differ from the value type that is assigned to that variable name by an earlier statement. For example, the free variables of the statement $y := x_{OclAny}.\text{isDefined}$ are $\{x_{OclAny}\}$. Nevertheless, the compound statement $x := 1; y := x_{OclAny}.\text{isDefined}$ is in Stat, without free variables. Similar, non-binding assignments can assign values of a more specific type than an earlier binding, such as $x := a;$ if $1 < 2$ then $x := b$ end with expressions $a \in I(t)$ and $b \in I(t')$, and $t' \leq t$.

Finally, notice that a variable name may be bound multiple times in a sequence of statements, with different types. We illustrated this 'rebinding' of variables informally in Fig. 4.2 on page 71 in the first section of this chapter. For example, consider $x := 1; y := x_{Integer} + 1; x := \text{new Worker}; x_{typeOf(Worker)}.\text{salary} := 15; y := x_{typeOf(Worker)}.\text{salary}$. The old binding $\{x_{Integer}, y_{Integer}\}$ is removed from the bound and replaced by $\{x_{typeOf(Worker)}, y_{Integer}\}$ by the third statement. Therefore, the following example $x := 1; y := x_{Integer} + 1; x := \text{new Worker}; y := x_{Integer} + 1$ is not a valid statement (there exists no operation $+ : typeOf(Worker) \times \text{Integer} \to T$).

4.3.2 Semantics of Statements

We now define the semantics of statements. Later in Sect. 4.5 we will prove that this definition is consistent with the syntax of SOIL, i.e., that every $s \in \text{Stat}$ has a well-defined meaning.

Definition 4.8 (Semantics of Statements). Let $\mathrm{Env}_{\mathrm{OCL}}$ be the set of all environments (σ, β). The semantics of an expression $e \in \mathrm{Expr}_t$ is a function $I[\![\, e \,]\!] : \mathrm{Env}_{\mathrm{OCL}} \to I(t)$, as defined in Sect. 3.3.2. Let $\mathrm{Env}_{\mathrm{Stat}}$ be the set of all pairs (σ, ζ) of a system state σ and variable stack ζ over σ. If $\forall v_t : v_t \in \mathrm{free}(s) \to \mathrm{val}(\zeta, v) \in I(t)$, the semantics of a statement $s \in \mathrm{Stat}$ is a function $I[\![\, s \,]\!] : \mathrm{Env}_{\mathrm{Stat}} \to \mathrm{Env}_{\mathrm{Stat}}$.

   i. (empty statement)

$$I[\![\, \Diamond \,]\!](\sigma, \zeta) := (\sigma, \zeta)$$

  ii. (sequence)

$$I[\![\, s_1; s_2 \,]\!](\sigma, \zeta) := I[\![\, s_2 \,]\!]\big(I[\![\, s_1 \,]\!](\sigma, \zeta)\big)$$

 iii. (variable assignment)

$$I[\![\, v := e \,]\!](\sigma, \zeta) := \Big(\sigma, \zeta\{v/I[\![\, e \,]\!](\sigma, \mathrm{binding}(\zeta))\}\Big)$$

 iv. (attribute assignment)

$$I[\![\, e_1.a := e_2 \,]\!](\sigma, \zeta) := \begin{cases} (\sigma', \zeta) & \text{if } I[\![\, e_1 \,]\!]\big(\sigma, \mathrm{binding}(\zeta)\big) \neq \bot \\ (\sigma, \zeta) & \text{otherwise} \end{cases}$$

where $\sigma' := \sigma$ except
$\sigma'_{\mathrm{ATT}}(a) := \sigma_{\mathrm{ATT}}(a)\big\{I[\![\, e_1 \,]\!]\big(\sigma, \mathrm{binding}(\zeta)\big) \,/\, I[\![\, e_2 \,]\!]\big(\sigma, \mathrm{binding}(\zeta)\big)\big\}$

 v. (object creation)

$$I[\![\, v := \mathrm{new}\ c \,]\!](\sigma, \zeta) := (\sigma', \zeta')$$

where $\sigma' := \sigma$ except $\sigma'_{\mathrm{CLASS}}(c) := \sigma_{\mathrm{CLASS}}(c) \cup \{\mathrm{newobj}\}$ with $\mathrm{newobj} \notin \sigma_{\mathrm{CLASS}}(c)$ and $\zeta' := \zeta\{v/\mathrm{newobj}\}$.

 vi. (object destruction)
    Let $\zeta = \langle b_1, \ldots, b_n \rangle$. Let $x = I[\![\, e \,]\!]\big(\sigma, \mathrm{binding}(\zeta)\big)$.

$$I[\![\, \mathrm{destroy}\ e \,]\!](\sigma, \zeta) := \begin{cases} (\sigma', \zeta') & \text{if } I[\![\, e \,]\!]\big(\sigma, \mathrm{binding}(\zeta)\big) \neq \bot \\ (\sigma, \zeta) & \text{otherwise} \end{cases}$$

where $\sigma' := \sigma$ except

$$\sigma'_{\text{CLASS}}(c) := \sigma_{\text{CLASS}}(c) - \{x\},$$
$$\sigma'_{\text{ASSOC}}(a) := \sigma_{\text{ASSOC}}(a)$$
$$- \{(o_1, \ldots, o_n) \mid \exists i : 1 \leq i \leq n \wedge o_i = x\},$$
$$\text{for } a \in \text{ASSOC}$$
$$\sigma'_{\text{ATT}}(a) := \sigma_{\text{ATT}}(a) - \{o_1 \mapsto o_2 \mid o_1 = x \vee o_2 = x\},$$
$$\text{for } a \in \text{ATT}$$

and $\zeta' := \langle b'_1, \ldots, b'_n \rangle$ where
$b'_i := b_i\{v/\bot, \text{ if } b_i(v) = I[\![e]\!](\sigma, \text{binding}(\zeta))\}.$

vii. (link insertion)
Let $x_1, \ldots, x_n = I[\![e_1]\!](\sigma, \text{binding}(\zeta)), \ldots, I[\![e_n]\!](\sigma, \text{binding}(\zeta)).$

$$I[\![\text{insert}(e_1, \ldots, e_n) \text{ into } a]\!](\sigma, \zeta)$$
$$:= \begin{cases} (\sigma', \zeta) & \text{if } \forall i : 1 \leq i \leq n \rightarrow x_i \neq \bot \\ (\sigma, \zeta) & \text{otherwise} \end{cases}$$

where $\sigma' := \sigma$ except
$\sigma'_{\text{ASSOC}}(a) := \sigma_{\text{ASSOC}}(a) \cup \{(x_1, \ldots, x_n)\}.$

viii. (link deletion)
Let $x_1, \ldots, x_n = I[\![e_1]\!](\sigma, \text{binding}(\zeta)), \ldots, I[\![e_n]\!](\sigma, \text{binding}(\zeta)).$

$$I[\![\text{delete}(e_1, \ldots, e_n) \text{ from } a]\!](\sigma, \zeta) := (\sigma', \zeta)$$

where $\sigma' := \sigma$ except
$\sigma'_{\text{ASSOC}}(a) := \sigma_{\text{ASSOC}}(a) - \{(x_1, \ldots, x_n)\}.$

ix. (conditional execution)

$$I[\![\text{if } e \text{ then } s_1 \text{ else } s_2 \text{ end}]\!](\sigma, \zeta)$$
$$:= \begin{cases} I[\![s_1]\!](\sigma, \zeta) & \text{if } I[\![e]\!](\sigma, \text{binding}(\zeta)) = \text{true} \\ I[\![s_2]\!](\sigma, \zeta) & \text{otherwise} \end{cases}$$

$$I[\![\text{if } e \text{ then } s_1 \text{ end}]\!](\sigma, \zeta) := I[\![\text{if } e \text{ then } s_1 \text{ else } \Diamond \text{ end}]\!](\sigma, \zeta)$$

x. (iteration)
Given $I[\![r]\!](\sigma, \text{binding}(\zeta)) = \langle x_1, \ldots, x_n \rangle,$

$$I[\![\text{for } v \text{ in } r \text{ do } s \text{ end}]\!](\sigma, \zeta) := \begin{cases} (\sigma, \zeta) & \text{if } I[\![r]\!](\sigma, \beta(\zeta)) = \langle \rangle \\ I[\![s']\!](\sigma', \zeta') & \text{otherwise} \end{cases}$$

where $s' = \text{for } v \text{ in Sequence}\{x_2, \ldots, x_n\} \text{ do } s \text{ end}$
and $(\sigma', \zeta') = I[\![s]\!](\sigma, \zeta\{v/x_1\}).$

xi. (operation call without result)

Let $\overline{\omega} : (v_1 : t_1, \ldots, v_n : t_n) \in \overline{\Omega}_{\mathcal{M}}$.

Let $x_1, \ldots, x_n = I[\![\, e_1 \,]\!](\sigma, \text{binding}(\zeta)), \ldots, I[\![\, e_n \,]\!](\sigma, \text{binding}(\zeta))$.

$$I[\![\, \overline{\omega}(e_1, \ldots, e_n) \,]\!](\sigma, \zeta) := I(\overline{\omega})(\sigma, \zeta, x_1, \ldots, x_n)$$

xii. (operation call with result)

Let $\overline{\omega} : (v_1 : t_1, \ldots, v_n : t_n \to t) \in \overline{\Omega}_{\mathcal{M}}$.

Let $x_1, \ldots, x_n = I[\![\, e_1 \,]\!](\sigma, \text{binding}(\zeta)), \ldots, I[\![\, e_n \,]\!](\sigma, \text{binding}(\zeta))$.

$$I[\![\, v := \overline{\omega}(e_1, \ldots, e_n) \,]\!](\sigma, \zeta) := (\sigma', \zeta'\{v/z\})$$

where $(\sigma', \zeta', z) = I(\overline{\omega})(\sigma, \zeta, x_1, \ldots, x_n)$

$\square$

Examples for the evaluation of statements can be found in Sect. 4.4. The interpretation of the empty statement (i) does not change the system state or the variable stack in any way. It is required to define empty bodies as part of other statements or operation definitions.

Sequential execution (ii) interprets the second statement in the system state and environment which result from the interpretation of the first.

Variable assignment (iii) binds the value of an OCL expression to a variable in the environment. The expression is interpreted in the most recent frame of the variable stack. The value of the expression is stored in ζ.

Attribute assignment (iv) binds the value of an OCL expression to an attribute of an object identified by another OCL expression. By the definition of the syntax, the expression is always of an object type. If the object expression evaluates to the undefined value ($\bot$), no assignment happens.

Object creation (v) inserts a new object of the specified class into the system state and stores it in the variable v. Object destruction (vi) removes an object specified by an OCL expression from the system state. If there is no such object, the state is not changed. Otherwise, σ' is cleared from all occurrences of the destroyed object: all variables that are bound to the value of the destroyed object are set to $\bot$ and all links containing the object are removed from their link sets. Furthermore, all occurrences of the destroyed object as a value of any attribute assignment are removed, as well as the attribute assignments for the object itself. As for (iv), the object expression is guaranteed to be of an object type, but the interpretation can be the undefined value. If the expression evaluates to the undefined value ($\bot$), no assignment happens.

Link insertion (vii) inserts a link into the link set of an association. The link ends are specified by OCL expressions. If the link already exists in the link set, the link set remains unchanged. For link insertion the same remark holds regarding undefined values as for (iv) and (vi). Link deletion (viii) removes a link from the link set of an association. The link ends are specified by OCL expressions. If the link is not present in the link set, the link set remains unchanged.

Conditional execution (ix) interprets one of two statements depending on the evaluation of a boolean OCL expression. Notice that an undefined value also leads to the interpretation of the second statement. If the *else* part is omitted, it is implicitly assumed to be the empty statement.

Iteration (x) interprets a body statement for each element of an OCL sequence expression. The ordering is as follows: first, the range expression is evaluated, then, the body statement is executed once for each element of the range value. Prior to each execution of the body statements, a new element of the range values is assigned to the iterator variable.

An operation call (xi) yields a new system state and a new variable stack by applying the interpretation of the operation. An operation call with a result value (xii) furthermore binds the result value to a variable. Examples for the evaluation of operation calls can be found in Sect. 4.4.3. Notice that, by Def. 4.4, the interpretation of the object always returns a variable stack ζ' that is unchanged from ζ except for the replacement of some values by $\bot$.

4.3.3   Comparison of One-Step and Step-wise Treatment of Statement Sequences

We want to point out a property which holds for every sequence statement $s_1; \ldots; s_n \in$ Stat. Given a system state σ and a variable stack ζ over σ containing all free variables of $s_1; \ldots; s_n$, the effect (σ', ζ') of $s_1; \ldots; s_n$ is determined by $(\sigma', \zeta') = I[\![s_1; \ldots; s_n]\!](\sigma, \zeta)$.

For any such $s_1; \ldots; s_n \in$ Stat we also have $s_1, \ldots, s_n \in$ Stat and $(\sigma', \zeta') = I[\![s_n]\!]\Big(\ldots I[\![s_2]\!]\big(I[\![s_1]\!](\sigma, \zeta) \big) \ldots \Big)$ is well-defined.

Thus, any one-step treatment of a sequence of statements $s_1, \ldots, s_n$ always has a corresponding step-wise treatment. The reverse direction is not true in general. This has important consequences for the implementation of SOIL in interactive environments. In anticipation of our implementation of SOIL in the UML-based Specification Environment, assume a notation '!s', meaning 'syntax check and execute s in the current environment and make the resulting environment the current environment'. Assume furthermore an initial system state σ and an initial variable stack $\zeta = \langle \emptyset \rangle$. Consider the following example:

```
1   !x := 'Hello'
2   !if Sequence{1,2,3}->sum > 4 then x := 1 end
3   !y := x + 1
```

The example consists of three statement executions. All three statements are in Stat (can be derived syntactically). For any execution, the requirement that all free variables are bound in a type-consistent way is fulfilled. Thus, the three statements can be executed in a row, yielding a final variable stack $\zeta = \langle\{x \mapsto 1, y \mapsto 2\}\rangle$. However, the following statement execution is not valid:

```
1   !x := 'Hello'; if Sequence{1,2,3}->sum then x :=1 end; y := x + 1
```

Both kinds of a step-wise execution and a one-step execution of a sequence of statements are realized in the UML-based Specification Environment, which we explain later in Sect. 5.1.

4.3.4 Defining Operations with Side-Effects by Statements

In Sect 3.3.2.3 we defined a partial mapping oclexp : $\mathrm{OP}_c \to$ Expr that assigns OCL expressions to query operations in OP_c. For all operations op in this mapping, an interpretation for the corresponding operation ω in $\Omega_\mathcal{M}$ is defined. In the same manner, we define a partial mapping stat : $\mathrm{OP}_C \to$ Stat to determine the effect of operations with side-effects by SOIL statements. In Fig. 4.3 on page 81, the mapping oclexp can realize the left-hand side of OP_c in $\Omega_\mathcal{M}$, and the mapping stat can realize the right-hand side of OP_C in $\overline{\Omega}_\mathcal{M}$. The statement associated by stat must contain no free variables other than the formal parameters of $\overline{\omega}$. If $\overline{\omega}$ is an operation with return value, the statement must further have bound variable result_t of the result type t.

Definition 4.9 (Association of operations with side-effects with statements). The partial mapping stat : $\mathrm{OP}_c \to$ Stat associates statements with operations with side-effects where (for operations without result value)

$$\forall w, t : w_t \in \mathrm{free}(s) \to \exists t' : \left[w_{t'} \in \{v_1, \ldots, v_n\} \ \wedge \ t' \leq t \right]$$

must hold for each $\overline{\omega}(v_1 : t_1, \ldots, v_n : t_n) \to s \in$ stat, and (for operations with result value) $\mathrm{result}_t \in \mathrm{bound}(s)$ and

$$\forall w, t : w_t \in \mathrm{free}(s) \to \exists t' : \left[w_{t'} \in \{v_1, \ldots, v_n\} \ \wedge \ t' \leq t \right]$$

must hold for each $\overline{\omega}(v_1 : t_1, \ldots, v_n : t_n \to t) \to s \in$ stat.

For the operations mapped by stat, the semantics is defined as follows. For an operation with side-effects without return value $\overline{\omega}(v_1 : t_1, \ldots, v_n : t_n)$ with

$\overline{\omega}(v_1 : t_1, \ldots, v_n : t_n) \to s \in \text{stat}$, the interpretation of $\overline{\omega}(v_1 : t_1, \ldots, v_n : t_n)$
is defined as

$$I\big(\overline{\omega}(v_1 : t_1, \ldots, v_n : t_n)\big) := \lambda(\sigma, \zeta, x_1, \ldots, x_n) \;.\; (\sigma', \uparrow\zeta')$$

where $(\sigma', \zeta') = I[\![\, s \,]\!](\sigma, \downarrow\zeta \; \{v_1/x_1, \ldots, v_n/x_n\})$.

For an operation with side-effects with return value $\overline{\omega}(v_1 : t_1, \ldots, v_n : t_n \to t)$
with $\quad \overline{\omega}(v_1 : t_1, \ldots, v_n : t_n \to t) \to s \in \text{stat}, \qquad$ the $\quad$ interpretation $\quad$ of
$\overline{\omega}(v_1 : t_1, \ldots, v_n : t_n \to t)$ is defined as

$$I\big(\overline{\omega}(v_1 : t_1, \ldots, v_n : t_n \to t)\big) := \lambda(\sigma, x_1, \ldots, x_n) \;.\; (\sigma', \uparrow\zeta', y)$$

where $(\sigma', \zeta') = I[\![\, s \,]\!](\sigma, \downarrow\zeta \; \{v_1/x_1, \ldots, v_n/x_n\})$ and $y = \text{binding}(\zeta')(\text{result}_t)$. $\qquad\square$

For a well-defined semantics, we need to make sure that there is no infinite
recursion resulting from an expansion of the operation call. A strict solution
that can be statically checked is to forbid any potentially recursive invoca-
tions. This can be done by constructing a directed graph over $\overline{\Omega}_{\mathcal{M}}$ as follows:

Algorithm 4.1 Decide if stat contains recursive invocations

$\quad (V, E) \leftarrow (\overline{\Omega}_{\mathcal{M}}, \emptyset)$
$\quad \textbf{for all } \overline{\omega} \mapsto s \in \text{stat } \textbf{do}$
$\quad\quad \textbf{for all } \text{invocations of } \overline{\omega}' \text{ in } s \textbf{ do}$
$\quad\quad\quad (V, E) \leftarrow (V, E \cup (\overline{\omega}, \overline{\omega}'))$
$\quad\quad \textbf{end for}$
$\quad \textbf{end for}$
$\quad \textbf{if } (V, E) \text{ contains a cycle } \textbf{then}$
$\quad\quad \textbf{return } \text{true}$
$\quad \textbf{else}$
$\quad\quad \textbf{return } \text{false}$
$\quad \textbf{end if}$

We could extend the previous definition such that 'V is cycle-free' has to be
fulfilled. However, allowing recursive operation calls considerably adds to the
expressiveness of SOIL. We therefore allow recursive invocations as long as
the recursion is finite. Unfortunately, this property is generally undecidable.

4.3.5   Summary of the Formalization

In this section we have defined the interpretation of SOIL statements. As OCL
expressions are part of SOIL statements, the definition of the interpretation

of statements refers to the definition of the interpretation of expressions. To summarize the definitions of this section, we put all mathematical objects involved in the formal semantics into Fig. 4.4.

The figure shows the three different layers of semantics for system states, expressions, and statements. Only the last layer has been defined in this section, the other two layers are unchanged from [Ric02] (c. f. Chap.3) with respect to SOIL (the addenda we provided are of general nature).

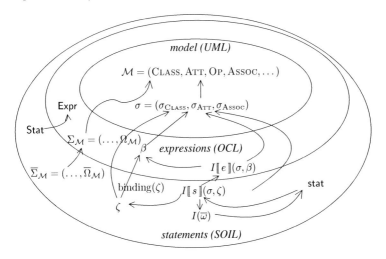

Figure 4.4: Overview: mathematical objects involved in the formal semantics

In the innermost layer (system) we have the model $\mathcal{M}$, containing classes, associations, attributes, etc., and the system state σ, containing objects, links, attribute values, and links for associations. This layer is defined in Sect. 3.2.

In the next layer (expressions) we have a data signature $\Sigma_{\mathcal{M}}$ for expressions over $\mathcal{M}$ that contains the set of query operations $\Omega_{\mathcal{M}}$. We have the set Expr of all OCL expressions that can be syntactically constructed over $\Sigma_{\mathcal{M}}$. We have the function $I[\![e]\!]$ that provides the interpretation for each expression $e \in$ Expr, given a system state σ and a binding function β that provides values for all free variables in e. This layer is defined in Sect. 3.3.

In the outermost layer (statements) we have an extended data signature $\overline{\Sigma}_{\mathcal{M}}$ for statements over $\mathcal{M}$ (Def. 4.5), where we added a set of imperative operations with side-effects $\overline{\Omega}_{\mathcal{M}}$ (Def. 4.4). We have the set of statements Stat that can be syntactically constructed over $\overline{\Sigma}_{\mathcal{M}}$ (Def. 4.7). The interpretation of statements (Def. 4.8) requires the notion of a variable stack ζ (Def. 4.1) which provides a sequence of mappings from variable names to values (stack frames). The function binding(ζ) is a helper which converts the most recent frame in a variable stack in a mapping from typed variables to values. We have the formal interpretation $I(\overline{\omega})$ of an operation $\overline{\omega}$ which is a mapping from a system state, a variable stack and zero or more parameters to a new system state, a new variable stack and (optionally) a return value (Def. 4.4). Based on these definitions we introduced the function $I[\![\,s\,]\!]$ which provides the interpretation for each statement $s \in$ Stat given a system state σ and a variable stack ζ (Def. 4.8). Within the definition of $I[\![\,s\,]\!]$ the interpretation of any expression e in s is given by $I[\![\,e\,]\!]$. Finally, we defined a mapping stat that allows us to define the interpretation of operations with side-effects using statements (Def. 4.9).

4.4 Examples

In this section, we illustrate the formal definitions for the syntax and semantics of statements by several examples. Each example consists of a model $\mathcal{M}$, an initial system state σ, an initially empty environment ζ, and a SOIL statement s. We illustrate the syntactic derivation of s and the derivation of $I[\![\,s\,]\!](\sigma,\zeta)$.

The first example (Sect. 4.4.1) demonstrates the derivation of iterations, sequences, and variable assignments. The second example (Sect. 4.4.2) shows how the state manipulation commands for objects, links and attributes are derived. Finally, the third example (Sect. 4.4.3) illustrates the invocation of operations that are implemented by SOIL statements.

4.4.1 Simple Calculations

The first example is a program that performs arithmetic operations (additions and multiplications) in a loop. Let $\mathcal{M}$ be the empty model (i. e., without classes), and σ be the (empty) system state of $\mathcal{M}$. Let $\zeta = \langle \emptyset \rangle$ be the empty variable stack. Listing 4.4 shows the program (i. e., the SOIL statement) s.

```
1   i:=5;
2   for j in Sequence{1,2,3} do
3     k := i * j;
4     i := i + k
5   end
```

Listing 4.4: First simple calculation

4.4.1.1 Syntactic Derivation

The formal derivation of s is as follows. We use the abbreviations Seq for Sequence and Int for Integer. Notice that the formal representation of an OCL expression requires the usage of typed variables (e. g., $i_{Integer}$), whereas the variable assignment, as defined by SOIL, does not require a type index. Therefore, we have to add type indexes to the variables that occur as part of OCL expressions in the following.

$$\underbrace{i := 5}_{s_1}; \text{ for j in Seq}\{1,2,3\} \text{ do } \underbrace{\underbrace{k := i_{Int} * j_{Int}}_{s_4}; \underbrace{i := i_{Int} + k_{Int}}_{s_5} \text{ end}}_{s_3}}_{s_2}$$

s is a sequence of two statements s_1 and s_2. s_1 is a variable assignment. s_2 is an iteration containing the OCL range expression Seq$\{1,2,3\}$. The body of s_2 is again a sequence of two variable assignments s_4 and s_5.

We have the following assigned, bound, and free sets.

	assigned	bound	free
s	$\{i_{Int}, j_{Int}, k_{Int}\}$	$\{i_{Int}\}$	$\emptyset$
s_1	$\{i_{Int}\}$	$\{i_{Int}\}$	$\emptyset$
s_2	$\{i_{Int}, j_{Int}, k_{Int}\}$	$\emptyset$	$\{i_{Int}\}$
s_3	$\{i_{Int}, k_{Int}\}$	$\{i_{Int}, k_{Int}\}$	$\{i_{Int}, j_{Int}\}$
s_4	$\{k_{Int}\}$	$\{k_{Int}\}$	$\{i_{Int}, j_{Int}\}$
s_5	$\{i_{Int}\}$	$\{i_{Int}\}$	$\{i_{Int}, k_{Int}\}$

We can read this table as follows: s binds i to Integer, meaning that the evaluation of $I[\![s]\!]$ will always produce a guaranteed Integer typed assignment to i. It may furthermore change the variables i, j and k to Integer values. No other variables will be changed to a new value that is different from $\bot$ by s. The statement s does not have any free variables. Looking at the two top-most sub-statements of s, s_1 and s_2, we see that s_2 – viewed in isolation – has a free variable i (Integer typed). The concatenation of both statements is valid according to the requirements in Def. 4.7ii, meaning that all non-binding assignments of s_2 are type consistent with the bound set of s_1 (Def. 4.7iib), and that all non-binding assignments of s_1 are type consistent with the free variables of s_2 (Def. 4.7iic).

Notice that s_3 (the body of the iteration) binds k and i (i. e., makes guaranteed assignments to k and i) but these bindings are not propagated to the bound set of s_2 (according to Def. 4.7x, iterations never bind any variables). The reason is, that, regarding s_2, the variables k, j and i may change but not necessarily (if the interpretation of the range expression of s_2 evaluates

to the empty sequence). The fact, that s_2 may change i, j and j to any value
of type Integer is reflected by the assigned set of s_2.

In s_3 we can see how the concatenation of statements eliminates free variables. Although s_5 has two free variables, i and k, only i is propagated to
the free variables of s_3. The variable k is removed from the free set of the
compound statement because it is bound (in a type consistent way) by s_4.

4.4.1.2   Semantic Derivation

The interpretation of s is as follows (Sequence abbreviated as Seq):

$$I[\![\, s \,]\!](\sigma, \zeta)$$
$$= \quad I[\![\, s_2 \,]\!]\big(I[\![\, i := 5 \,]\!](\sigma, \langle \emptyset \rangle)\big)$$
$$= \quad I[\![\, s_2 \,]\!](\sigma, \langle \{i \mapsto 5\} \rangle)$$
$$= \quad I[\![\, \underbrace{\text{for } j \text{ in } \text{Seq}\{2,3\} \text{ do } s_4; s_5 \text{ end}}_{s_2'} \,]\!]\big(I[\![\, s_4; s_5 \,]\!](\sigma, \langle \{i \mapsto 5\} \rangle \{j/1\})\big)$$
$$= \quad I[\![\, s_2' \,]\!]\big(I[\![\, s_5 \,]\!](I[\![\, s_4 \,]\!](\sigma, \langle \{i \mapsto 5, j \mapsto 1\} \rangle))\big)$$
$$= \quad I[\![\, s_2' \,]\!]\big(I[\![\, s_5 \,]\!](\sigma, \langle \{i \mapsto 5, j \mapsto 1, k \mapsto 5\} \rangle)\big)$$
$$= \quad I[\![\, s_2' \,]\!]\big(\sigma, \langle \{i \mapsto 10, j \mapsto 1, k \mapsto 5\} \rangle\big)$$
$$\ldots$$
$$= \quad I[\![\, \text{for } j \text{ in } \text{Seq}\{3\} \text{ do } s_4; s_5 \text{ end} \,]\!](\sigma, \langle \{i \mapsto 30, j \mapsto 2, k \mapsto 20\} \rangle)$$
$$\ldots$$
$$= \quad I[\![\, \text{for } j \text{ in } \text{Seq}\{\} \text{ do } s_4; s_5 \text{ end} \,]\!](\sigma, \langle \{i \mapsto 120, j \mapsto 3, k \mapsto 90\} \rangle)$$
$$\ldots$$
$$= \quad \big(\sigma, \langle \{i \mapsto 120, j \mapsto 3, k \mapsto 90\} \rangle\big)$$

This example shows the unfolding of the iteration (Definition 4.8x). Jumping
to the last line (the evaluated interpretation of s), we can see the result of
$I[\![\, s \,]\!](\sigma, \zeta)$: The system state σ is unchanged by s, and the variable stack
contains values for the variables i, j and k.

Notice that the resulting variable stack is consistent with the bound and
assigned sets of s: An Integer value is assigned in $I[\![\, s \,]\!](\sigma, \zeta)$ for variable i –
as required by bound(s) –, and no other variables than i, j and k are assigned
in $I[\![\, s \,]\!](\sigma, \zeta)$ – as required by assigned(s).

4.4.2   Modifying System States

The second example modifies a system state (object creation, link insertion,
attribute value assignment).

Let σ be an empty initial system state of $\mathcal{M}$ and $\zeta = \langle \emptyset \rangle$ be our initial variable stack. Listing 4.5 shows a program (i.e., a SOIL statement) s.

```
1   c := new Company;
2   w := new Worker;
3   insert (c,w) into Employs;
4   w.salary := 12000;
5   destroy w
```

Listing 4.5: A Startup

4.4.2.1 Syntactic Derivation

The derivation of s is as follows (using the following abbreviations for space reduction reasons: 'C' for Company, 'W' for Worker, 'E' for Employs).

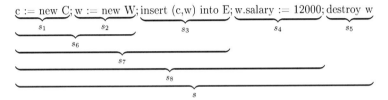

The following table shows the assigned, bound, and free sets of s and its sub-statements.

	assigned	bound	free
s	$\{c_{\text{Company}}, w_{\text{Worker}}\}$	$\{c_{\text{Company}}, w_{\text{Worker}}\}$	$\emptyset$
s_1	$\{c_{\text{Company}}\}$	$\{c_{\text{Company}}\}$	$\emptyset$
s_2	$\{w_{\text{Worker}}\}$	$\{w_{\text{Worker}}\}$	$\emptyset$
s_3	$\emptyset$	$\emptyset$	$\{c_{\text{Company}}, w_{\text{Worker}}\}$
s_4	$\emptyset$	$\emptyset$	$\{w_{\text{Worker}}\}$
s_5	$\emptyset$	$\emptyset$	$\{w_{\text{Worker}}\}$
s_6	$\{c_{\text{Company}}, w_{\text{Worker}}\}$	$\{c_{\text{Company}}, w_{\text{Worker}}\}$	$\emptyset$
s_7	$\{c_{\text{Company}}, w_{\text{Worker}}\}$	$\{c_{\text{Company}}, w_{\text{Worker}}\}$	$\emptyset$
s_8	$\{c_{\text{Company}}, w_{\text{Worker}}\}$	$\{c_{\text{Company}}, w_{\text{Worker}}\}$	$\emptyset$

The statement s is a concatenation of 4 statements (s_1, s_2, s_3 and s_4). This concatenation is syntactically derived by three applications of the sequence constructor ($s \rightsquigarrow s_8; s_5, s_8 \rightsquigarrow s_7; s_4, s_7 \rightsquigarrow s_6; s_3, s_6 \rightsquigarrow s_1; s_2$).

From the syntactic point of view, object creation, link insertion, and attribute assignment are simple. The object creation statements s_1 and s_2 do not have any free variables, and they bind and assign the variables c_{Company} resp. w_{Worker}. In contrast, the insert statement s_3 does not bind or assign any variables, but it has the free variables from all of its tuple component expressions, c_{Company} and w_{Worker}. Similarly, the attribute assignment s_4 does not bind or assign, but it has the free variables from its object and value expressions (only one in this example, w_{Worker}). Similarly, the destroy statement s_5 has one free variable.

Notice that the link insertion statement requires that the component expressions are typed consistently with $\mathcal{M}$ (i. e., consistent with associates(Employs) – Def. 4.7vii), and that attribute assignment requires that the object and value expressions are typed consistently with $\mathcal{M}$ (i. e., consistent with $\text{ATT}_{\text{Worker}}$ – Def. 4.7iv).

4.4.2.2 Semantic Derivation

We illustrate the step-wise evaluation of the interpretation of s.

We assume $\sigma_{\text{CLASS}}(\text{Company}) = \emptyset$ and $\sigma_{\text{CLASS}}(\text{Worker}) = \emptyset$ and $\zeta = \langle \emptyset \rangle$.

The interpretation of s is as follows:

$$I[\![\, s \,]\!](\sigma, \zeta) = I[\![\, s_5 \,]\!]\left(I[\![\, s_4 \,]\!]\left(I[\![\, s_3 \,]\!]\left(I[\![\, s_2 \,]\!]\left(I[\![\, s_1 \,]\!](\sigma, \zeta) \right) \right) \right) \right)$$

We use σ_1, ζ_1 to denote the system state and variable stack after the evaluation of s_1 and σ_2, ζ_2 to denote the system state and variable stack after s_2 and so on. We look at the intermediate result after s_1.

$$(\sigma_1, \zeta_1) = I[\![\, c := \text{ new Company} \,]\!](\sigma, \zeta)$$

We get $\sigma_{1,\text{CLASS}}(\text{Company}) = \{\underline{Company}_1\}$ (σ_1 unchanged otherwise) and $\zeta_1 = \langle \{c \mapsto \underline{Company}_1\} \rangle$.

Notice that the object identifier $\underline{Company}_1$ itself is not accessible as a variable in the variable stack. Only variables referencing the object can be used (c. f. Sect. 4.1.5 about garbage collection).

The next intermediate result after s_2 follows straightforward.

$$(\sigma_2, \zeta_2) = I[\![\, w := \text{ new Worker} \,]\!](\sigma_1, \zeta_1).$$

We get $\sigma_{2,\text{CLASS}}(\text{Worker}) = \{\underline{Worker}_1\}$ (σ_2 unchanged otherwise) and $\zeta_2 = \langle \{c \mapsto \underline{Company}_1, w \mapsto \underline{Worker}_1\} \rangle$.

The third intermediate result after s_3 brings us our first link.

$$(\sigma_3, \zeta_3) = I[\![\, \text{insert } (c, w) \text{ into Employs} \,]\!](\sigma_2, \zeta_2)$$

We get $\sigma_{3,\text{Assoc}}(\text{Employs}) = \{(\underline{Company}_1, \underline{Worker}_1)\}$ (σ_3 unchanged otherwise and $\zeta_3 = \zeta_2$ unchanged).

The fourth intermediate result after s_4 now assigns a value for $\underline{Worker}_1$ in the attribute mapping $\sigma_{4,\text{ATT}}(\text{salary})$.

$$(\sigma_4, \zeta_4) = I[\![\,w_{\text{Worker}}.\text{salary} := 12000\,]\!](\sigma_3, \zeta_3)$$

We get $\sigma_{4,\text{ATT}}(\text{salary}) = \{I[\![\,c\,]\!](\sigma_3, \text{binding}(\zeta_3)) \mapsto I[\![\,12000\,]\!](\sigma_3, \text{binding}(\zeta_3))\} = \{\underline{Worker}_1 \mapsto 12000\}$ (σ_4 unchanged otherwise) and $\zeta_4 = \zeta_3$ (unchanged).

Finally some noteworthy things happen in the final result after executing s_5.

$$(\sigma_5, \zeta_5) = I[\![\,\text{destroy } c\,]\!](\sigma_4, \zeta_4)$$

We get $\sigma_{5,\text{CLASS}}(\text{Worker}) = \emptyset$ and $\sigma_{5,\text{Assoc}}(\text{Employs}) = \emptyset$ (σ_5 unchanged otherwise) and $\zeta_5 = \langle\{c \mapsto \underline{Company}_1, w \mapsto \bot\}\rangle$.

The first noteworthy aspect we can see is that all variables referencing the destroyed object $\underline{Worker}_1$ have been set to $\bot$ (there is just one such variable in this example). Furthermore, all links have been removed in which the object participated. Cf. with Sect. 4.1.5 about garbage collection.

Finally, our program terminates with a state containing just one Company object.

4.4.3 Invoking Operations With Side-Effects that are Implemented by Statements

The following example illustrates how to evaluate invocations of operations which are implemented by SOIL statements. This especially shows the binding of actual parameters and the behavior of the variable stack. Furthermore, we see an example of how the variable stack is affected at deeper levels than the current binding when objects are destroyed (by changing all previous references to this object to $\bot$).

As our project world example does not contain appropriate operations to demonstrate nested operation invocations in a concise way, we use a special model for this example. We assume $\mathcal{M} = (\text{CLASS}, \text{ATT}, \text{ASSOC}, \text{associates}, \text{multiplicities})$ with

$$
\begin{aligned}
\text{CLASS} &= \{C\} \\
\text{ATT}_C &= \{\text{r} : C \rightarrow \text{Integer}\} \\
\text{ASSOC} &= \emptyset \\
\text{associates} &= \emptyset \\
\text{multiplicities} &= \emptyset
\end{aligned}
$$

and

$$\overline{\Omega}_\mathcal{M} = \{f() : C, g(c : C, n : \text{Integer}), h(c : C)\}$$

and

$$\text{stat}\big(f() : C\big) \quad = \quad \underbrace{\text{result} := \text{new C}}_{s_f}$$

$$\text{stat}\big(g(c : C, n : \text{Integer})\big) \quad = \quad \underbrace{\text{c.r} := \text{n}}_{s_g}$$

$$\text{stat}\big(h(c : C)\big) \quad = \quad \underbrace{\text{destroy c}}_{s_h}\}$$

We will skip the syntactic derivation for s_f, s_g, s_h, and s, as it is straightforward and has been explained in the previous examples already. We have

$$\begin{aligned}
\text{free}(s_f) &= \emptyset \\
\text{free}(s_g) &= \{\text{c}_\text{C}, \text{n}_\text{Integer}\} \\
\text{free}(s_h) &= \{\text{c}_\text{C}\} \\
\text{free}(s) &= \emptyset
\end{aligned}$$

By Def. 4.9 [stat], the stat mapping defines the following interpretation functions for $f() : C$, $g(c : C, n : \text{Integer})$, and $h(c : C)$ for us.

$$I\big(f() : C\big) := \lambda\sigma_a, \zeta_a \; . \; (\sigma_b, \uparrow\zeta_b, y)$$
$$\text{where } (\sigma_b, \zeta_b) = I[\![\, \text{result} \; := \; \text{new } C \,]\!](\sigma_a, \downarrow\zeta_a)$$
$$\text{and } y = \text{binding}(\zeta_b)(\text{result}_C)$$

$$I\big(g(\text{c} : C, \text{n} : \text{Integer})\big) := \lambda\sigma_a, \zeta_a, c_a, n_a \; . \; (\sigma_b, \uparrow\zeta_b)$$
$$\text{where } (\sigma_b, \zeta_b) = I[\![\, \text{c.r} := \text{n}_\text{Integer} \,]\!](\sigma_a, \downarrow\zeta_a\{\text{c} \mapsto c_a, \text{n} \mapsto n_a\})$$

$$I\big(g(\text{c} : C)\big) := \lambda\sigma_a, \zeta_a, c_a \; . \; (\sigma_b, \uparrow\zeta_b)$$
$$\text{where } (\sigma_b, \zeta_b) = I[\![\, \text{destroy } c \,]\!](\sigma_a, \downarrow\zeta_a\{\text{c} \mapsto c_a\})$$

In these interpretation functions, the environments ζ_b still contain the added variable binding (stack frame) in which the operation call is evaluated. This binding is finally removed in the interpretation function of the operation by the $\uparrow$ operator.

In the following we will consider the SOIL statement

$$\underbrace{x := f(); y := f(); g(x, 5); h(x)}_{s} \, .$$

4.4.3.1   Semantic Derivation

As before, we look at the step-wise evaluation of s, following the structure of s:

$$\underbrace{\underbrace{x := f();}_{s_1}\underbrace{y := f();}_{s_2}\underbrace{g(x,5);}_{s_3}\underbrace{h(x)}_{s_4}}$$

$$\underbrace{}_{s_5}$$

$$\underbrace{}_{s_6}$$

We assume $\sigma_{\text{CLASS}}(C) = \emptyset$ and $\zeta = \langle \emptyset \rangle$.

The interpretation of s is as follows. We use (σ_1, ζ_1) to denote the system state and variable stack after the evaluation of s_1 and (σ_2, ζ_2) to denote the system state and variable stack after s_2 and so on.

$$I[\![\, s \,]\!](\sigma, \zeta) = I[\![\, s_3 \,]\!]\Big(I[\![\, s_2 \,]\!]\big(I[\![\, s_1 \,]\!](\sigma, \zeta) \big) \Big)$$

We look at the intermediate result $(\sigma_1, \zeta_1) = I[\![\, s_1 \,]\!](\sigma, \zeta)$. We have $(\sigma_1, \zeta_1) = (\sigma', \zeta'\{x/w\})$ where $(\sigma', \zeta', w) = I(f)(\sigma, \zeta)$ by Def. 4.8 (semantics of operation call) and $(\sigma', \zeta', w) = (\sigma'', \uparrow\zeta'', w)$ where

$$(\sigma'', \zeta'') = I[\![\, \text{result} := \text{ new } C \,]\!](\sigma, \downarrow\zeta) \text{ and}$$
$$w = \text{binding}(\zeta'')(\text{result}_C)$$

by applying the λ function which is given for f by Def. 4.9 [stat].

This yields $\sigma_{1, \text{CLASS}(C)} = \{c_1\}$ and $\zeta_1 = \langle \{x \mapsto c_1\}\rangle$. We have $\zeta'' = \langle \emptyset, \{\text{result} \mapsto c_1\}\rangle$ within the interpretation of f. Notice how the evaluation of f takes place in a fresh variable frame and how the result value in that frame is finally assigned to x in the caller's frame.

The intermediate result $(\sigma_2, \zeta_2) = I[\![\, s_2 \,]\!](\sigma_1, \zeta_1)$ is done analogously. We have $\sigma_{2, \text{CLASS}(C)} = \{c_1, c_2\}$ and $\zeta_2 = \langle \{x \mapsto c_1, y \mapsto c_2\}\rangle$.

The next step gives us

$$(\sigma_3, \zeta_3) = I(g)\big(\sigma_2, \zeta_2, I[\![\, x \,]\!](\sigma_2, \zeta_2), I[\![\, 5 \,]\!](\sigma_2, \zeta_2)\big) = I(g)(c_1, 5) = (\sigma', \uparrow\zeta')$$

where
$$(\sigma', \zeta') = I[\![\, \text{c.r} := \text{n} \,]\!](\sigma_2, \downarrow\zeta_2\{c \mapsto c_1, n \mapsto 5\}).$$

This yields $\sigma_{3, \text{ATT}}(r) = \{c_1 \mapsto 5\}$ (σ_3 unchanged otherwise) and $\zeta_3 = \langle \{x \mapsto c_1, y \mapsto c_2\}\rangle$. We have $\zeta' = \langle \{x \mapsto c_1, y \mapsto c_2\}, \{c \mapsto c_1, n \mapsto 5\}\rangle$ within the interpretation of g. Notice how the actual parameter values for c and n are still in ζ' before the variable binding is removed ('popped') in ζ_3 (removal of dangling object references, c.f. Sect. 4.1.5).

We evaluate the final environment

$$(\sigma_4, \zeta_4) = I(h)(\sigma_3, \zeta_3, I[\![x]\!](\sigma_3, \zeta_3)) = I(h)(\sigma_3, \zeta_3, \underline{c_1}) = (\sigma', \uparrow\zeta')$$

where

$$(\sigma', \zeta') = I[\![\text{destroy c}]\!](\sigma_3, \downarrow\zeta_3\{c \mapsto \underline{c_1}\}).$$

This yields $\sigma_{4,\text{CLASS}(C)} = \{\underline{c_1}\}$ and $\zeta_4 = \langle\{x \mapsto \bot, y \mapsto \underline{c_2}\}\rangle$. We have $\zeta' = \langle\{x \mapsto \bot, y \mapsto \underline{c_2}\}, \{c \mapsto \bot\}\rangle$ within the interpretation of h. Notice how a different variable frame than the current one is affected in ζ' by the destruction statement. Our program terminates with a state containing just one object, which is not referenced by any variable any more.

4.5   Type-Soundness and Consistency Revisited

We already stated informally in Sect. 4.1 that the language SOIL is type-safe in the sense that every syntactically correct statement has a well-defined meaning. This proposition is formalized in this chapter by the following theorem.

Theorem 4.10 ($I[\![s]\!]$ is well-defined). Given $s \in$ Stat, a system state σ of $\mathcal{M}$, and a variable stack $\zeta = \langle b_1, \ldots, b_n \rangle$ over σ with

$$\forall v, t : v_t \in \text{free}(s) \rightarrow \text{val}(\zeta, v) \in I(t)$$

(i.e., a variable stack containing correctly typed valued for all free variables of s), then the interpretation $(\sigma', \zeta') = I[\![s]\!](\sigma, \zeta)$ is well-defined, i.e., σ' is a system state of $\mathcal{M}$ and $\zeta' = \langle b'_1, \ldots, b'_m \rangle$ is a variable stack over σ', $n = m$, and

$$\forall i, v : 1 \leq i \leq (n-1) \rightarrow \big(b'_i(v) = b_i(v) \ \vee \ b'_i(v) = \bot\big).$$

$\square$

Remark. The last proposition in Theorem 4.10 is not strictly required for the well-definedness of $I[\![s]\!]$. This property is required, however, in order to use a statement to define the interpretation of an operation with side-effects (c.f. Thm. 4.11).

In addition to the semantics of statements, we also provided a way to give interpretations for operations by means of statements (Def. 4.9 [stat]). These interpretations are sound w.r.t. the definition of the interpretation of operations with side-effects (Def. 4.4), if there are no recursive invocations of operations in the statements that are associated by stat (as statically determined by Algorithm 4.3.4 on page 94).

Theorem 4.11 (Interpretations provided by stat are interpretations for operations with side-effects). Given stat contains no recursive operation invocations, as determined by Algorithm 4.3.4 on page 94.

1. Then the λ-function given by Def. 4.9 [stat] for each $\bar{\omega}(v_1 : t_1, \ldots, v_n : t_n) \rightarrow s \in$ stat is an interpretation for an operation without result value as defined in Def. 4.4.

2. Then the λ-function given by Def. 4.9 [stat] for each $\bar{\omega}(v_1 : t_1, \ldots, v_n : t_n) : t \rightarrow s \in$ stat is an interpretation for an operation with result value as defined in Def. 4.4.

$\square$

The proofs for both theorems are space-consuming and are therefore provided in Appendix A. We want to emphasize that the formalization of the above theorems and the corresponding proofs have contributed a lot to the quality of the definitions of the formal syntax and semantics of SOIL. We had to make several revisions of SOIL during the prove process, to fix, one after the other, all of the small and hidden pitfalls in the language design, w. r. t. the type system as well as w. r. t. the semantics of statements. Although being quite time-consuming, this approach led to definitions that could be implemented more or less one-to-one in the UML-based Specification Environment (USE) as a subject of a M. Sc. thesis (c. f. Sect. 5.1). This work could be done in a straight, top-down manner. No unexpected problems w. r. t. the type systems and the semantics of statements have been found in the practical work. Thus, we believe that the efforts for the following proofs have been well-invested in total.

4.6 Extending SOIL by Error Handling

As said in Sect. 4.1.4, the semantics of SOIL could be extended to achieve a more sophisticated treatment of errors.

We leave this extension as future work and only sketch in this section how it could be done.

The idea is to define a new set of error conditions ERR. Let us assume we have

$$\text{ERR} \ = \{ \quad \text{UndefLinkComponent},$$
$$\text{UndefSourceObject},$$
$$\text{NonExistingLink},$$
$$\text{DuplicateLink} \ \}.$$

The interpretation of statements from Def. 4.8 could then be extended by
error propagation clauses as follows.

Definition 4.12 (Semantics of Statements (with error handling)). Let
Env_{OCL} be the set of environments (σ, β). The semantics of an expression $e \in \text{Expr}_t$ is a function $I[\![e]\!] : \text{Env}_{\text{OCL}} \to I(t)$, as defined in [Ric02].
Let Env_{Stat} be the set of triples $(\sigma, \zeta, \text{Err})$ of a system state σ, a variable stack ζ over σ, and a set of error conditions $\text{Err} \subseteq \text{ERR}$. Given
$\forall v_t : v_t \in \text{free}(s) \to \exists x : (v_t, x) \in \text{binding}(\zeta)$, the semantics of a statement $s \in \text{Stat}$ is a function $I[\![s]\!] : \text{Env}_{\text{Stat}} \to \text{Env}_{\text{Stat}}$.

i. (empty statement)

$$I[\![\Diamond]\!](\sigma, \zeta, \text{Err}) := (\sigma, \zeta, \text{Err})$$

ii. (sequence)

$$I[\![s_1; s_2]\!](\sigma, \zeta, \emptyset) := I[\![s_2]\!](I[\![s_1]\!](\sigma, \zeta, \emptyset))$$

$$I[\![s_1; s_2]\!](\sigma, \zeta, \text{Err}) := (\sigma, \zeta, \text{Err}) \text{ for } \text{Err} \neq \emptyset$$

iii. (variable assignment)

$$I[\![v := e]\!](\sigma, \zeta, \emptyset) := (\sigma, \zeta\{v/I[\![e]\!](\sigma, \text{binding}(\zeta))\}, \emptyset)$$

$$I[\![v := e]\!](\sigma, \zeta, \text{Err}) = (\sigma, \zeta, \text{Err}) \text{ for } \text{Err} \neq \emptyset$$

iv. (attribute assignment)

$$I[\![e_1.a := e_2]\!](\sigma, \zeta, \emptyset) := \begin{cases} (\sigma', \zeta, \emptyset) \\ \quad \text{if } I[\![e_1]\!](\sigma, \text{binding}(\zeta)) \neq \bot \\ (\sigma, \zeta, \{\text{UndefSourceObject}\}) \\ \quad \text{otherwise} \end{cases}$$

where $\sigma' := \sigma$ except
$\sigma'_{\text{ATT}}(a) := \sigma_{\text{ATT}}(a)\{I[\![e_1]\!](\sigma, \text{binding}(\zeta)) \ / \ I[\![e_2]\!](\sigma, \text{binding}(\zeta))\}$

$$I[\![e_1.a := e_2]\!](\sigma, \zeta, \text{Err}) = (\sigma, \zeta, \text{Err}) \text{ for } \text{Err} \neq \emptyset$$

v. (object creation)

$$I[\![\, v := \text{new } c \,]\!](\sigma, \zeta, \emptyset) := (\sigma', \zeta', \emptyset)$$

where $\sigma' := \sigma$ except
$\sigma'_{\text{CLASS}}(c) := \sigma_{\text{CLASS}}(c) \cup \{\text{newobj}\}$, $\text{newobj} \notin \sigma_{\text{CLASS}}(c)$
and $\zeta' := \zeta\{v/\text{newobj}\}$.

$$I[\![\, v := \text{new } c \,]\!](\sigma, \zeta, \text{Err}) = (\sigma, \zeta, \text{Err}) \;\; \text{for Err} \neq \emptyset$$

vi. (object destruction)
Let $\zeta = \langle b_1, \ldots, b_n \rangle$.

$$I[\![\, \text{destroy } e \,]\!](\sigma, \zeta, \emptyset)$$

$$:= \begin{cases} (\sigma', \zeta', \emptyset) & \text{if } I[\![\, e \,]\!]\big(\sigma, \text{binding}(\zeta)\big) \neq \bot \\ (\sigma, \zeta, \{\text{UndefSourceObject}\}) & \text{otherwise} \end{cases}$$

where $\sigma' := \sigma$ except

$$\sigma'_{\text{CLASS}}(c) := \sigma_{\text{CLASS}}(c) - \big\{ I[\![\, e \,]\!]\big(\sigma, \text{binding}(\zeta)\big) \big\},$$
$$\sigma'_{\text{ASSOC}}(a) := \sigma_{\text{ASSOC}}(a)$$
$$- \big\{ \langle o_1, \ldots, o_n \rangle \;\big|\; \exists i : 1 \leq i \leq n \wedge o_i = I[\![\, e \,]\!]\big(\sigma, \text{binding}(\zeta)\big) \big\},$$
$$\text{for } a \in \text{ASSOC}$$

and $\zeta' := \langle b'_1, \ldots, b'_n \rangle$ where
$b'_i := b_i \big\{ v / \bot, \text{ if } \text{binding}(\zeta)(v) = I[\![\, e \,]\!]\big(\sigma, \text{binding}(\zeta)\big) \big\}.$

$$I[\![\, \text{destroy } e \,]\!](\sigma, \zeta, \text{Err}) = (\sigma, \zeta, \text{Err}) \;\; \text{for Err} \neq \emptyset$$

vii. (link insertion)
Let $x_1, \ldots, x_n = I[\![\, e_1 \,]\!]\big(\sigma, \text{binding}(\zeta)\big), \ldots, I[\![\, e_n \,]\!]\big(\sigma, \text{binding}(\zeta)\big).$

$$I[\![\, \text{insert}(e_1, \ldots, e_n) \text{ into } a \,]\!](\sigma, \zeta)$$

$$:= \begin{cases} (\sigma, \zeta, \{\text{UndefLinkComponent}\}) & \text{if } \exists i : 1 \leq i \leq n \wedge x_i = \bot \\ (\sigma, \zeta, \{\text{DuplicateLink}\}) & \text{if } (x_1, \ldots, x_n) \in \sigma_{\text{ASSOC}}(A) \\ (\sigma', \zeta, \emptyset) & \text{otherwise} \end{cases}$$

where $\sigma' := \sigma$ except
$\sigma'_{\text{ASSOC}}(a) := \sigma_{\text{ASSOC}}(a) \cup \{(x_1, \ldots, x_n)\}.$

$$I[\![\, \text{insert}(e_1, \ldots, e_n) \text{ into } a \,]\!](\sigma, \zeta, \text{Err}) = (\sigma, \zeta, \text{Err}) \;\; \text{for Err} \neq \emptyset$$

viii. (link deletion)

Let $x_1, \ldots, x_n = I[\![\, e_1 \,]\!]\big(\sigma, \text{binding}(\zeta)\big), \ldots, I[\![\, e_n \,]\!]\big(\sigma, \text{binding}(\zeta)\big)$.

$I[\![\, \text{delete}(e_1, \ldots, e_n) \text{ from } a \,]\!](\sigma, \zeta)$

$$:= \begin{cases} (\sigma, \zeta, \{\text{UndefLinkComponent}\}) & \text{if } \exists i : 1 \leq i \leq n \wedge \; x_i = \bot \\ (\sigma, \zeta, \{\text{NonExistingLink}\}) & \text{if } (x_1, \ldots, x_n) \notin \sigma_{\text{Assoc}}(A) \\ (\sigma', \zeta, \emptyset) & \text{otherwise} \end{cases}$$

where $\sigma' := \sigma$ except
$\sigma'_{\text{Assoc}}(a) := \sigma_{\text{Assoc}}(a) - \{(x_1, \ldots, x_n)\}).$

$I[\![\, \text{delete}(e_1, \ldots, e_n) \text{ from } A \,]\!](\sigma, \zeta, \text{Err}) = (\sigma, \zeta, \text{Err}) \;\; \text{for } \text{Err} \neq \emptyset$

ix. (conditional execution)

Let $b = I[\![\, e \,]\!]\big(\sigma, \text{binding}(\zeta)\big)$

$$I[\![\, \text{if } e \text{ then } s_1 \text{ else } s_2 \text{ end} \,]\!](\sigma, \zeta) := \begin{cases} I[\![\, s_1 \,]\!](\sigma, \zeta) & \text{if } b = \text{true} \\ I[\![\, s_2 \,]\!](\sigma, \zeta) & \text{otherwise} \end{cases}$$

$I[\![\, \text{if } e \text{ then } s_1 \text{ end} \,]\!](\sigma, \zeta) := I[\![\, \text{if } e \text{ then } s_1 \text{ else } \Diamond \text{ end} \,]\!](\sigma, \zeta)$

$I[\![\, \text{if } e \text{ then } s_1 \text{ else } s_2 \text{ end} \,]\!](\sigma, \zeta, \text{Err}) = (\sigma, \zeta, \text{Err}) \;\; \text{for } \text{Err} \neq \emptyset$

x. (iteration)

Given $I[\![\, r \,]\!]\big(\sigma, \beta(\zeta)\big) = \langle x_1, \ldots, x_n \rangle$,

$$I[\![\, \text{for } v \text{ in } r \text{ do } s \text{ end}) \,]\!](\sigma, \zeta, \emptyset)$$

$$:= \begin{cases} (\sigma, \zeta, \emptyset) & \text{if } I[\![\, r \,]\!]\big(\sigma, \beta(\zeta)\big) = \langle \rangle \\ I[\![\, s' \,]\!](\sigma', \zeta', \emptyset) & \text{otherwise} \end{cases}$$

where $s' = \text{for } v \text{ in Sequence}\{x_2, \ldots, x_n\} \text{ do } s \text{ end}$
and $(\sigma', \zeta') = I[\![\, s \,]\!](\sigma, \zeta\{v/x_1\}).$

$I[\![\, \text{for } v \text{ in } r \text{ do } s \text{ end}) \,]\!](\sigma, \zeta, \text{Err}) = (\sigma, \zeta, \text{Err}) \;\; \text{for } \text{Err} \neq \emptyset$

xi. (operation call without result)

Let $\overline{\omega} : (v_1 : t_1, \ldots, v_n : t_n) \in \overline{\Omega}_{\mathcal{M}}$.

Let $x_1, \ldots, x_n = I[\![\, e_1 \,]\!]\big(\sigma, \text{binding}(\zeta)\big), \ldots, I[\![\, e_n \,]\!]\big(\sigma, \text{binding}(\zeta)\big)$.

$I[\![\, \overline{\omega}(e_1, \ldots, e_n) \,]\!](\sigma, \zeta, \emptyset)$

$$:= \begin{cases} I(\overline{\omega})\big(\sigma, \zeta, x_1, \ldots, x_n)\big) & \text{if } I[\![\, e_1 \,]\!]\big(\sigma, \text{binding}(\zeta)\big) \neq \bot \\ (\sigma, \zeta, \{\text{UndefSourceObject}\}) & \text{otherwise} \end{cases}$$

$$I[\![\,\overline{\omega}(e_1, \ldots, e_n)\,]\!](\sigma, \zeta, \text{Err}) = (\sigma, \zeta, \text{Err}) \quad \text{for } \text{Err} \neq \emptyset$$

xii. (operation call with result)

Let $\overline{\omega} : (v_1 : t_1, \ldots, v_n : t_n \rightarrow t) \in \overline{\Omega}_\mathcal{M}$.

Let $x_1, \ldots, x_n = I[\![\,e_1\,]\!]\big(\sigma, \text{binding}(\zeta)\big), \ldots, I[\![\,e_n\,]\!]\big(\sigma, \text{binding}(\zeta)\big)$.

$$I[\![\,v := \overline{\omega}(e_1, \ldots, e_n)\,]\!](\sigma, \zeta) := \begin{cases} (\sigma', \zeta'\{v/y\}) \\ \quad \text{if } I[\![\,e_1\,]\!]\big(\sigma, \text{binding}(\zeta)\big) \neq \bot \\ (\sigma, \zeta, \{\text{UndefSourceObject}\}) \\ \quad \text{otherwise} \end{cases}$$

where $(\sigma', \zeta', y) = I(\overline{\omega})(\sigma, \zeta, x_1, \ldots, x_n)$.

$$I[\![\,v := \overline{\omega}(e_1, \ldots, e_n)\,]\!](\sigma, \zeta, \text{Err}) = (\sigma, \zeta, \text{Err}) \quad \text{for } \text{Err} \neq \emptyset$$

$\square$

In this extended definition, error conditions are propagated by all statements: if there is an error already, the system state and the variable stack are unchanged and the error conditions is returned. Furthermore, the aforementioned statements object destruction, attribute assignment, link creation, link deletion, and operation invocation now raise such an error condition when undefined values occur. Using this extended definition, these error conditions are no longer silently ignored.

In addition to this extended semantics, new syntactical elements for handling errors could be added to Stat. For example, in the form of try-catch constructions as in Java or C++. However, as mentioned in the beginning of this section, this is left for future work.

4.7 Comparison to Related Languages

In the beginning of this thesis we referred to ImperativeOCL in MOF QVT, and UML Actions for Executable UML. In this section we compare SOIL to both approaches.

4.7.1 ImperativeOCL

We have presented ImperativeOCL and its pitfalls in Chap. 2. The most important difference between SOIL and ImperativeOCL is, that SOIL matches our definition of a modular embedding of OCL (Def. 2.1), whereas Imperative-OCL does not.

Apart from minor syntactical differences, where are the differences on the user level? The most noticeable difference for the user surely is the compute statement. While both languages allow the embedding of OCL in imperative statements, only ImperativeOCL allows the embedding of statements in expressions. This is the price, we have to pay for a modular embedding. Constructions such as

```
1    mySeq := Sequence{1,2,3}->collect( x |
2       compute(y:Integer) {
3          y := <y calculated imperatively from x>
4       })
```

are not possible in SOIL and have to be decomposed into several steps in SOIL:

```
1    mySeq := Sequence{};
2    for x in Sequence{1,2,3} do
3       y := <y calculated imperatively from x>;
4       mySeq := mySeq.append(y)
5    end
```

Notice furthermore, that in our definition, we only presented a way to use SOIL statements to define operations with side-effects. We provided no way to define side-effect free query operations with SOIL. Therefore, the following statement is not a valid statement in our approach, so far, although the operation factorial surely is a side-effect free operation w.r.t. the system state and the environment.

```
1    class C
2       factorial(n : Integer) : Integer
3       begin
4          result := 1;
5          if n > 1 then
6             result := n * self.factorial(n - 1);
7          end;
8       end
```

In our approach, we have to express the previous statement as follows (notice the difference in lines 6–7)

```
1    class C
2       factorial(n : Integer) : Integer
3       begin
4          result := 1;
5          if n > 1 then
6             tmp := self.factorial(n - 1);
7             result := n * tmp;
```

```
8     end;
9   end
```

The reason is that C.factorial is not a query operation (formally, it is part of $\overline{\Omega}_{\mathcal{M}}$ and not of $\Omega_{\mathcal{M}}$). Therefore, it cannot occur in OCL expressions. By storing the intermediate result in a variable tmp (notice that tmp := self.factorial(n - 1) is an operation call statement with result value assignment, not an assignment of an expression value to a variable), it is available in expressions in subsequent statements.

However, this restriction (statements can never define query operations) could be weakened. It would be possible to provide a mapping querystat that provides an interpretation for a side-effect free operation (c. f. Def. 3.15 on page 47) for certain statements. Therefore, we would need to define a restricted set of statements RStat that only contains statements that do not modify the system state. Given such an extension, operations such as factorial could be implemented as side-effect free operations with SOIL statements. While not present in this thesis, such an extension has been made in the implementation of SOIL in the UML-based Specification Environment (USE), as explained in Sect. 5.1.

Another major difference between ImperativeOCL and SOIL is the treatment of variables. Both languages are statically typed languages. In ImperativeOCL, variables have to be declared before they can be used. SOIL provides sophisticated type inference, making explicit variable declarations superfluous.

Apart from the aforementioned language constructs, ImperativeOCL comprises a sophisticated exception-style error treatment, whereas the presented version of SOIL deals with errors in a rather naive approach. We address this by an extended version of SOIL as sketched in Sect. 4.6.

4.7.2   UML Actions

The UML specification provides metamodel packages for the behavioral aspects of models [OMG07, Chapters 11ff]. This metamodel packages cover different aspects and different layers of behavior modeling. Figure 4.5 on the following page depicts the packages and their relationships.

FundamentalActivities The fundamental level defines activities as containing nodes, which includes actions. This level is shared between the flow and structured forms of activities.

BasicActivities This level includes control sequencing and data flow between actions, but explicit forks and joins of control, as well as decisions

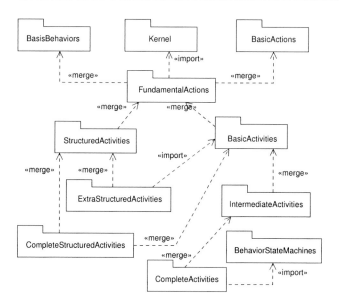

Figure 4.5: Package overview of UML Actions metamodel

and merges, are not supported. The basic and structured levels are orthogonal. Either can be used without the other or both can be used to support modeling that includes both flows and structured control constructs.

IntermediateActivities The intermediate level supports modeling of activity diagrams that include concurrent control and data flow, and decisions. It supports modeling similar to traditional Petri nets with queuing. It requires the basic level. The intermediate and structured levels are orthogonal. Either can be used without the other or both can be used to support modeling that includes both concurrency and structured control constructs.

CompleteActivities The complete level adds constructs that enhance the lower level models, such as edge weights and streaming.

StructuredActivities The structured level supports modeling of traditional structured programming constructs, such as sequences, loops, and conditionals, as an addition to fundamental activity nodes. It requires the fundamental level. It is compatible with the intermediate and complete levels.

CompleteStructuredActivities This level adds support for data flow output pins of sequences, conditionals, and loops. It depends on the basic layer for flows.

ExtraStructuredActivities The extra structure level supports exception handling as found in traditional programming languages and invocation of behaviors on sets of values. It requires the structured level.

We only regard a small subset of the metaclasses provided by all these packages. One fundamental class is the class *Action*, as depicted in Fig. 4.6. Actions, InputPins, and OutputPins are abstract constructs, which are described as follows in [OMG07]: "An action is a named element that is the fundamental unit of executable functionality. The execution of an action represents some transformation or processing in the modeled system, be it a computer system or otherwise. [...] An input pin is a pin that holds input values to be consumed by an action. [...] An output pin is a pin that holds output values produced by an action." As *Action* is the basis for all kinds of behavioral modeling, the definitions of *Action*, *InputPin*, and *OutputPin* are very generic descriptions.

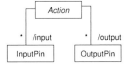

Figure 4.6: Actions, Input Pins, and Output Pins

The UML specification comprises 178 metaclasses for the specification of behavior. These classes are defined in a complex structure of definitions and redefinitions of their features and semantics. In Fig. 4.7 on the following page, we present a flattened subset which contains the classes required to realize the atomic SOIL operations.

The atomic statements of SOIL (variable assignment, attribute assignment, object creation, object destruction, link insertion, link deletion, operation call) can be mapped on the UML metaclasses as follows. An important prerequisite is that the input pins of an action can be given by OCL expressions (as *ValuePin* objects that contain a *ValueSpecification*, which contains an *Expression* object).

- Variable assignments $v := e$ can be modeled by a *WriteVariableAction* metaobject, referencing a *Variable* object for v with a *ValuePin* as input and a *ValueSpecification* containing the expression e.

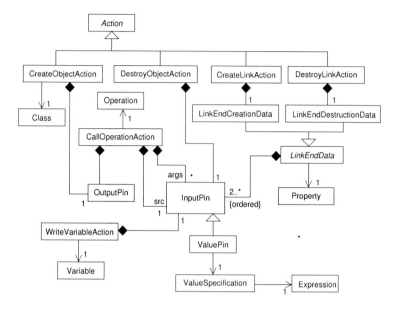

Figure 4.7: Relevant Actions from Intermediate and Structured Actions

- Object creations $v :=$ new C can be modeled by an *ObjectCreation-Action* metaobject in conjunction with a *WriteVariableAction* to store the new object (the output of *CreateObjectAction*) in a variable.

- Object destruction destroy e can be modeled by an *DestroyObjectAction* metaobject with a *ValuePin* as input and a *ValueSpecification* containing the expression e.

- Link insertion insert $(e_1, \ldots, e_n)$ into a and link deletion delete $(e_1, \ldots, e_n)$ from a can be modeled by the *CreateLinkAction* resp. *DestroyLinkAction* metaclasses. A *LinkEndDataObject* is required to capture the expressions $e_1, \ldots, e_n$ as individual *ValuePins* with *ValueSpecifications*.

- Operation calls $\overline{\omega}(e_1, \ldots, e_n)$ without result value can be modeled by *CallOperationActions* referencing the corresponding *Operation* object. As for link manipulation, the individual argument expressions are represented by *ValuePins*.

- Operation calls with result $v := \overline{\omega}(e_1, \ldots, e_n)$ can be modeled analogously, but require an additional *WriteVariableAction* to store the result in the *Variable* object for v.

The construction of more complex statements from basic statements (sequential execution, iteration, conditional execution) can be mapped on other metaclasses of UML, too. We do not show the corresponding metaclasses here for brevity. These complex statements can be represented visually in UML as activity diagram.

Thus, similar to Mellor's Object Action Language (OAL) [Mel02], SOIL could be directly used as-is to imperatively formulate the basic elements of executable UML models. Whereas OAL uses a proprietary notation for expression, SOIL builds on standard OCL. Therefore, in our opinion, the use of the atomic statements of SOIL in Executable UML should be considered. As more complex behavior is defined by means of state machines in Executable UML, iteration and conditional execution would not strictly be required.

However, notice that there is no real assurance for type-safety in these constructions in UML. Thus, not every instance of the metaclasses presented above constitutes a valid SOIL instance. Future work should investigate whether a sound system such as the one from SOIL could be formulated for UML Actions by means of a UML profile. Such a profile could enforce the typing rules for statements that contain OCL expressions by well-formedness rules.

Chapter 5

Applications of our Approach

In the preceding chapters we studied the reuse of OCL in imperative languages. We illustrated several problems that arise from a non-modular embedding of OCL, and therefore developed a definition of a modular embedding in Chap. 2. In Chap. 4 we then provided informal and formal definitions for a concrete imperative language SOIL that matches our requirements.

The results from Chapters 2 and 4 have been put into practice in two projects. The first project is the incorporation of SOIL into the UML-based Specification Environment (USE). The second application took part in an industrial development project for the eGovernment MDA tool 'XGenerator2'. In the following two sections, we provide details about both applications.

5.1   Extension of USE

The UML-based Specification Environment (USE) is a tool for the validation of UML models and OCL constraints, based on animation. Its first versions were developed by Mark Richters in 2001 as part of his work on the formalization of OCL. Later on, it has been maintained and extended by the Research Group Database Systems at the University of Bremen. Extensions were contributed by several diploma and M. Sc. projects.

The language SOIL that we defined in our work has been incorporated into USE as a diploma project by Daniel Gent under our supervision. This extension of USE resulted in a new major version of USE (USE 3.0) with substantial new features. The diploma thesis will be published prior to the final version of this thesis.

In the following, we describe this extension of USE. We first extend our running example 'Project World' by several constraints in Sect. 5.1.1. We illustrate the features of the previous version of USE in Sect. 5.1.2. Then, we explain the new features that are available in USE due to the integration of SOIL in Sect. 5.1.3. In Sect. 5.1.4 we discuss compatibility issues. Section 5.1.5 explains extensions of the implementation w. r. t. the formalizations provided in our work. Finally, we give a summary in Sect. 5.1.7.

5.1.1   Running Example

We will use our running example 'Project World' again, as introduced in Sect. 3.2.1.1. In addition to the structures depicted in Fig. 3.1 on page 34, extra constraints apply to 'Project World' now. In this section, we illustrate some of these constraints, Appendix B contains the complete example.

The first constraint is a structural one (a class invariant) that, analogously to association multiplicities, has to be fulfilled for a valid state. The others are pre- and postconditions describing the operations 'hire' and 'fire'.

Invariant 'OnlyOwnEmployeesInProjects' : Only own employees can be connected to the projects of a company. This is a classical example of an inclusion constraint in database modeling (c. f. [EN10] for a detailed discussion of inclusion constraints).

Precondition 'OnlyNonEmployeesCanBeHired' for 'hire' : No one can be hired twice.

Postcondition 'Hired' for 'hire' : If the management orders 'hire', the worker is hired. This constraint describes the main effect of 'hire'.

Precondition 'OnlyEmployeesCanBeFired' for 'fire' : Only workers connected to this company can be fired.

Postcondition 'Fired' for 'fire' : If the management orders 'fire', the worker has to go. This constraint describes the main effect of 'fire'.

Postcondition 'ProjectsStillHappy' for 'fire' : After an employee has been fired, all projects, that are still active, must have all the qualifications that they require (if some qualification could not be replaced, the project could be set to suspended, for example).

Postcondition 'NoOneOverloaded' for 'fire' : After an employee has been fired, none of the remaining workers must be overloaded with work, due to a rescheduling or project memberships.

We will use this example in the following subsections to introduce the USE system and to explain the extensions that have been made by incorporating SOIL into USE.

5.1.2   USE 2

Figure 5.1 depicts the features of the USE system. The main use cases of USE are: (1) to specify a model, (2) to instantiate system states of this model, (3) to animate operational scenarios, (4) to query the system state, and (5) to validate system states and scenarios. We will explain each of these use cases. A complete technical documentation of the USE systems is bundled with the distribution ([USE10]). A detailed presentation of USE can also be found in [GBR07b].

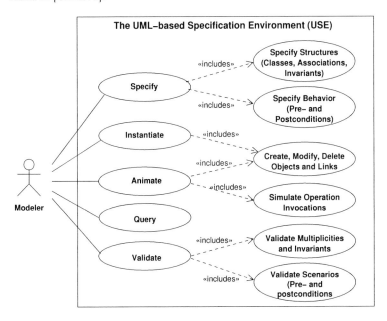

Figure 5.1: Use Cases of USE

Model Specification

The first task to use the system is to specify a model. The model has to be provided in a textual syntax as the USE specification file (.use file). The specification file comprises structural and behavioral definitions. The top level entities in the specification file are classes and associations.

The Listing 5.1 on the next page shows an excerpt of the USE specification for our model from Fig. 3.1. The complete listing is printed in Appendix B.

```
1    model Projects
2
3    enum ProjectSize {small,medium,big}
4    enum ProjectStatus {planned, active, finished, suspended}
5
6    class Company
7    attributes
8      name : String
9    operations
10     fire(w : Worker)
11       pre OnlyEmployeesCanBeFired: employees->includes(w)
12       post Fired: employees->excludes(w)
13       post ProjectsStillHappy: projects->forAll(p|
14         p.status = #active implies p.missingQualifications()->isEmpty)
15       post NoEmployeeOverloaded:
16         employees->forAll(e|not e.isOverloaded())
17     constraints
18       inv OnlyOwnEmployeesInProjects:
19         employees->includesAll(projects.members->asSet)
20     end
21
22   class Worker
23   attributes
24     nickname : String
25     salary : Integer
26   operations
27     isOverloaded() : Boolean =
28       let active = projects->select(p|p.status = #active) in
29         active->select(p|p.size=#big)->size * 2 +
30         active->select(p|p.size=#medium)->size > 3
31     end
32
33   class Project
34   attributes
35     name : String
36     size : ProjectSize
37     status : ProjectStatus
38   operations
39     missingQualifications() : Set(Qualification) = requirements->select(q|
40       not members->exists(m | m.qualifications->includes(q)))
41     isHelpful(w : Worker) : Boolean =
42         missingQualifications()->exists(q|w.qualifications->includes(q))
43     end
44
45   association Employs between
46    Company[0..1] role employer
47    Worker[1..*] role employees
48   end
     -- ...
```

Listing 5.1: USE specification for Project World (excerpt)

The 'model' keyword in the first line sets the name of our model. The following two 'enum' lines declare the enumerations for project statuses and project sizes. Then the 'class' definition for Company follows. Attributes are defined in the 'attributes' section. The Company class has only a single String typed attribute 'name'. In the 'operations' section, the operations for Company are declared. The declaration consists of a name for the operation and a signature of parameter names and types, and an optional return type. The Company class declares one operations 'fire' (the complete example declares all four operations from Fig. 3.1 on page 34). For each operation, pre- and postconditions can be declared. We can find the four conditions for 'fire' that we introduced in Sect. 5.1.1. For each pre- and postcondition, an OCL expression has to be defined. This expression must be true prior to resp. after an invocation of this operation.

Operations can also be defined as query operations, as the operations 'isOverloaded' in class Worker and 'hasAllQualification' in class Project. These operations are side-effect free and can be used within OCL expressions, such as in the postconditions 'ProjectsStillHappy' and 'NoEmployeeOverloaded' in class Company.

The last ingredient in class definitions are invariant constrains. The only invariant constraint in our example is 'OnlyOwnEmployeesInProjects'. Unlike pre- and postconditions, invariants are part of the structural definition of a model, as they have to be fulfilled for any valid system state.

The listing shows the class definitions for Company, Worker, and Project. After the class definitions, the association definitions follow. For brevity, we included only one association (Employs) in Listing 5.1 on the preceding page. For each association, the name and two or more association ends have to be supplied. For the association ends, multiplicities and role names need to be given. If there is no role name given, the lower case class name of this association end is used implicitly as its role name.

State Instantiation

We can start the USE system with our specification file. USE provides a graphical user interface (GUI) as well as a command line interface. The GUI visualizes the model, i. e., classes, associations, and all constraints, as well as the system state. The main visualizations of the system state are object diagrams (these diagrams are configurable in what kinds of objects and links they display). Figure 5.2 on the following page shows a screenshot of the GUI. On the left-hand side we can see the model explorer, showing a tree-like representation of our model in the top and a detailed view of the selected tree element in the bottom. On the right-hand side we can see our example

class diagram in the background and an object diagram showing a system
state in the foreground.

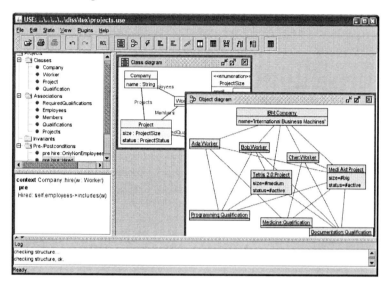

Figure 5.2: The UML-based Specification Environment (now supporting SOIL)

The system state can be instantiated by executing state manipulation commands. This can be done via the GUI or on the command
line. In the following, we will stick to the command line. USE always
starts with an empty state. Prior to SOIL, the command line comprised
five state manipulation commands: (1) `create <objName> : <clsName>`,
to create an instance of a class, (2) `destroy <objExpr>`, to destroy an instance of a class, identified by an object expression,
(3) `insert (<objExpr1>, ... <objExprN>) into <assocName>` and (4)
`delete (<objExpr1>, ... <objExprN>) from <assocName>`, to insert and
delete links into and from an association extent, and finally (5)
`set <objExpr>.<attrName> := <expr>` to manipulate attribute values of
an object.

These state manipulation commands can be issued on the command line
directly, or they can be placed in a command file which can be read in
one step via the 'read' command. Listing 5.2 on the next page shows the
state manipulation commands required to create the system state depicted
in the screenshot in Fig. 5.2. We have the company IBM employing the
three workers Ada, Bob, and Cher. IBM carries out two projects. The large
project MediAid requires qualifications in programming, documentation, and

```
 1  !create IBM : Company
 2  !set IBM.name := 'International Business Machines'
 3
 4  !create Programming : Qualification
 5  !create Documentation : Qualification
 6  !create Medicine : Qualification
 7
 8  !create MediAid : Project
 9  !set MediAid.name := 'Medi Aid'
10  !set MediAid.size := #big
11  !set MediAid.status := #active
12  !insert (IBM,MediAid) into CarriesOut
13
14  !create Tetris2 : Project
15  !set Tetris2.name := 'Tetris 2.0'
16  !set Tetris2.size := #small
17  !set Tetris2.status := #active
18  !insert (IBM,Tetris2) into CarriesOut
19
20  !insert (MediAid, Programming) into Requires
21  !insert (MediAid, Documentation) into Requires
22  !insert (MediAid, Medicine) into Requires
23
24  !insert (Tetris2, Programming) into Requires
25  !insert (Tetris2, Documentation) into Requires
26
27  !create Ada : Worker
28  !set Ada.nickname := 'Ada Amazing'
29  !insert (Ada,Programming) into IsQualified
30  !insert (Ada,Medicine) into IsQualified
31
32  !create Bob : Worker
33  !set Bob.nickname := 'Bob the Builder'
34  !insert (Bob,Programming) into IsQualified
35  !insert (Bob,Documentation) into IsQualified
36
37  !create Cher : Worker
38  !insert (Cher,Documentation) into IsQualified
39  !insert (Cher,Medicine) into IsQualified
40
41  !insert (IBM,Ada) into Employs
42  !insert (IBM,Bob) into Employs
43  !insert (IBM,Cher) into Employs
44
45  !insert (MediAid,Ada) into Member
46  !insert (MediAid,Cher) into Member
47  !insert (Tetris2,Bob) into Member
```

Listing 5.2: System State Creation for Project World

medicine. The small project Tetris2 only requires programming and documentation. Currently, Ada and Cher work in MediAid whereas Bob handles
Tetris2 alone.

Structural Validation

Having instantiated our model, we can check the structural constraints, i. e.,
if the links adhere to the association multiplicities, and if all invariant constraints are fulfilled. The validation of the structural constraints can be done
using the GUI or by issuing the 'check' command on the command line.
For our example state, the 'check' command confirms that all structural
constraints are fulfilled. For example, if we removed (IBM, Ada) from the
Employs association, the 'check' command would tell us that the invariant
'OnlyOwnEmployeesInProjects' was violated.

Queries

Both the USE command line and the GUI allow us to evaluate free stand-
ing OCL expressions. An extended evaluation command is provided that
displays a sophisticated evaluation tree of an expression. This is useful for
understanding the result of a complex expression. We do not go into details
of the query evaluation features of USE in this work.

Animation

Beside the structural validation of states explained above, animations of
operation invocations can be validated as well. These animations can be
seen as a replaying of scenarios: The modeler tells USE what is happening,
and USE tells the modeler if this animation is valid w. r. t. the model.

Considering the system state in Fig. 5.2 on page 122, we now want to fire
Ada. We can animate the invocation of the 'fire' operation by providing what
is happening inside the operation. USE will check all pre- and postconditions
and tell us, if our animation of this operation is valid.

The following listing shows our interaction with USE on the command line.
Our inputs start with 'USE>', everything else is output of USE.

```
1  USE> !openter IBM fire(Ada)
2  precondition `OnlyEmployeesCanBeFired' is true
3  USE> !delete (IBM,Ada) from Employs
4  USE> !delete (MediAid,Ada) from Members
5  USE> check
6  checking structure...
```

```
 7  checking invariants...
 8  checking invariant (1) `Company::OnlyOwnEmployeesInProjects': OK.
 9  USE> !opexit
10  postcondition `Fired' is true
11  postcondition `ProjectsStillHappy' is false
12  postcondition `NoEmployeeOverloaded' is true
13  Error: postcondition false in operation call `Company::fire(self:@IBM,
       w:@Ada)'.
```

The 'openter' (enter operation) command in the first line tells USE we are now simulating an operation invocation of 'fire' on the object IBM with the worker parameter Ada. USE then checks all preconditions for 'fire' (namely, 'OnlyEmployeesCanBeFired', which is fulfilled, as Ada is an employee of IBM).

In the next two lines (3 – 4) we are providing the effect of 'fire' in this scenario by entering state manipulation commands. We are removing the Employs and Members link that connect Ada and IBM resp. Ada and the project MediAid. We make sure to still have a structurally valid state by issuing a 'check' command (line 5). USE tells us that all multiplicity constraints and all invariants are fulfilled.

Finally, we are done with the animation of this operation invocation and finish by issuing the 'opexit' (exit operation) command. Now, USE checks if all postconditions of 'fire' are fulfilled for this invocation. Actually, as we see, this is not the case. While 'Fired' and 'NoEmployeeOverloaded' are fulfilled, 'ProjectsStillHappy' is not. The project MediAid is left without any programmer, but it requires one. Thus, our scenario animation is not valid with respect to the model.

We can fix our scenario to make it valid. The simplest modification is to suspend the MediAid project (until more workers are employed):

```
 1  USE> !openter IBM fire(Ada)
 2  precondition `OnlyEmployeesCanBeFired' is true
 3  USE> !delete (IBM,Ada) from Employs
 4  USE> !delete (MediAid,Ada) from Members
 5  USE> !set MediAid.status = #suspended
 6  USE> !opexit
 7  postcondition `Fired' is true
 8  postcondition `ProjectsStillHappy' is true
 9  postcondition `NoEmployeeOverloaded' is true
```

However, a more sophisticated check of resources would reveal that the programmer Bob could be assigned to MediAid, because he is only working in one small sized project so far. This will be a much better animation from the perspective of business.

```
1   USE> !openter IBM fire(Ada)
2   precondition `OnlyEmployeesCanBeFired' is true
3   USE> !delete (IBM,Ada) from Employs
4   USE> !delete (MediAid,Ada) from Members
5   USE> !insert (MediAid,Bob) into Members
6   USE> !opexit
7   postcondition `Fired' is true
8   postcondition `ProjectsStillHappy' is true
9   postcondition `NoEmployeeOverloaded' is true
```

This example illustrates that pre- and postconditions do not fully determine an operation. Several different implementations for 'fire' would be possible that fulfill the specified pre- and postconditions.

Notice that operation invocations can be generally nested to any depth in the validation of more complex scenarios. Thus, USE allows further 'openter' commands within an active operation invocation. It keeps track of all nested invocations using a call stack.

5.1.3   USE 3

We now explain how USE has been extended by SOIL. Figure 5.3 on the facing page picks up the use case diagram from Fig. 5.1 on page 119. New and extended use cases are depicted in thick lines. The addition of SOIL affected USE in the following features: (1) the specification of models, (2) the instantiation of models, (3) the animation of models, and (4) the validation of these animations.

Model Specification (as Extended)

In USE 3, operations can now be defined by SOIL statements. This reflects the connection of imperative operations and statements we drew by the stat mapping in Def. 4.9 on page 93. Listing 5.3 on page 128 provides an extended version of the Company class, now with an imperative definition of 'fire' (the complete listing in Appendix B includes imperative definitions for all four operations of the Company class). The imperative definition is enclosed by 'begin' and 'end'. The requirements with respect to free and bound variables from Def. 4.9 apply to the statements. In addition to the operational definition of 'fire', we still have the pre- and postconditions that we had in the previous version of Company. As in USE 2, we can still declare operations without imperative definitions. Table 5.1 on page 129 displays all kinds of operation definitions that are possible in USE 3. The first four lines show those combinations that were possible in USE 2 already. We have not regarded the

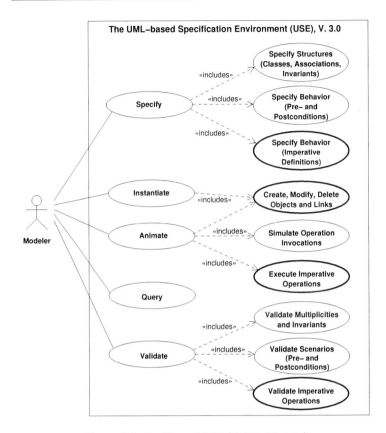

Figure 5.3: Use Cases of USE (V. 3.0 with SOIL)

```
1   class Company
2   attributes
3     name : String
4   operations
5     fire(w : Worker)
6       begin
7         delete (self,w) from Employs;
8         for p in w.projects do
9           delete (p,w) from Member;
10          if not p.missingQualifications()->isEmpty then
11            p.status := #suspended
12          end
13        end
14      end
15      pre OnlyEmployeesCanBeFired: employees->includes(w)
16      post Fired: employees->excludes(w)
17      post ProjectsStillHappy: projects->forAll(p|
18        p.status = #active implies p.missingQualifications()->isEmpty)
19      post NoEmployeeOverloaded:
20        employees->forAll(e|not e.isOverloaded())
21  constraints
22    inv OnlyOwnEmployeesInProjects:
23      employees->includesAll(projects.members->asSet)
24  end
```

Listing 5.3: USE 3.0 specification for class Company (excerpt)

first line (declaration only) in this work. We used OCL-defined query operations (line 2) throughout the work at several places. USE furthermore allows
the additional specification of pre- and postconditions for these queries (line
3). Thus, further assertions can be put on the functional definition. Notice,
that this may violate the functional character of a query operation (the operation may abort with an error). Nevertheless, this can be helpful in validating
and 'debugging' a model. In the validation of concrete scenarios (sequences
of actions), operations having pre- and postconditions but no OCL expression (line 4) can be validated. The next two lines show the construction,
animation, and validation of system states by SOIL-implemented operations.
These use cases are discussed in detail in the next two sections. It is not possible in USE to provide a SOIL and a OCL definition for an operation (rows
7–8 in Tab. 5.1). If we want to give a complemental functional definition for
an imperative operation, we have to provide the functional definition as a
postcondition.

OCL expression given	Pre- and postconditions given	Imperative definition given	Purpose
			Declaration only; Creation of class and sequence diagrams in the GUI.
✓			Side-effect free query operation to be used in other OCL expressions
✓	✓		Side-effect free query operation with further assertions (to be checked in query evaluation)
	✓		Validation of scenarios (by open-ter and opexit)
		✓	Construction and animation of system states (by operation invocations)
	✓	✓	Construction and animation; Validation of implementations by scenarios (by operation invocations)
✓		✓	(not supported in USE)
✓	✓	✓	(not supported in USE)

Table 5.1: Operation descriptions in USE models

State Instantiation (as Extended)

The six basic state manipulation commands of USE 2 have been completely replaced by SOIL (we make some remarks about compatibility later). This enables much more concise sequences of state manipulation commands, in order to instantiate a model. For example, we can create a much more compact and less error prone version of Listing 5.2 on page 123 if we add some small helper operations in class Company (Listing 5.4 on the following page). The same state as in Listing 5.2 can then be created as shown in Listing 5.5 on the next page. This version provides a higher level of abstraction, is less redundant, and requires less lines of code. This representation of the system state is much more concise and, thus, less error prone. If we think of larger system states, or families of system states, we can estimate that using SOIL statements or SOIL implemented operations can simplify the description of system states.

```
 1   class Company
 2     -- other definitions omitted
 3
 4     createWorker(qs : Set(Qualification)) : Worker begin
 5         w := new Worker;
 6         insert (self,w) into Employees;
 7         for q in qs do insert (w,q) into Qualifications end;
 8         result := w
 9       end
10
11     createProject(n : String, ws : Set(Worker), qs : Set(Qualification), s
           : ProjectSize) : Project begin
12         p := new Project;
13         insert (self, p) into Projects;
14         for w in ws do insert (p,w) into Members end;
15         for q in qs do insert (p,q) into RequiredQualifications end;
16         p.status := #active;
17         p.size := s;
18         p.name := n;
19         result := p
20       end
21   end
```

Listing 5.4: USE 3.0 specification for class Company with state instantiation helpers (excerpt)

```
 1   !create IBM : Company
 2   !IBM.name := 'International Business Machines'
 3
 4   !create Programming : Qualification
 5   !create Documentation : Qualification
 6   !create Medicine : Qualification
 7
 8   !Ada := IBM.createWorker(Set{Programming,Documentation,Medicine})
 9   !Bob := IBM.createWorker(Set{Programming,Documentation})
10   !Cher := IBM.createWorker(Set{Documentation,Medicine})
11
12   !MediAid := IBM.createProject('Medi Aid',
         Set{Ada,Bob},Set{Programming,Documentation,Medicine},#big)
13   !Tetris2 := IBM.createProject('Tetris 2.0', Set{Bob,
         Cher},Set{Programming,Documentation},#small)
```

Listing 5.5: System State Creation for Project World really using SOIL

Validation (as Extended)

The commands 'openter' and 'opexit' are not available for operations that
are defined by a SOIL statement. Instead, these operations are invoked using
the corresponding operation call statement. After having instantiated the
system state described by one of the Listings 5.2 and 5.5, we can fire Ada
using the command line by issuing !IBM.fire(Ada).

All pre- and postconditions are checked. As no pre- or postcondition viola-
tions are reported, the operation invocation conformed to its specification.
If we try to fire Ada a second time, we get the following output:

```
1  use> !IBM.fire(Ada)
2  [Error] 1 precondition in operation call `Company::fire(self:@IBM,
       w:@Worker1)' does not hold:
3    OnlyEmployeesCanBeFired: self.employees->includes(w)
4      self : Company = @IBM
5      self.employees : Set(Worker) = Set{@Worker2,@Worker3}
6      w : Worker = @Worker1
7      self.employees->includes(w) : Boolean = false
8
9    call stack at the time of evaluation:
10      1. Company::fire(self:@IBM, w:@Worker1) [caller:
           IBM.fire(Ada)@<input>:1:0]
11
12   +----------------------------------------------------------------+
13   | Evaluation is paused. You may inspect, but not modifiy the state. |
14   +----------------------------------------------------------------+
15
16   Currently only commands starting with `?', `help' or `info' are
       allowed.
17   `c' continues the evaluation (i.e. unwinds the stack).
```

In this case, the precondition 'OnlyEmployeesCanBeFired' was not fulfilled.
The user is asked if he wants to continue despite of this violation. Similarly,
the system reports if any postcondition is not fulfilled when exiting an operation. These checks are carried out for any operation invocation. Thus, in
nested operation calls, all preconditions are checked while descending down
the nested invocations, and all postconditions are checked while winding back
up the call stack.

If a postcondition is violated and the user decides to abort, any state manip-
ulations made so far are rolled back, leaving the system state in the condition
it was before executing the statement containing the offending operation call.

Our implementation of 'fire' is very simple and it will fulfill the postconditions
of 'fire' for all scenarios. A more sophisticated version with rescheduling of
project members, as sketched in the beginning, will be more complicated

and error prone though (the rescheduling problem seems to be an instance of
the NP-complete Knapsack problem, c.f. [MT90]). Thus, when developing
this implementation, we will much likely see violated postconditions several
times.

Notice that invariants are not checked during the execution of SOIL-
implemented operations. While there is a clear point in time for the validation of pre- and postconditions (before and after each invocation of an
operation), there is no clear point in time for the validation of invariants.
The OCL specification says "An OCL expression is an invariant of the type
and must be true for all instances of that type at any time" [OMG06, p.7],
but leaves the interpretation of 'any time' open. As computers are discrete
machines, we could render 'at any time' more specifically as "in any state
that we have between the execution of any two consecutive atomic actions".
However, such an interpretation would not be very practical. For example, it
would never be possible to change the link of an association with multiplicity 1, as removal and insertion are two separate actions. In whatever order we
execute them, we have a state in between that is structurally invalid. For the
same reason, we might want to have helper operations that carry out repeat-
ing sub-tasks. We may want such helper operations to create intermediate
system states that are structurally invalid. Thus, further context information
would be required in order to decide when to check which invariant.

The SQL standard for database systems solves this problem by allowing the
database developer to explicitly specify for each constraint, if it is to be
checked at statement or transaction level. USE does not comprise transactions in the current version. Therefore, we leave the decision when to check
class invariants to the modeler.

5.1.4 Compatibility

The six basic state manipulation commands from USE 2.0 are still supported
as legacy synonyms on the USE command line. They are mapped on SOIL
statements as show in Tab. 5.1.4

Legacy command and SOIL translation	Remarks
create <objName> : <clsName> ⤳ <anonymousVar> := new clsName(objName)	The parenthesis after the class name are an extension of SOIL, they allow to specify the object name, see next section.
destroy <expr> ⤳ destroy <expr>	(unchanged)
insert (<expr>,...<expr>) into A	(unchanged)
delete (<expr>,...<expr>) from A	(unchanged)
set <objExpr>.<attr> := <expr> ⤳ <objExpr>.<attr> := <expr>	
let <var> = <expr> ⤳ <var> := <expr>	

Table 5.2: Implicit Mapping of USE 2 commands on SOIL in USE 3

This mapping does not apply to the definition of operations by SOIL. Thus, `create Ada : Worker` is not valid between 'begin' and 'end'. Notice that the last line (the 'let') command is not a really one of the state manipulation commands of USE. Nevertheless, it has been used in several applications to store intermediate results for further expressions. It is mapped on the variable assignment statement in SOIL.

Within his diploma thesis, Daniel Gent performed extensive regression tests with a large number of USE command files to assure that the new version is backward compatible with the new version.

5.1.5 Extensions

In addition to the aspects we have formalized in Sect. 4.3, some extensions have been added to USE.

Error Handling

Unlike our formal definition, USE will abort with an error, if any of the error conditions described in Sect. 4.1.4 occurs. A more sophisticated error handling approach like the one we described in Sect. 4.6, however, is still left as future work (and should be in accordance with a corresponding formal definition).

SOIL-defined Query Operations

We explained in our motivation why we do not allow to use operations with side-effects as part of OCL expressions. Consequently, operations with an imperative definition cannot occur in OCL expressions in USE. This restriction can be softened by starting the system with a switch '-XsoilOpInOCL' which allows certain imperatively defined operations to be called. These operation must neither use any of the state manipulation statements from SOIL (e. g., attribute assignment), nor call any operations that contain such state manipulation statements (such operations are can be guaranteed to be side-effect free).

Object Names, Implicit Variables for Objects, and @-Syntax

The legacy version of object creation of the form `create Bob : Worker` did two things. First, it created an object named Bob in the system state, and second it assigned this object value to a variable of the same name. USE 2 disallowed further assignments to this variable. Thus, the object Bob was always reachable using the variable Bob. USE 3 mirrors this behavior on the command line by binding all objects in the system state to equally named variables. However, as there are no read-only variables in SOIL (and, thus, in USE 3), these variables can be overridden now, leaving objects without any reference to them by links or variables. As a solution to this situation, a new (proprietary) syntax extension `@<objName>` is available on the command line to safely refer to objects under all circumstances (nevertheless, '@Bob' is not a variable). Furthermore, the new object creation statement has an optional string parameter `x := new Worker('Bob')` to provide the object name in object creation. The string parameter can be any String typed OCL expression that creates a value that matches the form of an object identifier. Notice that, if the object name is already in USE, or the object name is of the wrong form (e. g., contains white spaces), the system aborts with an error. The following listing shows how these concepts interrelate:

```
1   -- This is almost the same as `create Bob : Worker'
2   x := new Worker('Bob')
3   -- now we have two variables, x and Bob,
4   -- pointing to the object Bob
5   x := 42
6   -- now only Bob refers to the object Bob
7   Bob := 43
8   -- No more variables pointing to Bob
9   -- But it always possible to use the @-Syntax
10  z := Set{@Bob}
```

Iteration over sets

In the formal description of SOIL, iteration requires a range expression of type Sequence. To iterate over a set, an explicit conversion '->asSequence' is required. This conversion is applied implicitly in USE. Thus, the following statement is valid:

```
1  for emp in Worker.allInstances do
2    emp.salary := 1000
3  end
```

5.1.6 Comparison to the Generator Extension

In [GBR03] and [GBR05], Gogolla et al. introduced an extension of USE, providing a snapshot generator. Today, this extension is bundled with USE. The motivation for this extension is to construct snapshots (system states) in a more declarative way by specifying properties that the desired snapshot has to fulfill. For this means, they developed the language ASSL (A Snapshot Sequence Language) allowing the construction of snapshots apart from giving command sequences. Thus, one can specify properties the resulting snapshots have to satisfy.

With the old command language being replaced by SOIL, we need to investigate how ASSL relates to SOIL, in order to avoid undesired redundancies in USE.

The main function of the snapshot generator is to execute an ASSL procedure. Such a procedure *tries* to construct or extend a certain system state by means of new objects, links, or attribute values. Listing 5.6 on the following page shows an ASSL procedure 'createActiveSetting'. Given a Company object as a parameter, this procedure tries to connect employees of the company to the projects of the company, such that all projects have all the qualifications they require and can become active.

Despite a slightly different syntax, ASSL contains the same basic state manipulation commands as the old (CMD) and new (SOIL) command languages. For technical reasons, OCL expressions have to be enclosed in brackets in ASSL files. The procedure 'createActiveSetting' (starting at line 1) loops over all projects of the company (lines 4–12). For each project, a second inner loop (lines 5–10) regards all required qualifications of this project. If the qualification is missing for the project (if-statement in lines 6–9), an employee is selected that is not yet a member of the project, and which is helpful for the project (line 7). For now, we assume that an arbitrary element of this sequence is selected. This selected worker is inserted in the 'Member' association (line 8). Finally, each project is set to active (line 11).

The power of ASSL lays in the 'Try' directive in line 7. To demonstrate it, we extend our 'Project World' model by two more invariants, as shown in Listing 5.7 on the next page. In this extended version, we used the query

```
1    procedure createActiveSetting(c : Company)
2      var w : Worker;
3    begin
4      for p : Project in [c.projects->asSequence] begin
5        for q : Qualification in [p.requirements->asSequence] begin
6          if [not p.members.qualifications->includes(q)] then begin
7            w := Try([(c.employees - p.members)->select(w |
                   p.isHelpful(w))->asSequence]);
8            Insert(Member,[p],[w]);
9          end;
10       end;
11       [p].status := [#active];
12     end;
13   end;
```

Listing 5.6: ASSL procedure 'createActiveSetting'

```
1    class Worker
2      // ... omitted
3    constraints
4      inv notOverloaded: not isOverloaded()
5    end
6
7    class Project
8      // ... omitted
9    constraints
10     inv AllQualificationsForActiveProject: status = #active implies
           missingQualifications()->isEmpty
11   end
```

Listing 5.7: 'Project World' extended by two more invariants

operations 'isOverloaded' and 'missingQualifications' to formulate two invariants. Let us assume we started USE with the system state in Listing 5.2 on page 123, with the exception that we omitted lines 45–47. Thus, we omitted all initial assignments of employees to projects. Furthermore, we will set both projects to size 'big' later.

Obviously, if we now started 'createActiveSetting' and selected an arbitrary employee in line 7, we could end up with an invalid state, for example, because employees are overloaded with work. This is were the 'Try' directive comes into play. It initiates a backtracking search. All elements of the sequence line 7 are tried, in order to construct a valid system state, i.e., a state that fulfills all structural constraints, including all invariants.

The following lines show our interaction with USE on the command line:

```
 1  use> Tetris2.size := #big
 2  USE> gen start -r 1 projects.assl createActiveSetting(IBM)
 3  USE> gen result
 4  Random number generator was initialized with 1.
 5  Checked 14 snapshots.
 6  Result: Valid state found.
 7  Commands to produce the valid state:
 8  !insert (MediAid,Cher) into Member
 9  !insert (MediAid,Ada) into Member
10  !set @MediAid.status := #active
11  !insert (Tetris2,Bob) into Member
12  !set @Tetris2.status := #active
13  USE> gen result accept
14  Generated result (system state) accepted.
```

First we set the Tetris2 project to size big. Then, we start the procedure named 'createActiveSetting' in the file 'projects.assl' in line 1. The object IBM is passed as the Company parameter to the procedure. The switch '-r 1' sets a fixed seed for the generation of random numbers. This is done to get repeatable results for the examples. As there is no further output from the 'gen start' command, the generator has found a valid system state using our procedure. The next command 'gen result' (line 3) tells the snapshot generator to display us the commands necessary to create this state. The tool tells us it had to check 14 snapshots to find a valid one. This means, the 'Try' directive induced 13 backtracking steps in order to find a state. The result shows us, that Ada and Cher will be assigned to the MediAid project, whereas Bob will be assigned to Tetris2. We can accept this system state (make it the current one) by issuing the 'gen result accept' command in line 13.

We can make the business situation even harder by removing Bob from the employees of IBM. In this case, the generator cannot find any valid system

state. Obviously, it is not possible to make both projects active with just
Ada and Cher:

```
1  USE> Tetris2.size := #big
2  USE> delete (IBM,Bob) from Employs
3  USE> gen start -r 1 projects.assl createActiveSetting(IBM)
4  USE> gen result
5  Random number generator was initialized with 1.
6  Checked 4 snapshots.
7  Result: No valid state found.
```

The examples demonstrate that ASSL procedures can used to specify effects
on UML models. Nevertheless, there are some important differences. Table 5.3 shows the major differences between the old command line language
CMD, ASSL and SOIL. Both ASSL and SOIL completely cover the expres-

	CMD	ASSL	SOIL
Basic state manipulations	✓	✓	✓
Flow control		✓	✓
Explicit variable declarations required		✓	
Implementations of UML operations by state-ments			✓
Recursive invocations of operations			✓
Declarative creation of states by backtracking		✓	

Table 5.3: Differences between ASSL and SOIL

siveness of the old command line language (as explained in Sect. 5.1.4, the
old syntax is still working on the command line; internally it is mapped on
SOIL statements). Furthermore, both languages support flow control. Apart
from syntactical differences (we could eliminate the need to put all OCL
expressions in brackets in the SOIL implementation), there is no differences
between both languages. All languages support the notion of variable. In
ASSL, variables have to be declared before they can be used. In SOIL variable
declarations are implicitly inferred. The CMD language requires no variable
declaration either. However, as there are no compound statements in CMD,
there was no type checking required. Only SOIL statements can be used to
define an operation for a class in the model specification. ASSL procedures
are not related to classes, and there is no implicit parameter *self* available.
The most important difference in expressiveness is depicted in the last two
lines. Only SOIL supports the (recursive) invocation of operations from operations. In ASSL, one cannot call an ASSL procedure from within another
ASSL procedure. On the contrary, ASSL supports the declarative specification of system states by the backtracking directive 'Try'. In SOIL, we have
to fully implement such search operations by hand.

In summary, none of the languages ASSL and SOIL completely covers the other. The strength of ASSL lays in the declarative *construction* of states, whereas the strength of SOIL lays in the specification of *behavior*.

We believe, that ASSL is even more useful than before, in USE 3, due to the extended validation capabilities of the new version. In USE 3, not only certain scenarios can be validated (by openter/opexit) but complete implementations can be validated. We illustrated this by the operation 'fire'. In USE 2, we could check certain sequences of basic state manipulation commands to see, if they constitute a valid instantiation of the 'fire' operation w. r. t. the pre- and postconditions. In USE 3, we can furthermore check for an actual implementation of 'fire' if it is valid under a certain initial system state, or not. A proper validation of operations in this sense requires a proper set of initial system states, e. g., a large set of combinations of big/medium/small projects, few and many employees, and different constellations of qualifications. The snapshot generator is perfectly suited to create such system states.

With respect to the syntax, we think the syntax of ASSL should be aligned to the syntax of SOIL in a future work.

5.1.7   Conclusions

In this section we summarized how the theoretical considerations of our work could be translated into the UML-based Specification Environment as part of a diploma thesis. This extension could be realized in a backward compatible manner. We explained how the features of the USE system were extended for the modeling and validation of imperative operations as well as for a more concise treatment of system state modifications. We believe that this yields an even more versatile USE than before. Now, a whole refinement process from classes and associations over constraints towards implementations can be represented in USE, with validation at all stages. We finally compared the language SOIL with the snapshot generator and the language ASSL. We explained why both languages are still required in the future, and how ASSL can help in the validation of operations which are implemented by SOIL statements.

A last remark on validation: The USE system has never been a model checker or a theorem prover, nor is it now. Thus, for system states, it can tell us if a certain state is valid w. r. t. the model, it cannot tell us, if there exists a state of the model, in general. Analogously, USE can tell us if a certain interaction (in the sense of operation invocations) is valid w. r. t. the model. It cannot tell us if a certain implementation of method is sound with respect to its pre- and postconditions. This work is left for theorem proving approaches such as [BW08].

5.2   XGenerator2

The XGenerator2 is a software tool that constitutes one of the core elements of a model-driven architecture which is applied in several eGovernment projects in Germany in the context of DOL (Deutschland OnLine, Germany online). In 2010, its application has been made mandatory for eGovernment projects in Germany in order to achieve the 'XÖV conformance certificate' from the Bundesministerium des Innern (German for Federal Ministry of Interior) and the OSCI Leitstelle (OSCI coordination office), c. f. [BCC$^+$10].

As a member of the Research Group Database Systems, the author of this thesis has been actively engaged in the development of this tool, as well as in the definition of the XÖV conformance criteria. The work was carried out as a joined project of the]init[AG, Berlin and the Technologie-Zentrum Informatik und Informationstechnik (TZI).

DOL and XÖV in general span a really large field, including technical and organizational aspects, and a lot more infrastructure than just XGenerator2. In this work, however, we focus on XGenerator2 only. We have published a much more detailed view on DOL and XÖV in [BKG$^+$08].

XGenerator2 performs several tasks with respect to model validation and model transformation. OCL expressions are employed (1) to enforce modeling constraints and (2), within the model transformation tasks, to query UML input models. These queries are embedded into an imperative template language that is used to render several textual outputs from the input model. While syntactically different from SOIL, the embedding of OCL into this template language follows the requirements that we developed in Chap. 2. The template language resembles SOIL but is more restricted.

5.2.1   Context: MDA Employed in a Joint eGovernment Strategy

DOL is a joint eGovernment strategy by the federal government, federal-state governments, and municipalities in Germany [DOL]. Its objectives include the provision of a standardization infrastructure to support the development and deployment of semantic standards for electronic data exchange between and with public authorities, so-called XÖV standards (XML in der Öffentlichen Verwaltung, XML in public authorities). Several concrete ongoing XÖV projects (including civil status registration, data exchange for immigration offices, data exchange in the judiciary domain, and municipal citizens registration) have been realized as DOL projects on top of this infrastructure.

An important task of XÖV projects is to specify the electronic processes between communication partners describing which data has to (resp. is allowed to) be transmitted, and when. In most projects, this is set on an abstract level by specific laws. All this information is collected in conceptual models. The resulting data transmission models have to be translated into precise technical specifications (published by the respective authorities). These specifications, containing XML schemas, documentation, and WSDL files, are required later on by tool vendors to implement interoperable solutions for the public administration. The development of such specifications is time and resource consuming. Therefore, in addition to concrete technological recommendations (e. g., for using XML on top of the secure OSCI Transport [OSC02] protocol), the initiative also aims to standardize the definition process of electronic data exchange specifications. The specifications of an XÖV project are frequently called the XÖV standards.

On the technical level, the infrastructure of DOL and XÖV includes (requires) UML models, UML profiles, and an MDA tool, to provide a unifying production chain for XÖV standards. Automated profile validation is employed to ensure standardized UML models for individual XÖV projects, and correct usage of information core components in the domain models of XÖV projects. Model transformation is employed to generate standardized products from the UML models, such as XML Schema files, web service definition (WSDL) files, and documentation.

The MDA tool XGenerator2 has been developed in DOL to perform the profile validation and transformation tasks for XÖV projects. A specific UML profile, the XÖV UML profile, has been developed to enforce several modeling rules for the UML domain models and to attach platform-specific information to the models. This additional information is used by XGenerator2 to produce the various products that are required to publish an XÖV specification. XGenerator2 is based on OCL to configure the validation and transformation tasks. OCL is employed to describe the well-formedness rules in the UML profiles and to formulate query expressions within the transformation language.

The model-driven architecture of DOL, including the XÖV UML profile and XGenerator2, has been developed in cooperation between government, public authorities, industry, and academia. The DOL project shows a successful transfer of MDA technology into "real world" projects. The XGenerator has been released under the GNU public license on [SF] and we encourage employment in other projects.

In the following, we focus only on the way OCL is used in XGenerator2, and how the imperative model-to-text transformation language embeds OCL. More details about the 'bigger picture' of the technical aspects of XÖV standardization can be found in [BKG+08, BCC+10].

5.2.2   The XGenerator2 Tool

The XGenerator2 is the central MDA ingredient in DOL. It supports the model-driven development process of an XÖV project in two major activities, *model validation* and *model transformation*. The tool is utilized in domain working groups (to check model validity) as well as in the final generation of the specification products (XML Schema, Documentation, WSDL files).

Figure 5.4 shows a data flow perspective of the XGenerator. Basically, the tool reads a UML model and produces several output documents; in case of any problem, it produces an error report instead. A more detailed description follows:

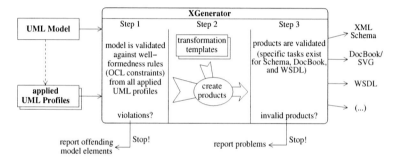

Figure 5.4: The XGenerator: Validation and Transformation

Initially, the UML model is read from a corresponding XMI (XML Metadata Interchange) file. This file is exported from a CASE tool. The EMF UML2 XMI importer, used here, supports a wide range of UML tools. All UML profiles that are applied to this model are read as well (in this case, the XÖV profile, other profiles may apply as well, such as the Core Components Profile, c.f. [UN06]). As the first step, the tool validates the model against its profiles. This means, all well-formedness rules from the profiles are checked by evaluating their OCL invariants. If any well-formedness rule is violated, a detailed list of the violated rules and the offending UML model elements is reported to the user and the tool stops.

If the model has been successfully validated, the XGenerator generates its outputs. The tool supports the generation of arbitrary textual output formats. A future version might also support other transformation paradigms, such as model-to-model transformations. The generation process is configured by means of *transformation templates*. The current projects employ transformation templates for XML Schema, DocBook (including SVG for graphics), and WSDL. Transformation templates can be developed and maintained without modifications of the tool. Well-formedness rule specification and the transformation language are described in detail below.

For the aforementioned output formats, the XGenerator further supports a final format-specific validation of the results. This is a built-in addition to the tool. Ideally, a valid UML model never produces invalid output documents. However, to detect bugs in the development of transformation templates, Step 3 in Fig. 5.4 on the facing page has proven to be a quality assurance measure to catch errors that result from unexpected model constellations. Often, such errors led to further OCL well-formedness rules in the XÖV profile, to prevent such constellations in future developments.

5.2.2.1 Well-formedness rule validation

UML profiles define well-formedness rules to control their correct application (e. g., correct usage of stereotypes). The XGenerator supports the automatic validation of well-formedness rules if they are specified as OCL invariants. To validate a UML profile, these OCL invariants have to be specified in the context of a UML metaclass or a stereotype.

OCL invariants can be provided as an external XML file to the XGenerator. A (constructed) example well-formedness rule looks as follows:

```
<invariant context='Class' name='propsUniqueInClass'>
  <body>
    self.ownedAttribute->forAll(p1,p2 |
      p1.extensionMyStereo.prop = p2.extensionMyStereo.prop
        implies (p1=p2) )
  </body>
  <documentation>
    Prop values must be unique in each class!
  </documentation>
</invariant>
```

The semantics of invariants is as usual. The XGenerator internally uses the UML-based Specification Environment (USE) [GBR07b] as its OCL evaluation and validation engine.

5.2.2.2 Transformation templates

The XGenerator currently provides model-to-text transformations (a comparison to other approaches follows in the next subsection). The transformation templates are operational descriptions that, given a UML model as input, produce one or more text files as output. Similar to template processors such as JSP or Apache Velocity (which is actually used internally by the

XGenerator), the transformation templates consist of fragments of the result
document which are surrounded by template language directives. Compared
with conventional programming languages, the output data is contained directly whereas transformation and template logic is escaped (indicated by
'#' or '$' in Fig. 5.5).

The XGenerator uses only a few processing directives: conditional output,
iteration (foreach), sub-template evaluation, and evaluation of expressions.
The templates use OCL as an expression language to query and navigate
through the UML model. Applied profile stereotypes and their properties
are available as specified by the OMG.

Figure 5.5 provides a small example to illustrate the XGenerator transformation templates. The example template generates a simple model summary
(classes and attributes). On the left-hand side there is a UML model (which
consists of only two classes). The model uses a single stereotype «MyStereo»
from a UML profile (constructed for this example, not shown in this figure).
«MyStereo» introduces a single stereotype property *prop* that can be set
wherever this stereotype is applied. (In UML 2, stereotype properties replace
UML 1.x tagged values that could be applied independently of stereotypes.)
On top of the figure, we see a transformation template which is parametrised
with a single package typed parameter *p*. Let us assume that this template
is invoked with our complete UML model (such a root template has to be
specified in the XGenerator configuration).

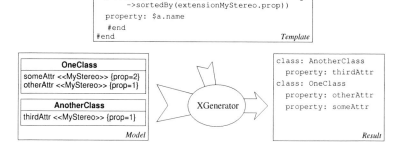

Figure 5.5: Transformation Template Example

The template evaluation will produce the output shown on the right-hand
side. The evaluation consists of two nested foreach-loops, the outer iterates
over all classes, the inner iterates over the attributes of each class. The outer

loop uses an additional operation *hlpAllClasses()* in the metaclass Package in its range expression. The XGenerator supports the definition of such additional OCL operations for all metaclasses. Let us assume that *hlpAllClasses()* returns all classes contained in this package in alphabetical ordering. Additional operations allow us to factor out common methods of transformation templates. In contrast, the inner loop uses an inline OCL expression to sort a set of attributes by their *prop* values.

Notice that three different languages are used in the template depicted in Fig. 5.5 on the facing page: (1) the template control language consisting of operational constructs (they all start with a hash sign), (2) embedded OCL as a side-effect free expression language, and (3) fragments in the actual output language (e. g., XML Schema or DocBook).

At the time of writing, the XÖV transformation templates consist of approximately 1200 lines of code. These include only simple OCL expressions. Complex logic is factored out into additional operations of approx 230 lines of OCL.

5.2.3   Relationship between the XGenerator Template Language and SOIL

Table 5.4 on the next page shows the language elements of the XGenerator template language and SOIL. We can summarize the relationships as follows:

- **Flow control:** Both languages have the same flow control capabilities: sequential execution, conditional execution, iteration, and sub-routine calls.

- **Variable assignments:** Both languages provide assignments to variables, which are visible in OCL expressions within the corresponding frame (i. e., the remainder of a template, the scope of an iteration).

- **Operation calls:** Both languages provide the invocation of operations (resp. templates). The XGenerator2 does not support return values.

- **State manipulation:** The template language has no capabilities to change the system state. In XGenerator2, the system state is read-only, the (textual) output is kept separately from the (model) input.

- **Generating output:** There is no direct correspondence for textual output in SOIL.

If we look at generating output as 'syntactic sugar' for accumulating a String expression (we made a similar consideration for Model-to-Text in Sect. 2.3.2), we could regard the XGenerator2 template language as a direct subset of SOIL. However, there is no static type-checking for templates. Referencing an unbound variable from within an OCL expression produces a runtime error in XGenerator2. Thus, in comparison to SOIL, executing a template resembles executing several SOILstatements interactively (c.f. Sect. 4.3.3 about step-wise execution of statements).

Although we defined no formal semantics for the template language, we can say it fulfills the requirements we set in Chap. 2. We embedded the USE tool as a library in XGenerator2, without any modifications. There were no extensions to the set of OCL expressions, OCL expressions are still side-effect free, and statements in the template language are disjoint from expressions.

XGenerator2 template	SOIL
n/a	$\Diamond$
#s1 #s2	$s_1; s_2$
#set($v = e)	$v := e$
n/a	$e_1.\text{attr} := e_2$
n/a	v := new C
n/a	destroy e
n/a	insert$(e_1, \ldots, e_n)$ into A
n/a	delete$(e_1, \ldots, e_n)$ from A
#if(e) ... #else ... #end	if e then ... else ... end
#foreach($v in e) ... #end	for v in e do ... end
$template.call(t, $e_1, \ldots, e_n$)	$t(e_1, \ldots, e_n)$
n/a	$v := t(e_1, \ldots, e_n)$
⟨text⟩	n/a

Table 5.4: Comparison of XGenerator template language and SOIL

5.2.4   Conclusions

We shortly sketched the employment of MDA technology in the context of eGovernment in Germany. The model-driven architecture provides three major benefits for XÖV projects: (1) The separation of conceptual model-ing from technical details (e.g., XML Schema) allows a closer integration of non-technical domain experts into the modeling process. (2) The integrated generation of the various parts of an XÖV specification (documentation, XML Schema, WSDL) has proven to be a time-saving and, in particular, consistent way to deal with the inherent redundancies between them. (3) Most rules regarding the standardization of standards (e.g., uniform struc-tures and namings for XML schema, reuse of standardized data types) are implicitly enforced by the production chain.

Within the MDA tool XGenerator2, OCL has been successfully employed in model validation and transformation. Especially, OCL has been embedded into the template language of XGenerator2. Unlike MOF Model-to-Text, the XGenerator2 template language is a full-fledged imperative programming language in the sense that it provides variable assignments. However, there are no state manipulation capabilities in the language. Although there is no formal semantics for the language, it fulfills the requirements of a modular embedding of OCL as postulated in Sect. 2.5.

Chapter 6

Conclusion

In this thesis, we investigated the reuse of the Object Constraint Language (OCL) as part of imperative programming languages. The results are summarized in Sect. 6.1. In Sect. 6.2 we draw some conclusions and outline future work.

6.1 Summary

In Chapters 1 and 2 we put our work in the context of Executable UML, the Model-Driven Architecture (MDA) and ImperativeOCL. While the side-effect free language OCL has already been successfully employed in the specification of models, many variants of the Executable UML and MDA approaches require a further side-effected textual language to express certain behavioral aspects of models, and to describe model processing operations such as model transformations.

It is obvious to employ OCL as the foundation for these side-effected languages, and several approaches use extended versions of OCL, most prominently the "official" OMG MDA language ImperativeOCL, which is part of the Query, Views, Transformations (QVT) standard.

We explained that – unfortunately – most of these approaches extend OCL in a way that leads into inconsistencies on the semantics level. By identifying expressions and statements in the extended languages, aspects such as strict or non-strict evaluation of logical connectives suddenly become relevant. This not only renders the language definition incomplete, it also yields to possible incompatibilities between OCL tools. Furthermore, the addition of new imperative language constructs such as loops yield redundancies with existing OCL constructs that could be (mis-)used for the same purposes.

Apart from the semantic issues, we showed that these approaches extend
OCL in a way that conflicts with a modular reuse of OCL components (or
libraries) on the implementation level. Seeing the increasing number of UML
modeling tools, OCL tools, and corresponding libraries, this is a real problem
in practice and could constitute an obstacle in further standardization and
tool interoperability.

Therefore, we formulated the requirement of a modular reuse of OCL in
the definition of imperative languages. This requirement of modularity holds
for the formal level (assuming a denotational semantics for both OCL and
the imperative language) as well as for the implementation level (w. r. t. the
interfaces to OCL evaluation components and libraries).

Before we could introduce the language SOIL in Chap. 4 we had to provide several foundations regarding the formal semantics of UML and OCL
in Chap. 3. While we followed Richters' definitions straightforward in general, we had to make some modifications or extensions at some points. These
modifications were not related to SOIL, but regarded the adherence to the
current OCL standard. Especially, we provided a clarification regarding the
treatment of polymorphic applications of collection constructors, and we introduced the OCL 2 type OclVoid. The inclusion of the OclVoid type, yielding a lattice in the OCL type hierarchy, had impacts on the undefined value
as well. It is noteworthy that these modifications have been implemented in
the UML tool USE as well.

With this background we could then introduce our own language SOIL in
Chap. 4 . SOIL is a simple, yet complete imperative programming language
which is based on OCL as its core for expressions. We first introduced the
language informally, then we provided formal syntax and denotational semantics. These formal definitions are based on the formal definitions for
OCL, in a modular way. Thus, we did not change any of the definitions of
OCL when we described SOIL. We presented examples for the informal and
for the formal parts. Our language provides sophisticated type inference and
does not require explicit variable declarations.

We formally investigated the type-soundness of SOIL. We proved a theorem
stating that no (syntactically derivable) SOIL statement has an undefined
or inconsistent interpretation. We furthermore proved, that SOIL statements
can be safely used to define imperative operations (unless there is recursion
involved, which always leaves a back door for undefined semantics). We want
to stress that the extensive proofs of these theorems have not been an end of
its own. They have rather been a valuable quality assurance instrument that
grew along with the actual definitions of the syntax and semantics. We had
to make several revisions of the definitions as a direct result of (a dead end)
in the process of proving. We believe that the definitions have a high quality
now. However, the development of the soundness proofs for SOIL required

more effort than initially planned and the proofs got quite lengthy. A proof environment such as the Isabelle HOL-OCL [BW08] should be considered for future extensions of SOIL.

In the following we discussed how SOIL's treatment of errors could be improved in an exception handling style, and we related our language to UML's Action Semantics and the Object Action Language used in Executable UML by Mellor. We pointed out that SOIL could be used in Executable UML without any modification.

In Chap. 5 we presented two practical applications of our work. The first application is a major revision of USE. This revision has been done as part of a Master project which has been supervised by the author. Noteworthy, our definition of the language could be implemented in the USE tool in a straightforward manner. This is in contrast with previous experiences we made in similar projects. It underpins our opinion that the efforts for the soundness proofs where well-invested.

The language SOIL could be employed to fully replace the old command line language for state manipulation of USE. In the new version of USE, a much broader range of applications have been opened up. While the old command line language could only be used to replay predefined scenarios of basic state manipulation commands, the new USE allows real programming within an interactive visual environment. The interplay of descriptive behavioral modeling with pre- and postconditions on the one hand, and imperative definitions on the other hand, could be used to connect different stages of the model refinement process. We explained how SOIL relates to the snapshot generator language ASSL. We pointed out that both languages are still required in the future. The extension of USE by SOIL especially benefits from the snapshot generator w.r.t. the validation of imperatively defined operations.

The second application we presented is the model-to-text MDA tool XGenerator2 which has been successfully employed in several eGovernment projects in the past years. While XGenerator2 does not directly implement the full SOIL language, it still perfectly follows our requirement of a modular embedding of OCL into another imperative language.

6.2 Conclusions and Future Work

SOIL is meant to be a complete but simple (i. e., easy to understand) example of how to define a sound imperative language that includes OCL in a modular way.

While being simple, the language has proven practical enough to be added to the USE tool as an replacement for the command line language for state manipulation. This introduced a number of new applications for USE. The complementing aspects of declarative modeling (by pre- and postconditions) and imperative modeling (by providing a SOIL implementation) of behavior can now be investigated in USE side-by-side. Together with the visual and interactive character of USE we see a great potential for a step-wise refinement of declarative models into executable models. This could be used especially in teaching of software engineering (c.f. [EHLS05] for the use of UML in computer science education). We can clearly imagine how to start in class with a descriptive model of a domain (let us say, a project planning system), defining several invariants and pre-/postconditions. Then, step by step, the operations could be filled with SOIL implementations, transitioning from a simple scenario replaying to a full implementation. All work with the "model under refinement" could be done in the same environment, checking the descriptive model aspects at every time.

In this context, a final ingredient that should be added in the future, regards the interactive visualization of behavior. The USE environment should be extended in a way that SOIL implementations can be executed step-wise, or in slow speed. Such a feature should include appropriate visualizations for state changes and the operation invocations. We think an extends like this could be realized in a future student project.

Regarding the interplay of SOIL and the ASSL, we showed that ASSL contributes an important instrument to validate (i.e., test) imperative implementations of operations. However, in the current version, this is restricted to instantiating initial test states. An extension of ASSL should be considered which allows the actual invocation of SOIL-implemented operations. With this extension, complete scenarios of state instantiations and interacting objects could be created by the generator.

With respect to the language itself, an OMG compliant metamodel should be defined, as it has been done for OCL. This metamodel would build on the OCL metamodel as a module. The syntax of SOIL had to be embedded as well-formedness rules. Maybe this work could be done in a future B. Sc. project. Alternatively, a UML profile could be defined that allows to safely represent SOIL statements using UML Actions (we sketched this in Sect. 4.7).

A possible extension of SOIL itself that could be added for further practical use, is a more sophisticated error handling. SOIL is constructed in a way that no errors can occur in a formal sense – every syntactically correct statement can be interpreted, there is no error-state. For example, an empty link $(\perp, \perp)$ can be added to an association extent. Such a statement simply has no effect. However, a better handling of these situation is desirable for real applications. The formal semantics of SOIL could be improved by an exception-style error handling as sketched in Sect. 4.6. The signature of the interpretation function had to be extended by an error state which is propagated through the semantic derivation. This should be accompanied by further language elements for exception handling (try/catch constructs as we know them from other modern imperative object-oriented languages). If done, such an extension should be made on the formal level (including an extension of the proof of the type soundness theorem) as well as on the implementation level.

Finally, another possible variation of SOIL is explicit variable declaration. Although we decided to define an implicit declaration of variables by type inference for SOIL, an explicit declaration of variables seems to be desirable for some people. In fact, our type inference approach is stronger than an explicit variable approach. Thus, the formal definitions of the syntax and semantics of SOIL could be extended easily to support explicit variable declaration. To achieve this extension, another statement *define* would be required, and the syntax rules had to be changed to require explicit declaration. We assume that no changes would be required on the semantics level (except for the new *define* statement which would have identity semantics).

Bibliography

[AC96]   M. Abadi and L. Cardelli. *A Theory of Objects*. Springer-Verlag, New York, 1996.

[ALSU07] A. V. Aho, M. S. Lam, R. Sethi, and J. D. Ullman. *Compilers: Principles, Techniques, and Tools*. Addison-Wesley Longman, Amsterdam, 2nd edition, 2007.

[AP08]   D. Akehurst and O. Patrascoiu.   KMF (Kent Modeling Framework) OCL Library. website, http://www.cs.kent.ac.uk/projects/ocl/tools.html, last visited 10.02.2011, 2008.

[APW08] E. G. Aydal, R. F. Paige, and J. Woodcock.   Evaluation of OCL for Large-Scale Modelling: A Different View of the Mondex Purse. *ECEASST*, 9, 2008.

[AZH08] D. H. Akehurst, S. Zschaler, and W. G. J. Howells. OCL: Modularising the Language. *ECEASST*, 9, 2008.

[Baa05] T. Baar. OCL and graph-transformations - A symbiotic alliance to alleviate the frame problem. In J.-M. Bruel, editor, *MoDELS Satellite Events*, volume 3844 of *Lecture Notes in Computer Science*, pages 20–31. Springer, 2005.

[BB06]   F. Büttner and H. Bauerdick.   Realizing UML Model Transformations with USE.   In D. Chiorean, B. Demuth, M. Gogolla, and J. Warmer, editors, *UML/MoDELS Workshop on OCL (OCLApps'2006)*, pages 96–110. Technical University of Dresden, Technical Report TUD-FI06, 2006.

[BBG05] F. Büttner, H. Bauerdick, and M. Gogolla. Towards Transformation of Integrity Constraints and Database States. In D. C. Martin, editor, *Proc. Dexa'2005 Workshop Logical Aspects and Applications of Integrity Constraints (LAAIC'2005)*, pages 823–828. IEEE, Los Alamitos, 2005.

[BBG⁺06] J. Bezivin, F. Büttner, M. Gogolla, F. Jouault, I. Kurtev, and A. Lindow. Model Transformations? Transformation Models! In O. Nierstrasz, J. Whittle, D. Harel, and G. Reggio, editors, *Proc. 9th Int. Conf. Model Driven Engineering Languages and Systems (MoDELS'2006)*. LNCS 4199, Springer, Berlin, 2006.

[BCC⁺10] F. Büttner, N. Cordes, C. Crome, S. Drees, A. Franke, L. Hamann, J. Heins, C. Karich, Krolczyk, M. Kuhlmann, K. Lahmann, C. Lange, D. Lopes, Y. Rabenstein, C. Senf, F. Steimke, A. Stosiek, H. Weber, and W. Zimmer. *Handbuch zur Entwicklung XÖV-konformer IT-Standards*. OSCI-Leitstelle Bremen, Die Beauftragte der Bundesregierung für Informationstechnik, March 2010.

[BG04a] F. Büttner and M. Gogolla. On Generalization and Overriding in UML 2.0. In J. Bezivin, T. Baar, T. Gardner, M. Gogolla, R. Hähnle, H. Hußmann, O. Patrascoiu, P. H. Schmitt, and J. Warmer, editors, *Proc. UML'2004 Workshop OCL and Model Driven Engineering*, pages 69–69. In: UML - Modeling Languages and Applications. Nuno Jardim Nunes, Bran Selic, Alberto Rodrigues da Silva, Ambrosio Toval Alvarez (Eds). LNCS 3297, Springer Verlag. Long version: University of Kent, http://www.cs.kent.ac.uk/projects/ocl/oclmdewsuml04/, 2004.

[BG04b] F. Büttner and M. Gogolla. Realizing UML Metamodel Transformations with AGG. In R. Heckel, editor, *Proc. ETAPS Workshop Graph Transformation and Visual Modeling Techniques (GT-VMT'2004)*. Electronic Notes in Theoretical Computer Science (ENTCS), Elsevier, 2004.

[BG06] F. Büttner and M. Gogolla. Realizing Graph Transformations by Pre- and Postconditions and Command Sequences. In A. Corradini, H. Ehrig, U. Montanari, L. Ribeiro, and G. Rozenberg, editors, *Proc. 3rd Int. Conf. Graph Transformations (ICGT'2006)*, pages 398–412. LNCS 4178, Springer, Berlin, 2006.

[BGH⁺10] F. Büttner, M. Gogolla, L. Hamann, M. Kuhlmann, and A. Lindow. On Better Understanding OCL Collections *or* An OCL Ordered Set is not an OCL Set. In S. Ghosh, editor, *Workshops and Symposia at 12th Int. Conf. Model Driven Engineering Languages and Systems (MODELS'2009)*, pages 276–290. Springer, Berlin, LNCS 6002, 2010.

[BK09] F. Büttner and M. Kuhlmann. Shortcomings of the Embedding of OCL into QVT ImperativeOCL. In M. R. Chaudron, editor,

Workshops and Symposia at 11th Int. Conf. Model Driven Engineering Languages and Systems (MODELS'2008), pages 263–272. Springer, Berlin, LNCS 5421, 2009.

[BKG⁺08] F. Büttner, M. Kuhlmann, M. Gogolla, J. Dietrich, F. Steimke, A. Pankratz, A. Stosiek, and A. Salomon. MDA Employed in a Joint eGovernment Strategy: An Experience Report. In T. Bailey, editor, *Proc. 3rd ECMDA Workshop "From Code Centric To Model Centric Software Engineering" (2008)*. European Software Institute, http://www.esi.es/modelplex/c2m/program.php, 2008.

[Boo94] G. Booch. *Object-Oriented Analysis and Design with Applications*. Benjamin/Cummings, 1994.

[BRLG04] F. Büttner, O. Radfelder, A. Lindow, and M. Gogolla. Digging into the Visitor Pattern. In F. Maurer and G. Ruhe, editors, *Proc. IEEE 16th Int. Conf. Software Engineering and Knowlege Engineering (SEKE'2004)*. IEEE, Los Alamitos, 2004.

[Büt08] F. Büttner. OMG Issue Reporting Process, MOF QVT Issue 13082 (The current abstract syntax of ImperativeOCL introduces a couple of unclear situations). available online, http://www.omg.org/issues/issue13082.txt, 2008.

[Büt05] F. Büttner. Transformation-Based Structure Model Evolution. In J.-M. Bruel, editor, *Satellite Events at the MoDELS'2005 Conference*, pages 339–340. Springer, Berlin, LNCS 3844, 2005.

[BW08] A. D. Brucker and B. Wolff. HOL-OCL: A Formal Proof Environment for UML/OCL. In J. L. Fiadeiro and P. Inverardi, editors, *FASE*, volume 4961 of *Lecture Notes in Computer Science*, pages 97–100. Springer, 2008.

[Cab07] J. Cabot. From Declarative to Imperative UML/OCL Operation Specifications. In C. Parent, K.-D. Schewe, V. C. Storey, and B. Thalheim, editors, *ER*, volume 4801 of *Lecture Notes in Computer Science*, pages 198–213. Springer, 2007.

[Che76] P. P. Chen. The Entity-Relationship Model: Toward a Unified View of Data. *ACM Transactions on Database Systems*, 1:9–36, 1976.

[CJMB08] J. S. Cuadrado, F. Jouault, J. G. Molina, and J. Bézivin. Deriving OCL Optimization Patterns from Benchmarks. *ECEASST*, 15, 2008.

[Cod70]   E. F. Codd. A Relational Model of Data for Large Shared Data
            Banks. *Communications of the ACM*, 13(6):pages 377–387, June
            1970.

[CPC⁺04]   D. Chiorean, M. Pasca, A. Cârcu, C. Botiza, and S. Moldovan.
            Ensuring UML Models Consistency Using the OCL Environ-
            ment. *Electronic Notes in Theorethical Computer Science*,
            102:99–110, 2004.

[CT07]   J. Cabot and E. Teniente. Transformation techniques for OCL
            constraints. *Science of Computer Programming*, 68(3):179–195,
            2007.

[DKR00]   D. S. Distefano, J. P. Katoen, and A. Rensink. Towards model
            checking ocl. In *ECOOP 2000: Defining Precise Semantics for
            UML, Sophia Antipolis, France*. June 2000.

[DN66]   O. Dahl and K. Nygaard. SIMULA, an ALGOL-based simulation
            language. *Communications of the ACM*, 9(9):671–678, Septem-
            ber 1966.

[DOL]   Deutschland Online. Website, http://www.deutschland-online.
            de, last visited 10.02.2011.

[EHLS05]   G. Engels, J. H. Hausmann, M. Lohmann, and S. Sauer. Teaching
            UML Is Teaching Software Engineering Is Teaching Abstraction.
            In J.-M. Bruel, editor, *MoDELS Satellite Events*, volume 3844
            of *Lecture Notes in Computer Science*, pages 306–319. Springer,
            2005.

[Ehr92]   H. Ehrig. Introduction to graph grammars with applications to
            semantic networks. *Computer Mathematical Applications*, 23(6-
            9):557–5572, 1992.

[EN10]   R. Elmasri and S. B. Navathe. *Fundamentals of Database Sys-
            tems*. Addison Wesley, 6th edition, 2010.

[EPS]   Epsilon project page homepage. Website, http://www.eclipse.
            org/gmt/epsilon/, last visited 10.02.2011.

[F03]   S. Flake and W. M. 0003. Formal semantics of static and tempo-
            ral state-oriented OCL constraints. *Software and System Model-
            ing*, 2(3):164–186, 2003.

[FM08]   D. Flanagan and Y. Matsumoto. *The Ruby Programming Lan-
            guage*. O'Reilly Media, 2008.

[GBD08]   M. Gogolla, F. Büttner, and D.-H. Dang. From Graph Transformation to OCL using USE. In A. Schürr, M. Nagl, and A. Zündorf, editors, *Proc. 3rd Int. Workshop Applications of Graph Transformation with Industrial Relevance (AGTIVE '07)*, pages 585–586. Springer, Berlin, LNCS 5088, 2008.

[GBR03]   M. Gogolla, J. Bohling, and M. Richters. Validation of UML and OCL Models by Automatic Snapshot Generation. In G. Booch, P. Stevens, and J. Whittle, editors, *Proc. 6th Int. Conf. Unified Modeling Language (UML'2003)*, pages 265–279. Springer, Berlin, LNCS 2863, 2003.

[GBR05]   M. Gogolla, J. Bohling, and M. Richters. Validating UML and OCL Models in USE by Automatic Snapshot Generation. *Journal on Software and System Modeling*, 4(4):386–398, 2005.

[GBR07a] M. Gogolla, F. Büttner, and M. Richters. USE: A UML-Based Specification Environment for Validating UML and OCL. *Science of Computer Programming*, 69:27–34, 2007.

[GBR07b] M. Gogolla, F. Büttner, and M. Richters. USE: A UML-Based Specification Environment for Validating UML and OCL. *Science of Computer Programming*, 69:27–34, 2007.

[GBR07c] M. Gogolla, F. Büttner, and M. Richters. USE: A UML-Based Specification Environment for Validating UML and OCL. *Science of Computer Programming*, 2007.

[GFB05]   M. Gogolla, J.-M. Favre, and F. Büttner. On Squeezing M0, M1, M2, and M3 into a Single Object Diagram. In T. Baar, D. Chiorean, A. Correa, M. Gogolla, H. Hußmann, O. Patrascoiu, P. H. Schmitt, and J. Warmer, editors, *Proc. MoDELS'2005 Workshop Tool Support for OCL and Related Formalisms*. In: Satellite Events at MoDELS'2005 Conference. Jean-Michel Bruel (Ed.). Springer, LNCS 3844. Long Version: EPFL (Switzerland), Technical Report LGL-REPORT-2005-001, 2005.

[GKB08]   M. Gogolla, M. Kuhlmann, and F. Büttner. A Benchmark for OCL Engine Accuracy, Determinateness, and Efficiency. In K. Czarnecki, editor, *Proc. 11th Int. Conf. Model Driven Engineering Languages and Systems (MoDELS'2008)*, pages 446–459. LNCS 5301, Springer, Berlin, 2008.

[GRB+04] M. Gogolla, M. Richters, J. Bohling, A. Lindow, F. Büttner, and P. Ziemann. Werkzeugunterstützung für die Validierung von UML- und OCL-Modellen durch automatische Snapshot-Generierung. In B. Rumpe and W. Hesse, editors, *Proc. Modellierung'2004*, pages 281–282. Gesellschaft für Informatik, LNI P-45, 2004.

[Har87]   D. Harel. Statecharts: A Visual Formalism for Complex Systems. *Science of Computer Programming*, 8(3):231–274, June 1987.

[HDF02]   H. Hußmann, B. Demuth, and F. Finger. Modular architecture for a toolset supporting OCL. *Science of Computer Programming*, 44(1):51–69, 2002.

[Hud98]   P. Hudak. Modular Domain Specific Languages and Tools. In *Proceedings of the Fifth International Conference on Software Reuse*, pages 134–142. IEEE Computer Society Press, 1998.

[JABK08]   F. Jouault, F. Allilaire, J. Bézivin, and I. Kurtev. ATL: A model transformation tool. *Science of Computer Programming*, 72(1-2):31–39, 2008.

[Jac95]   I. Jacobson. Formalizing Use-Case Modeling. *JOOP*, 8(3):10–14, 1995.

[JRE91]   J. R. James Rumbaugh and F. Eddy. *Object-Oriented Modeling and Design*. Prentice-Hall, 1991.

[JZM08]   K. Jiang, L. Zhang, and S. Miyake. Using OCL in Executable UML. *ECEASST*, 9, 2008.

[Kay93]   A. C. Kay. The early history of Smalltalk. In *ACM SIGPLAN Notices*, volume 28, pages 69–95. ACM Press, March 1993.

[KHGB11]   M. Kuhlmann, L. Hamann, M. Gogolla, and F. Büttner. A Benchmark for OCL Engine Accuracy, Determinateness, and Efficiency. *Journal on Software and System Modeling, to be published*, 2011.

[KK08]   M. P. Krieger and A. Knapp. Executing Underspecified OCL Operation Contracts with a SAT Solver. *ECEASST*, 15, 2008.

[Kla05]   Klasse Objecten. The Klasse Objecten OCL Checker Octopus. website www.klasse.nl/english/research/octopus-intro.html, Klasse Objecten, 2005.

[Kle09]   A. Kleppe. Object Constraint Language: Metamodeling Semantics. In K. Lano, editor, *UML 2 Semantics and Applications*. John Wiley Sons, 2009.

[KPP06]   D. S. Kolovos, R. F. Paige, and F. Polack. The Epsilon Object Language (EOL). In A. Rensink and J. Warmer, editors, *ECMDA-FA*, volume 4066 of *Lecture Notes in Computer Science*, pages 128–142. Springer, 2006.

[KRP10]   D. Kolovos, L. Rose, and R. Paige.   *The Epsilon Book.* http://www.eclipse.org/gmt/epsilon/doc/book/, last visited 10.02.2011, 2010.

[KRV08]   H. Krahn, B. Rumpe, and S. Völkel. MontiCore: Modular Development of Textual Domain Specific Languages. In R. F. Paige and B. Meyer, editors, *TOOLS (46)*, volume 11 of *Lecture Notes in Business Information Processing*, pages 297–315. Springer, 2008.

[Lan66]   P. J. Landin. The next 700 programming languages. *Communications of the ACM*, 9(3):157–164, March 1966. Originally presented at the Proceedings of the ACM Programming Language and Pragmatics Conference, August 8–12, 1965.

[LW94]   B. H. Liskov and J. M. Wing. A behavioral notion of subtyping. *ACM Transactions on Programming Languages and Systems*, 16:1811–1841, 1994.

[Mar96a]   R. C. Martin. The Liskov substitution principle. *C++ Report*, 8(3):14, 16–17, 20–23, March 1996.

[Mar96b]   R. C. Martin. The open closed principle. *C++ Report*, 8, January 1996.

[MB08]   S. Markovic and T. Baar. Refactoring OCL annotated UML class diagrams. *Software and System Modeling*, 7(1):25–47, 2008.

[MDT]   Epsilon model development tools (mdt) project page. Website, http://www.eclipse.org/modeling/mdt/, last visited 10.02.2011.

[Mel02]   S. J. Mellor. *Executable UML: A Foundation for Model-Driven Architecture.* Addison-Wesley, 2002.

[Mey97]   B. Meyer. *Object-Oriented Software Construction.* Prentice Hall, second edition, 1997.

[MFJ05]   P.-A. Muller, F. Fleurey, and J.-M. Jézéquel. Weaving Executability into Object-Oriented Meta-languages. In L. C. Briand and C. Williams, editors, *MoDELS*, volume 3713 of *Lecture Notes in Computer Science*, pages 264–278. Springer, 2005.

[MSS04]   J. P. Mika Siikarla and P. Selonen. Combining OCL and Pro-
          gramming Languages for UML Model Processing. In P. Schmitt,
          editor, *Proceedings of the Workshop, OCL 2.0 – Industry Stan-
          dard or Scientific Playground*, volume 102, pages 175–194. Else-
          vier, 2004.

[MSUW04] S. J. Mellor, K. Scott, A. Uhl, and D. Weise. *MDA Dis-
          tilled: Principles of Model-Driven Architecture*. Addison-Wesley,
          Boston, 2004.

[MT90]   S. Martello and P. Toth. *Knapsack Problems: Algorithms and
          Computer Implementation*. John Wiley and Sons, 1990. Available
          online at http://www.or.deis.unibo.it/kp/KnapsackProblems.
          pdf.

[MTAL98] S. J. Mellor, S. R. Tockey, R. Arthaud, and P. Leblanc. An action
          language for UML: Proposal for a precise execution semantics. In
          J. Bézivin and P.-A. Muller, editors, *UML*, volume 1618 of *Lec-
          ture Notes in Computer Science*, pages 307–318. Springer, 1998.

[NS73]   I. Nassi and B. Shneiderman. Flowchart Techniques for Struc-
          tured Programming. *ACM Sigplan Notices*, 8(8):12–26, 1973.

[OMG99a] OMG. Object Constraint Language Specification. In *OMG Uni-
          fied Modeling Language Specification, Version 1.3, June 1999*
          [OMG99b], chapter 7.

[OMG99b] OMG. *OMG Unified Modeling Language Specification, Ver-
          sion 1.3, June 1999*. Object Management Group, Inc., Fram-
          ingham, Mass., Internet: http://www.omg.org, 1999.

[OMG03]   OMG. *MDA Guide Version 1.0.1*. Object Management Group,
          Inc., Framingham, Mass., Internet: http://www.omg.org, June
          2003.

[OMG06]   OMG. *Object Constraint Language Specification, version 2.0
          (Document formal/2006-05-01)*, June 2006.

[OMG07]   *OMG Unified Modeling Language Specification, version 2.1.2*.
          Object Management Group, Inc., Framingham, Mass., Internet:
          http://www.omg.org, November 2007.

[OMG08a] OMG. *Meta Object Facility (MOF) 2.0 Query/Views/Trans-
          formation Specification (Document formal/08-04-03)*. Object
          Management Group, Inc., Framingham, Mass., Internet: http:
          //www.omg.org, 2008.

[OMG08b] OMG. *MOF Model to Text Transformation Language, v1.0 (Document formal/2008-01-06).* Object Management Group, Inc., Framingham, Mass., Internet: http://www.omg.org, January 2008.

[OMG10] OMG. *Unified Modeling Language Specification, version 2.3 (Document formal/2010-05-03).* Object Management Group, Inc., Framingham, Mass., Internet: http://www.omg.org, 2010.

[OSC02] OSCI Transport 1.2 final specification. Technical report, OSCI Leitstelle, 2002. Available online http://www1.osci.de/sixcms/detail.php?gsid=bremen02.c.1205.de, last visited 10.02.2011.

[Rat97] S. C. Rational. Unified modeling language V. 1.0.1 - summary. Documentation available at http://www.rational.com, Rational Software Corp., 3/1997 1997.

[RG00] M. Richters and M. Gogolla. Validating UML Models and OCL Constraints. In A. Evans and S. Kent, editors, *Proc. 3rd Int. Conf. Unified Modeling Language (UML'2000)*, pages 265–277. Springer, Berlin, LNCS 1939, 2000.

[RGN10] L. Renggli, T. Girba, and O. Nierstrasz. Embedding languages without breaking tools. In T. D'Hondt, editor, *ECOOP*, volume 6183 of *Lecture Notes in Computer Science*, pages 380–404. Springer, 2010.

[Ric02] M. Richters. *A Precise Approach to Validating UML Models and OCL Constraints.* Ph.D. thesis, Universität Bremen, Fachbereich Mathematik und Informatik, Logos Verlag, Berlin, BISS Monographs, No. 14, 2002.

[Roz97] G. Rozenberg, editor. *Handbook of Graph Grammars and Computing by Graph Transformation. Vol. I: Foundations.* World Scientific, 1997.

[RT] RoclET-Team. Welcome to RoclET. Website, http://www.roclet.org/, last visited 10.02.2011.

[Rum96] J. E. Rumbaugh. To form a more perfect union: Unifying the OMT and booch methods. *JOOP*, 8(8):14–18, 65, 1996.

[Sch02] A. Schürr. A new type checking approach for OCL version 2.0 ? In T. Clark and J. Warmer, editors, *Object Modeling with the OCL: The Rationale behind the Object Constraint Language*, pages 21–41. Springer, 2002.

[SF]   The XGenerator project in the SourceForge OpenSource project
            repository. Website, http://www.sourceforge.net/projects/
            xgenerator2, last visited 10.02.2011.

[SLB04]   J. G. Süß, A. Leicher, and S. Busse. OCLPrime - Environment
            and Language for Model Query, Views and Transformations.
            Electronic Notes in Theoretical Computer Science, 102:133–153,
            2004.

[SM92]   S. Shlaer and S. J. Mellor. *Object Lifecycles: Modeling the World
            in States*. Yourdon Press, 1992.

[Str93]   B. Stroustrup. A history of C++: 1979–1991. *ACM SIGPLAN
            Notices*, 28(3):271–297, March 1993.

[Tur36]   A. M. Turing. On computable numbers, with an application to
            the entscheidungsproblem. *Procedings of the London Mathemat-
            ical Society*, 42(2):230–265, 1936.

[UN06]   UN/CEFACT UML Profile for Core Components Version 1.0
            (BCSS). Technical report, United Nations Centre for Trade
            Facilation and Electronic Business – Techniques and Methodolo-
            gies Group, Oct 2006. Available online at http://www.untmg.org.

[USE10]   The UML-based Specification Environment (USE) – Home
            Page. website, http://www.db.informatik.uni-bremen.de/
            projects/use/, Aug 2010.

[War00]   J. Warmer. Extending OCL to include Actions. In *UML 2000 -
            The Unified Modeling Language. Advancing the Standard*, pages
            440–450. Springer, 2000.

[WK03]   J. B. Warmer and A. G. Kleppe. *The Object Constraint Lan-
            guage: Getting Your Models Ready for MDA*. Addison-Wesley,
            2nd edition, 2003.

[WTEK08]   J. Winkelmann, G. Taentzer, K. Ehrig, and J. M. Küster. Trans-
            lation of Restricted OCL Constraints into Graph Constraints for
            Generating Meta Model Instances by Graph Grammars. *Elec-
            tronic Notes in Theorethical Computer Science*, 211:159–170,
            2008.

[Zie06]   P. Ziemann. *An Integrated Operational Semantics For a UML
            Core based on Graph Transformation*. Ph.D. thesis, Universität
            Bremen, Fachbereich Mathematik und Informatik, Logos Verlag,
            Berlin, BISS Monographs, No. 23, 2006.

Appendix A

Proofs for Type-Soundness and Consistency

This appendix contains the proofs for Thm. 4.10 [$I[\![s]\!]$ is well-defined] and Thm. 4.11 [Interpretations provided by stat are interpretations for operations with side-effects]. In order to prove Thm. 4.10, we first need to introduce Lem. A.1 [Only variables from the 'assigned' set are modified to non-nil values in the variable stack] and Lem. A.2 [the variable stack contains all bound variables]. All proofs are by natural induction over the structure of Stat. In the proof for Thm. 4.10 we assume both lemmas to hold for the sub-statements of a compound statement in the induction step. This is valid, as both proofs follow the same induction. Figure A.1 on the following page depicts the relationships between the theorems and lemmas in this appendix.

We silently assume the correctness of the definition of $I[\![e]\!]$ in [Ric02] in the following proofs: If we have an expression $e \in \mathrm{Expr}_t$, a system state σ and a binding β providing correctly typed values for all free variables in e, we assume $I[\![e]\!](\sigma, \beta)$ to be well-defined and $I[\![e]\!](\sigma, \beta) \in I(t)$.

Lemma A.1 (only variables from the 'assigned' set are modified to non-nil values in the variable stack). Given $s \in \mathrm{Stat}$, a system state σ of $\mathcal{M}$, a variable stack ζ, and $(\sigma', \zeta') = I[\![s]\!](\sigma, \zeta)$, the following property holds under the assumption that Thm. 4.10 [$I[\![s]\!]$ is well-defined] holds for s:

$$\forall v : [\mathrm{val}(\zeta, v) \neq \mathrm{val}(\zeta', v) \ \wedge \ \mathrm{val}(\zeta', v) \neq \bot] \rightarrow$$
$$\exists t : v_t \in \mathrm{assigned}(s) \wedge \mathrm{val}(\zeta', v) \in I(t)$$

$\square$

Proof for Lemma A.1. We prove the lemma by structural induction over the statement constructors (ii) [sequence], (ix) [conditional execution], and (x) [iteration] in definitions 4.7 and 4.8.

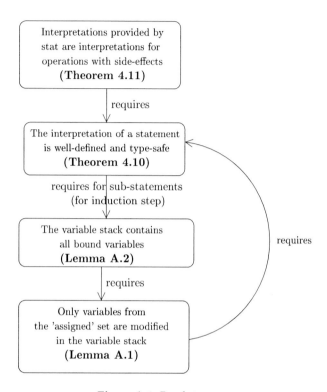

Figure A.1: Proof structure

Induction basis:

We need to show the lemma for the statements (i), (iii)–(viii), and (xi)–(xii).

(i) [empty statement, $(\sigma', \zeta') = I[\![\,\lozenge\,]\!](\sigma, \zeta) := (\sigma, \zeta)$]

By Def. 4.8i [semantics of empty statement] we have $\zeta' = \zeta$, and by Def. 4.7i [syntax of empty statement] we have assigned$(\lozenge) = \emptyset$. Therefore, we have to show

$$\forall v : \big[\,\mathrm{val}(\zeta, v) \neq \mathrm{val}(\zeta, v) \;\wedge\; \mathrm{val}(\zeta, v) \neq \bot\,\big] \rightarrow$$
$$\exists t : t \in \emptyset \wedge \mathrm{val}(\zeta, v) \in I(t)$$

which can be simplified by $\forall x : P(x) \rightarrow \mathrm{false} \;\Leftrightarrow\; \nexists x : P(x)$ to

$$\nexists v : \big[\,\mathrm{val}(\zeta, v) \neq \mathrm{val}(\zeta, v) \;\wedge\; \mathrm{val}(\zeta, v) \neq \bot\,\big]. \tag{A.1}$$

As $\mathrm{val}(\zeta, v) \neq \mathrm{val}(\zeta, v)$ cannot be true, Prop. A.1 holds.

(iii) [variable assignment, $(\sigma', \zeta') = I[\![\,\mathrm{v} := \mathrm{e}\,]\!](\sigma, \zeta)$]

By Def. 4.7iii [syntax of variable assignment] we have $e \in \mathrm{Expr}_t$ and assigned$(v := e) := \{v_t\}$. We have to show

$$\forall w : \big[\,\mathrm{val}(\zeta, w) \neq \mathrm{val}(\zeta', w) \;\wedge\; \mathrm{val}(\zeta', w) \neq \bot\,\big]$$
$$\rightarrow \exists t' : v_{t'} \in \{v_t\} \wedge \mathrm{val}(\zeta', w) \in I(t'),$$

which can be simplified to

$$\forall w : \big[\,\mathrm{val}(\zeta, w) \neq \mathrm{val}(\zeta', w) \;\wedge\; \mathrm{val}(\zeta', w) \neq \bot\,\big]$$
$$\rightarrow \mathrm{val}(\zeta', w) \in I(t). \tag{A.2}$$

By Def. 4.8iii [semantics of variable assignment] we have $\zeta' = \zeta\{v/y\}$ where $y \in I(t)$. For all $w \neq v$ it must be $\mathrm{val}(\zeta, w) = \mathrm{val}(\zeta, w')$ (contradiction). Therefore w can only be v in Prop. A.2. Thus, to show Prop. A.2, it is sufficient to show

$$\big[\,\mathrm{val}(\zeta, v) \neq \mathrm{val}(\zeta', v) \;\wedge\; \mathrm{val}(\zeta', v) \neq \bot\,\big] \rightarrow \mathrm{val}(\zeta', v) \in I(t).$$

We have $\mathrm{val}(\zeta', v) = y$ and $y \in I(t)$. Therefore, the previous proposition holds.

(iv) [attribute assignment, $(\sigma', \zeta') = I[\![\,e_1.a := e_2\,]\!](\sigma, \zeta)$]

By Def. 4.8iv [semantics of attribute assignment] we have $\zeta' = \zeta$. Thus, the proposition is true (see proof for empty statement).

(v) [object creation, $(\sigma', \zeta') = I[\![\, v := \text{new } c \,]\!](\sigma, \zeta)]$

By Def. 4.8v [semantics of object creation] we have $t = \text{typeOf}(c)$ and $\zeta' = \zeta\{v/o\}$, with $o \in I(t)$. By Def. 4.7v [syntax of object creation] we have assigned$(v := \text{new } c) = \{v_t\}$.

The proof step for object creation is analogous to the proof step for variable assignment.

(vi) [object destruction, $(\sigma', \zeta') = I[\![\, \text{destroy } e \,]\!](\sigma, \zeta)]$

By Def. 4.7vi [syntax of object destruction] we have $e \in \text{Expr}_t$ and assigned(destroy e) $= \emptyset$. We have to show

$$\forall v : \big[\, \text{val}(\zeta, v) \neq \text{val}(\zeta', v) \ \wedge \ \text{val}(\zeta', v) \neq \bot \,\big] \rightarrow$$
$$\exists t' : v_{t'} \in \emptyset \wedge \text{val}(\zeta', v) \in I(t')$$

which can be simplified by $\forall x : P(x) \rightarrow \text{false} \ \Leftrightarrow \ \nexists x : P(x)$ to

$$\nexists v : \big[\, \text{val}(\zeta, v) \neq \text{val}(\zeta', v) \ \wedge \ \text{val}(\zeta', v) \neq \bot \,\big] \qquad (A.3)$$

By Def. 4.8vi [semantics of object destruction] we have

$$\zeta' \ := \ \langle b_1', \ldots, b_n' \rangle,$$
$$b_i' := b_i\{w/\bot, \text{ where } b_i(w) = I[\![\, e \,]\!]\big(\sigma, \text{binding}(\zeta)\big)\}.$$

Therefore, we have either $\text{val}(\zeta, v) = \text{val}(\zeta', v)$ or $\text{val}(\zeta', v) = \bot$, and Prop. A.3 holds.

(vii) [link insertion, $(\sigma', \zeta') = I[\![\, \text{insert}(e_1, \ldots, e_n) \text{ into } a \,]\!](\sigma, \zeta)]$

By Def. 4.8vii [semantics of link insertion] we have $\zeta' = \zeta$. Thus, the proposition is true (see proof for empty statement).

(viii) [link deletion, $(\sigma', \zeta') = I[\![\, \text{delete}(e_1, \ldots, e_n) \text{ from } a \,]\!](\sigma, \zeta)]$

By Def. 4.8vii [semantics of link insertion] we have $\zeta' = \zeta$. Thus, the proposition is true (see proof for empty statement).

(xi) [operation call, $(\sigma', \zeta') = I[\![\, \overline{\omega}(e_1, \ldots, e_n) \,]\!](\sigma, \zeta)]$

By Def. 4.7xi [syntax of operation call] we have assigned$\big(\overline{\omega}(e_1, \ldots, e_n)\big) = \emptyset$. We have to show

$$\forall v : \big[\, \text{val}(\zeta, v) \neq \text{val}(\zeta', v) \ \wedge \ \text{val}(\zeta', v) \neq \bot \,\big] \rightarrow$$
$$\exists t' : v_{t'} \in \emptyset \wedge \text{val}(\zeta', v) \in I(t')$$

which can be simplified by $\forall x : P(x) \rightarrow \text{false} \ \Leftrightarrow \ \nexists x : P(x)$ to

$$\nexists v : \big[\, \text{val}(\zeta, v) \neq \text{val}(\zeta', v) \ \wedge \ \text{val}(\zeta', v) \neq \bot \,\big] \qquad (A.4)$$

By Def. 4.8xi [semantics of operation call] we have

$$(\sigma', \zeta') = I(\overline{\omega})\Big(\sigma, \zeta, I[\![e_1]\!](\sigma, \text{binding}(\zeta)), \dots, I[\![e_n]\!](\sigma, \text{binding}(\zeta))\Big).$$

Let $\zeta = \langle b_1, \dots, b_n \rangle$ and $\zeta' = \langle b'_1, \dots, b'_m \rangle$. By Def. 4.4 [Operation with side-effects] we have $n = m$ and

$$\forall v, i : 1 \leq i \leq n \rightarrow \big(b'_i(v) = b_i(v) \ \vee \ b'_i(v) = \bot\big).$$

Therefore, we have either $\text{val}(\zeta, v) = \text{val}(\zeta', v)$ or $\text{val}(\zeta', v) = \bot$, and Prop. A.4 holds.

(xii) [operation call with result, $(\sigma', \zeta') = I[\![v := \overline{\omega}(e_1, \dots, e_n)]\!](\sigma, \zeta)]$

By Def. 4.7xii [syntax of operation call with result] we have assigned$\big(v := \overline{\omega}(e_1, \dots, e_n)\big) = \{v_t\}$ with $\overline{\omega} : (v_1 : t_1, \dots, v_n : t_n) \rightarrow t \in \overline{\Omega}_{\mathcal{M}}$. We have to show

$$\forall w : \big[\text{val}(\zeta, w) \neq \text{val}(\zeta', w) \ \wedge \ \text{val}(\zeta', w) \neq \bot\big] \rightarrow$$
$$\exists t' : w_{t'} \in \{v_t\} \wedge \text{val}(\zeta', w) \in I(t'),$$

which can be simplified to

$$\forall w : \big[\text{val}(\zeta, w) \neq \text{val}(\zeta', w) \ \wedge \ \text{val}(\zeta', w) \neq \bot\big] \rightarrow$$
$$w = v \ \wedge \ \text{val}(\zeta', w) \in I(t). \tag{A.5}$$

By Def. 4.8xii [semantics of operation call with result] we have $(\sigma', \zeta') = (\sigma'', \zeta''\{v/y\})$ where

$$(\sigma'', \zeta'', y) = I(\overline{\omega})\Big(\sigma, \zeta, I[\![e_1]\!](\sigma, \text{binding}(\zeta)), \dots, I[\![e_n]\!](\sigma, \text{binding}(\zeta))\Big).$$

Let $\zeta = \langle b_1, \dots, b_n \rangle$, $\zeta' = \langle b'_1, \dots, b'_m \rangle$ and $\zeta'' = \langle b''_1, \dots, b''_p \rangle$. By Def. 4.4 [Operation with side-effects] we have $n = m$ and

$$\forall w, i : 1 \leq i \leq n \rightarrow \big(b''_i(w) = b_i(w) \ \vee \ b''_i(w) = \bot\big).$$

Thus we have either $\text{val}(\zeta, w) = \text{val}(\zeta', w)$ or $\text{val}(\zeta', w) = \bot$ (for $w \neq v$) or $\text{val}(\zeta', w) = y$ (for $w = v$). The first case contradicts the premise of Prop. A.5. In the second case, the proposition to be shown is fulfilled because we have $w = v$ and $\text{val}(\zeta', v) = y$ and $y \in I(t)$.

Induction step:

Given the lemma has already been shown for $s \in \text{Stat}$ resp. $s_1, s_2 \in \text{Stat}$, we need to show the lemma for the statements (ii), (ix), and (ix).

(ii) [sequence of statements, $(\sigma'', \zeta'') = I[\![s_1; s_2]\!](\sigma, \zeta)$]

By Def. 4.7ii [syntax of sequence] we have assigned$(s_1; s_2)$ = assigned$(s_1) \cup$ assigned(s_2). We have to show

$$
\begin{aligned}
\forall v : \big[\mathrm{val}(\zeta, v) \neq \mathrm{val}(\zeta'', v) \ \wedge \ \mathrm{val}(\zeta'', v) \neq \bot \big] \\
\rightarrow \exists t : v_t \in \mathrm{assigned}(s_1) \cup \mathrm{assigned}(s_2) \ \wedge \ \mathrm{val}(\zeta'')(v) \in I(t)
\end{aligned}
\tag{A.6}
$$

Let $(\sigma', \zeta') = I[\![s_1]\!](\sigma, \zeta)$. Then $(\sigma'', \zeta'') = I[\![s_2]\!](\sigma', \zeta')$. By the assumption of this lemma (the lemma has already been proved for s_1 and s_2) we have

$$
\begin{aligned}
\forall v : \big[\mathrm{val}(\zeta, v) \neq \mathrm{val}(\zeta', v) \ \wedge \ \mathrm{val}(\zeta', v) \neq \bot \big] \\
\rightarrow \exists t : v_t \in \mathrm{assigned}(s_1) \ \wedge \ \mathrm{val}(\zeta', v) \in I(t)
\end{aligned}
\tag{A.7}
$$

and

$$
\begin{aligned}
\forall v : \big[\mathrm{val}(\zeta', v) \neq \mathrm{val}(\zeta'', v) \ \wedge \ \mathrm{val}(\zeta'', v) \neq \bot \big] \\
\rightarrow \exists t : v_t \in \mathrm{assigned}(s_2) \ \wedge \ \mathrm{val}(\zeta'', v) \in I(t).
\end{aligned}
\tag{A.8}
$$

We rewrite Prop. A.6 to be shown by case distinction

$$
\begin{aligned}
\forall v : & \\
& \Big[\mathrm{val}(\zeta', v) = \mathrm{val}(\zeta'', v) \ \wedge \\
& \quad \big[\mathrm{val}(\zeta, v) \neq \mathrm{val}(\zeta'', v) \ \wedge \mathrm{val}(\zeta'', v) \neq \bot \\
& \qquad \rightarrow \exists t : v_t \in \mathrm{assigned}(s_1) \cup \mathrm{assigned}(s_2) \ \wedge \ \mathrm{val}(\zeta'', v) \in I(t) \big] \Big] \\
& \vee \\
& \Big[\mathrm{val}(\zeta', v) \neq \mathrm{val}(\zeta'', v) \ \wedge \\
& \quad \big[\mathrm{val}(\zeta, v) \neq \mathrm{val}(\zeta'', v) \ \wedge \mathrm{val}(\zeta'', v) \neq \bot \big] \\
& \qquad \rightarrow \exists t : v_t \in \mathrm{assigned}(s_1) \cup \mathrm{assigned}(s_2) \ \wedge \ \mathrm{val}(\zeta'', v) \in I(t) \big] \Big]
\end{aligned}
\tag{A.9}
$$

To proof Prop. A.9 we will proof the stronger proposition

$$\forall v :$$

$$\left[\mathrm{val}(\zeta', v) = \mathrm{val}(\zeta'', v) \ \wedge \right.$$
$$\left[\mathrm{val}(\zeta, v) \neq \mathrm{val}(\zeta'', v) \ \wedge \mathrm{val}(\zeta'', v) \neq \bot \right.$$
$$\left. \rightarrow \exists t : v_t \in \mathrm{assigned}(s_1) \ \wedge \ \mathrm{val}(\zeta'', v) \in I(t) \big] \right]$$
$$\vee$$
$$\left[\mathrm{val}(\zeta', v) \neq \mathrm{val}(\zeta'', v) \ \wedge \right.$$
$$\left[\mathrm{val}(\zeta, v) \neq \mathrm{val}(\zeta'', v) \ \wedge \mathrm{val}(\zeta'', v) \neq \bot \right]$$
$$\left. \rightarrow \exists t : v_t \in \mathrm{assigned}(s_2) \ \wedge \ \mathrm{val}(\zeta'', v) \in I(t) \big] \right] \tag{A.10}$$

In this proposition, the first part of the disjunction can be shown by applying Prop. A.7. The second part can be inferred by applying Prop. A.8.

(ix) [conditional execution, $(\sigma', \zeta') = I[\![\text{if } e \text{ then } s_1 \text{ else } s_2 \text{ end}]\!](\sigma, \zeta)]$

We have to show

$$\forall v : \left[\mathrm{val}(\zeta, v) \neq \mathrm{val}(\zeta', v) \ \wedge \ \mathrm{val}(\zeta', v) \neq \bot \right]$$
$$\rightarrow \exists t : v_t \in \mathrm{assigned}(s_1) \cup \mathrm{assigned}(s_2) \ \wedge \ \mathrm{val}(\zeta', v) \in I(t).$$

By Def. 4.8ix [semantics of conditional execution] we have

$$(\sigma', \zeta') = \begin{cases} I[\![s_1]\!](\sigma, \zeta) & \text{if } I[\![e]\!](\sigma, \mathrm{binding}(\zeta)) = \text{true} \\ I[\![s_2]\!](\sigma, \zeta) & \text{otherwise.} \end{cases}$$

In both cases the proposition to be shown follows directly from the assumption of the lemma for s_1 resp. s_2.

(x) [iteration, $(\sigma', \zeta') = I[\![\text{for } v \text{ in } e \text{ do } s \text{ end}]\!]]$ By Def. 4.7x [syntax of iteration], we have $e \in \mathrm{Expr}_{\mathrm{Sequence}(t)}$ and $\mathrm{assigned}(\text{for } v \text{ in } e \text{ do } s \text{ end}) = \mathrm{assigned}(s) \cup \{ v_{t'} | t \leq t' \}$.

We have to show

$$\forall w : \left[\mathrm{val}(\zeta, w) \neq \mathrm{val}(\zeta', w) \ \wedge \mathrm{val}(\zeta', w) \neq \bot \right]$$
$$\rightarrow \exists t' : w_{t'} \in \mathrm{assigned}(s) \cup \{ v_t \} \ \wedge \ \mathrm{val}(\zeta', w) \in I(t'). \tag{A.11}$$

By Def. 4.8x [semantics of iteration] we have

$$(\sigma', \zeta') = I[\![s]\!]\Big(\dots I[\![s]\!]\big(I[\![s]\!](\sigma, \zeta\{v/x_1\}) \{v/x_2\}\big) \dots \{v/x_n\} \Big)$$

and $\langle x_1, \ldots, x_n \rangle = I[\![\, e \,]\!](\sigma, \text{binding}(\zeta))$.

Let σ_i, ζ_i denote the intermediate result after the i-th application of $I[\![\, s \,]\!]$ such that $(\sigma_{i+1}, \zeta_{i+1}) = I[\![\, s \,]\!](\sigma_i, \zeta_i\{v/x_i\})$. We have $(\sigma', \zeta') = (\sigma_n, \zeta_n)$. We show Prop. A.11 by induction over i.

For the induction basis we have to show

$$\forall w : \big[\,\text{val}(\zeta, w) \neq \text{val}(\zeta_1, w) \ \wedge \text{val}(\zeta_1, w) \neq \bot\,\big]$$
$$\rightarrow \exists t' : w_{t'} \in \text{assigned}(s) \cup \{v_t\} \ \wedge \ \text{val}(\zeta_1, w) \in I(t'). \tag{A.12}$$

where $(\sigma_1, \zeta_1) = I[\![\, s \,]\!](\sigma, \zeta\{v/x_1\})$.

We have $\not\exists t' : v_{t'} \in \text{assigned}(s)$ by Def. 4.7x [syntax of iteration] and therefore $\neg\big[\text{val}(\zeta\{v/x_1\}, v) \neq \text{val}(\zeta_1, v) \wedge \ \text{val}(\zeta_1, v) \neq \bot\big]$. That Prop. A.12 is true can be shown by case decision. If we have $w = v$ then we have $\text{val}(\zeta_1, v) = x_1$ with $x_1 \in I(t)$ (because v cannot be changed by s). If we have $w \neq v$ then we must have $w_{t''} \in \text{assigned}(s)$ by Lem. A.1 [Only variables from the 'assigned' set are modified to non-nil values in the variable stack] for s because w is modified in the first iteration.

For the induction step we have to show

$$\forall w : \big[\,\text{val}(\zeta_i, w) \neq \text{val}(\zeta_{i+1}, w) \ \wedge \text{val}(\zeta_{i+1}, w) \neq \bot\,\big]$$
$$\rightarrow \exists t' : w_{t'} \in \text{assigned}(s) \cup \{v_t\} \ \wedge \ \text{val}(\zeta_{i+1}, w) \in I(t').$$

where $(\sigma_{i+1}, \zeta_{i+1}) = I[\![\, s \,]\!](\sigma_i, \zeta_i\{v/x_1\})$. That this proposition is true can be shown analogously to the induction basis by case decision.

$\square$

Lemma A.2 (the variable stack contains all bound variables). Given $s \in$ Stat, a system state σ of $\mathcal{M}$, a variable stack ζ, and $(\sigma', \zeta') = I[\![\, s \,]\!](\sigma, \zeta)$, the following property holds under the assumption that Thm. 4.10 ($I[\![\, s \,]\!]$ is well-defined) holds for s:

$$\forall v, t : v_t \in \text{bound}(s) \rightarrow \text{val}(\zeta', v) \in I(t)$$

$\square$

Proof for lemma A.2. We prove the lemma by structural induction over the statement constructors (ii) [sequence], (ix) [conditional execution], and (x) [iteration] in definitions 4.7 and 4.8.

Induction basis:

We need to show the lemma for the statements (i), (iii)–(viii), and (xi)–(xii).

(i) [empty statement, $(\sigma', \zeta') = I[\![\lozenge]\!](\sigma, \zeta) := (\sigma, \zeta)]$

By Def. 4.7i [syntax of empty statement] we have bound$(\lozenge) = \emptyset$. Therefore the proposition is true.

(iii) [variable assignment, $(\sigma', \zeta') = I[\![v := e]\!](\sigma, \zeta)]$

By Def. 4.7ii [syntax of sequence], we have $e \in \text{Expr}_t$ and bound$(v := e) := \{v_t\}$. We have to show

$$\forall w, t' : w_{t'} \in \{v_t\} \rightarrow \text{val}(\zeta', w) \in I(t')$$

which is equal to
$$\text{val}(\zeta', v) \in I(t).$$

By Def. 4.8iii [semantics of variable assignment] we have $(\sigma', \zeta') = (\sigma, \zeta\{v/y\})$ where $y = I[\![e]\!](\sigma, \text{binding}(\zeta))$ and therefore $y \in I(t)$ and $\text{val}(\zeta', v) = y$. Thus we have $\text{val}(\zeta', v) \in I(t)$.

(vi) [object destruction, $(\sigma', \zeta') = I[\![\text{destroy } e]\!](\sigma, \zeta)]$

By Def. 4.7vi [syntax of object destruction] we have bound(destroy e) = $\emptyset$. Therefore the proposition is true.

(vii) [link insertion, $(\sigma', \zeta') = I[\![\text{insert}(e_1, \ldots, e_n) \text{ into } a]\!](\sigma, \zeta)]$

By Def. 4.7vii [syntax of link insertion] we have bound(insert$(e_1, \ldots, e_n)$ into a) = $\emptyset$. Therefore the proposition is true.

(viii) [link deletion, $(\sigma', \zeta') = I[\![\text{delete}(e_1, \ldots, e_n) \text{ from } a]\!](\sigma, \zeta)]$

By Def. 4.7viii [syntax of link deletion] we have bound(delete$(e_1, \ldots, e_n)$ from a) = $\emptyset$. Therefore the proposition is true.

(xi) [operation call, $(\sigma', \zeta') = I[\![\overline{\omega}(e_1, \ldots, e_n)]\!](\sigma, \zeta)]$

By Def. 4.7xi [syntax of operation call] we have bound$(\overline{\omega}(e_1, \ldots, e_n)) = \emptyset$. Therefore the proposition is true.

(xii) [operation call with result, $(\sigma'', \zeta'') = I[\![v := \overline{\omega}(e_1, \ldots, e_n)]\!](\sigma, \zeta)]$

By Def. 4.7xii [syntax of operation call with result] we have $\overline{\omega} : (v_1 : t_1, \ldots, v_n : t_n \rightarrow t) \in \overline{\Omega}_{\mathcal{M}}$ and bound$(v := \overline{\omega}(e_1, \ldots, e_n)) = \{v_t\}$. Thus, we have to show

$$\forall w, t' : w_{t'} \in \{v_t\} \rightarrow \text{val}(\zeta', v) \in I(t)$$

which is equal to
$$\text{val}(\zeta', v) \in I(t).$$

By Def. 4.8(xii) we have $(\sigma'', \zeta'') = (\sigma', \zeta'\{v/y\})$ where

$$(\sigma', \zeta', y) = I(\overline{\omega})\Big(\sigma, \zeta, I[\![e_1]\!](\sigma, \text{binding}(\zeta)), \dots, I[\![e_n]\!](\sigma, \text{binding}(\zeta))\Big).$$

From Def. 4.4 [Operation with side-effects] we have $y \in I(t)$ and therefore $\text{val}(\zeta', v) \in I(t)$.

Induction step:

Assuming the lemma has already been shown for s resp. $s_1, s_2 \in \text{Stat}$, we need to show the lemma for the statements (ii), (ix), and (ix).

(ii) [sequence of statements, $(\sigma'', \zeta'') = I[\![s_1; s_2]\!](\sigma, \zeta)$]

By Def. 4.7ii [syntax of sequence] we have $\text{bound}(s_1; s_2) = \text{bound}(s_2) \cup \big(\text{bound}(s_1) \ominus \text{bound}(s_2)\big)$. Thus, we have to show

$$\forall v, t : v_t \in \text{bound}(s_2) \cup \big(\text{bound}(s_1) \ominus \text{bound}(s_2)\big) \rightarrow \text{val}(\zeta', v) \in I(t).$$

We proof the proposition by case distinction. Let $(\sigma', \zeta') = I[\![s_1]\!](\sigma, \zeta)$. Then $(\sigma'', \zeta'') = I[\![s_2]\!](\sigma', \zeta')$.

Case distinction: $v_t \in \text{bound}(s_2) \lor v_t \notin \text{bound}(s_2)$

Case 1: Assume $v_t \in \text{bound}(s_2)$. We have do show

$$\forall v, t : v_t \in \text{bound}(s_2) \rightarrow \text{val}(\zeta'', v) \in I(t).$$

This proposition holds by Lem. A.2 [the variable stack contains all bound variables] for s_2.

Case 2: Assume $v_t \notin \text{bound}(s_2)$. We have to show

$$\begin{aligned}
\forall v, t : v_t &\in \big(\text{bound}(s_1) \ominus \text{bound}(s_2)\big) \\
&\rightarrow \text{val}(\zeta'', v) \in I(t)
\end{aligned} \tag{A.13}$$

By Def. 4.6 of $\ominus$ we have $v_t \in \big(\text{bound}(s_1) \ominus \text{bound}(s_2)\big) \rightarrow v_t \in \text{bound}(s_1)$. Therefore we can apply Lem. A.2 [the variable stack contains all bound variables] for s_1 and get

$$\forall v, t : v_t \in \big(\text{bound}(s_1) \ominus \text{bound}(s_2)\big) \rightarrow \text{val}(\zeta', v) \in I(t).$$

We combine the two previous propositions and get

$$\begin{aligned}
\forall v, t : v_t &\in \big(\text{bound}(s_1) \ominus \text{bound}(s_2)\big) \\
&\rightarrow \text{val}(\zeta', v) \in I(t) \land \\
&\quad \big[\forall t' : v_{t'} \in \text{assigned}(s_2) \rightarrow \exists t'' : v_{t''} \in \text{bound}(s_1) \land t' \leq t''\big].
\end{aligned}$$

We insert a second case decision (disjunction):

$$\forall v, t : v_t \in \big(\mathrm{bound}(s_1) \ominus \mathrm{bound}(s_2)\big) \rightarrow \big[$$
$$\mathrm{val}(\zeta', v) \in I(t) \ \wedge \ \mathrm{val}(\zeta'', v) = \mathrm{val}(\zeta', v)$$
$$\vee$$
$$\mathrm{val}(\zeta', v) \in I(t) \ \wedge \ \mathrm{val}(\zeta'', v) \neq \mathrm{val}(\zeta', v) \ \wedge \ \mathrm{val}(\zeta'', v) \neq \bot \qquad (A.14)$$
$$\vee$$
$$\mathrm{val}(\zeta', v) \in I(t) \ \wedge \ \mathrm{val}(\zeta'', v) = \bot \ \big].$$

In the first and third case we obviously have $\mathrm{val}(\zeta'', v) \in I(t)$. Thus we have

$$\forall v, t : v_t \in \big(\mathrm{bound}(s_1) \ominus \mathrm{bound}(s_2)\big) \rightarrow \big[$$
$$\mathrm{val}(\zeta', v) \in I(t) \ \wedge \ \mathrm{val}(\zeta'', v) = \mathrm{val}(\zeta', v) \rightarrow \mathrm{val}(\zeta'', v) \in I(t)$$
$$\vee$$
$$\mathrm{val}(\zeta', v) \in I(t) \ \wedge \ \mathrm{val}(\zeta'', v) \neq \mathrm{val}(\zeta', v) \ \wedge \ \mathrm{val}(\zeta'', v) \neq \bot$$
$$\vee$$
$$\mathrm{val}(\zeta', v) \in I(t) \ \wedge \ \mathrm{val}(\zeta'', v) = \bot \ \wedge \ \mathrm{val}(\zeta'', v) \in I(t)\big].$$

To infer $\mathrm{val}(\zeta'', v) \in I(t)$ in the second case, we require the syntax restriction

$$\forall v, t : v_t \in \big(\mathrm{bound}(s_1) \ominus \mathrm{bound}(s_2)\big)$$
$$\rightarrow \big[\forall t' : v_{t'} \in \mathrm{assigned}(s_2) \rightarrow \exists t'' : v_{t''} \in \mathrm{bound}(s_1) \wedge \ t' \leq t''\big].$$

from Def. 4.7iib. As $\mathrm{val}(\zeta'', v) \neq \mathrm{val}(\zeta', v) \wedge \mathrm{val}(\zeta'', v) \neq \bot$ implies $v_t \in \mathrm{assigned}(s_2)$, we can infer the following from our previous proposition:

$$\forall v, t : v_t \in \big(\mathrm{bound}(s_1) \ominus \mathrm{bound}(s_2)\big) \rightarrow \big[$$
$$\mathrm{val}(\zeta', v) \in I(t) \ \wedge \ \mathrm{val}(\zeta'', v) = \mathrm{val}(\zeta', v) \ \wedge \ \mathrm{val}(\zeta'', v) \in I(t)$$
$$\vee$$
$$\mathrm{val}(\zeta', v) \in I(t) \ \wedge \ \mathrm{val}(\zeta'', v) \neq \mathrm{val}(\zeta', v) \ \wedge \ \mathrm{val}(\zeta'', v) \neq \bot \ \wedge$$
$$\big[\exists t' : v_{t''} \in \mathrm{bound}(s_1) \wedge \ t \leq t'\big]$$
$$\vee$$
$$\mathrm{val}(\zeta', v) \in I(t) \ \wedge \ \mathrm{val}(\zeta'', v) = \bot \ \wedge \ \mathrm{val}(\zeta'', v) \in I(t)\big].$$

By Lem. A.2 [the variable stack contains all bound variables] for s_1, we can infer $\mathrm{val}(\zeta'', v) \in I(t')$ from $\exists t' : v_{t''} \in \mathrm{bound}(s_1) \wedge \ t \leq t'$. By $I(t') \subseteq I(t)$ we can further infer $\mathrm{val}(\zeta'', v) \in I(t)$. Thus, we can infer $\mathrm{val}(\zeta'', v) \in I(t)$ in all three cases of our case decision. Therefore we can now get

$$\forall v, t : v_t \in \big(\mathrm{bound}(s_1) \ominus \mathrm{bound}(s_2)\big) \rightarrow$$
$$\big[\mathrm{val}(\zeta', v) \in I(t) \ \wedge \ \mathrm{val}(\zeta'', v) \in I(t)\big],$$

which proves Prop. A.13.

(ix) [conditional execution, $(\sigma', \zeta') = I[\![\text{if } e \text{ then } s_1 \text{ else } s_2 \text{ end}]\!](\sigma, \zeta)]$

   By Def. 4.7ix [syntax of conditional execution] we have bound(if e then s_1 else s_2 end) $= \emptyset$. Therefore, the proposition holds.

(x) [iteration, $(\sigma', \zeta') = I[\![\text{for } v \text{ in } e \text{ do } s \text{ end}]\!]]$

   By Def. 4.7x [syntax of iteration] we have bound(for v_t in e do s end) $= \emptyset$. Therefore, the proposition holds.

□

Having Lem. A.1 [Only variables from the 'assigned' set are modified to non-nil values in the variable stack] and Lem. A.2 [the variable stack contains all bound variables], we can now show that the interpretations of all OCL expressions contained in s are well-defined.

Proof for Thm. 4.10. We restate the proposition of Thm. 4.10: Given $s \in$ Stat, a system state σ of $\mathcal{M}$, and a variable stack $\zeta = \langle b_1, \ldots, b_n \rangle$ over σ with

$$\forall v, t : v_t \in \text{free}(s) \rightarrow \text{val}(\zeta, v) \in I(t)$$

(i.e., a variable stack containing correctly typed valued for all free variables of s), then the interpretation $(\sigma', \zeta') = I[\![s]\!](\sigma, \zeta)$ is well-defined, i.e., σ' is a system state of $\mathcal{M}$ and $\zeta' = \langle b'_1, \ldots, b'_m \rangle$ is a variable stack over σ', and

$$
\begin{aligned}
n = m \ \wedge \ \forall i, v : \\
1 \le i \le (n-1) \rightarrow \left(b'_i(v) = b_i(v) \ \vee \ b'_i(v) = \bot \right).
\end{aligned}
\tag{A.15}
$$

We prove this proposition by structural induction over the statement constructors (ii) [sequence], (ix) [conditional execution], and (x) [iteration] in Defs. 4.7 [syntax of statements] and 4.8 [semantics of statements].

We will use the following proof strategy: If s contains any expressions $e_1, \ldots, e_k$ then we will first show that all interpretations occurrences of $I[\![e_i]\!](\sigma_i, \beta_i)$ are well-defined in Def. 4.8 for $1 \le i \le k$. Therefore we need to show that σ_i is a system state of $\mathcal{M}$ and that all free variables of e_i are bound in β_i with the correct type for every expression e_i. Notice, that there is exactly one occurrence of $I[\![e_i]\!]$ for each expression e_i in each of the 12 statements in Def. 4.8. Therefore, it is sufficient to refer to σ_i and β_i. Then we will show that σ' is a system state of $\mathcal{M}$ and that ζ' is a variable stack over σ'. Proposition A.15, regarding the relationship between ζ' and ζ, follows last. To compact the proofs and increase readability, we use the convention validTransition(ζ, ζ') to state that Prop. A.15 holds.

Induction basis: We need to show the theorem for the statements (i), (iii)–(viii), and (xi)–(xii).

(i) [empty statement, $(\sigma', \zeta') = I[\![\, \Diamond \,]\!](\sigma, \zeta)$]

> σ is a system state of $\mathcal{M}$ and ζ is a variable stack over σ. We have $\sigma' = \sigma$ and $\zeta' = \zeta$ by Def. 4.8i [semantics of empty statement]. Therefore, σ' is a system state of $\mathcal{M}$, ζ' is a variable stack over σ', and validTransition(ζ, ζ').

(iii) [variable assignment, $(\sigma', \zeta') = I[\![\, v := e \,]\!](\sigma, \zeta)$]

> By Def. 4.7iii [syntax of variable assignment] we have free$(v := e) = $ free(e) and $e \in \mathrm{Expr}_t$. By Def. 4.8iii [semantics of variable assignment] we have $\sigma' = \sigma$ and $\zeta' = \zeta\{v/x\}$ where $x = I[\![\, e \,]\!](\sigma, \mathrm{binding}(\zeta))$.

> To show that $I[\![\, e \,]\!](\sigma, \mathrm{binding}(\zeta))$ is well-defined we have to show that

$$\forall w, t' : w_{t'} \in \mathrm{free}(e) \rightarrow \exists y : (w_{t'}, y) \in \mathrm{binding}(\zeta) \ \wedge \ x \in I(t),$$

> which follows directly from the assumption

$$\forall w, t' : w_{t'} \in \mathrm{free}(v := e) \rightarrow \mathrm{val}(\zeta, w) \in I(t').$$

> We have σ is a system state of $\mathcal{M}$. Therefore, σ' is a system state of $\mathcal{M}$. We have ζ is a variable stack over σ and $x \in I(t)$. If $x \in \sigma_{\mathrm{CLASS}}(c)$ for any class c with $c = \mathrm{classOf}(t)$, then it must be $x \in \sigma'_{\mathrm{CLASS}}(c)$. Therefore $\zeta' = \zeta(v/x)$ is a variable stack over σ'.

> Let $\zeta = \langle b_1, \ldots, b_n \rangle$ and $\zeta' = \langle b'_1, \ldots, b'_m \rangle$. We have $n = m$ and

$$\forall w, i : 1 \leq i \leq (n-1) \rightarrow b'_i(w) = b_i(w)$$

> by Def. 4.1 [Variable Stack]. Thus, we have validTransition(ζ, ζ').

(iv) [attribute assignment, $(\sigma', \zeta') = I[\![\, e_1.a := e_2 \,]\!](\sigma, \zeta)$]

> By Def. 4.7iv [syntax of attribute assignment] we have $e_1 \in \mathrm{Expr}_{t_1}$, $e_2 \in \mathrm{Expr}_{t_2}$, $c = \mathrm{classOf}(t_1)$, $a : t_1 \rightarrow t_2 \in \mathrm{ATT}_c^*$, and free$(e_1.a := e_2) = \mathrm{free}(e_1) \cup \mathrm{free}(e_2)$.

> By Def. 4.8iv [semantics of attribute assignment] we have

$$(\sigma', \zeta') = \begin{cases} (\sigma', \zeta) & \text{if } I[\![\, e_1 \,]\!](\sigma, \mathrm{binding}(\zeta)) \neq \bot \\ (\sigma, \zeta) & \text{otherwise} \end{cases}$$

> where $\sigma' = \sigma$ except $\sigma'_{\mathrm{ATT}}(a) := \sigma_{\mathrm{ATT}}(a)\{x/y\}$ where $x = I[\![\, e_1 \,]\!](\sigma, \mathrm{binding}(\zeta))$, $y = I[\![\, e_2 \,]\!](\sigma, \mathrm{binding}(\zeta))$, and $\sigma' = \sigma$

> To show that $I[\![\, e_1 \,]\!](\sigma, \mathrm{binding}(\zeta))$ and $I[\![\, e_2 \,]\!](\sigma, \mathrm{binding}(\zeta))$ are well-defined we have to show that

$$\forall v, t' : v_{t'} \in \mathrm{free}(e_1) \cup \mathrm{free}(e_2) \rightarrow \exists z : (v_{t'}, z) \in \mathrm{binding}(\zeta) \wedge z \in I(t'),$$

which follows directly from the assumption

$$\forall v, t : v_t \in \text{free}(e_1.a := e_2) \rightarrow \text{val}(\zeta, v) \in I(t).$$

Thus, $I[\![e_1]\!](\sigma, \text{binding}(\zeta))$ is well-defined and $x \in I(t_1)$ and $I[\![e_2]\!](\sigma, \text{binding}(\zeta))$ is well-defined and $y \in I(t_2)$.

σ is a system state of $\mathcal{M}$ and σ' is unchanged from σ except $\sigma'_{\text{ATT}}(a) := \sigma_{\text{ATT}}(a)\{x/y\}$. To show that σ' is a system of $\mathcal{M}$, we have to show that $\sigma'_{\text{ATT}}(a)$ is a mapping $\sigma'_{\text{ATT}}(a) : \sigma_{\text{CLASS}}(c) \rightarrow I(t_2)$. We already have $x \in I(t_1)$ and $y \in I(t_2)$. From $x \neq \bot$ we can infer $x \in \sigma_{\text{CLASS}}(c)$. Therefore σ' is a system state over $\mathcal{M}$. We have ζ is a variable stack over σ and $\zeta' = \zeta$ and $\sigma'_{\text{CLASS}} = \sigma_{\text{CLASS}}$. Therefore, is a variable stack over σ'. From $\zeta' = \zeta$ we have validTransition(ζ, ζ').

(v) [object creation $(\sigma', \zeta') = I[\![v := \text{new } c]\!](\sigma, \zeta)]$

By Def. 4.7v [syntax of object creation] we have $t = \text{typeOf}(c)$. By Def. 4.8v [semantics of object creation] we have $\sigma'_{\text{CLASS}}(c) = \sigma_{\text{CLASS}}(c) \cup \{\text{newobj}\}$ and newobj $\in I(t)$. Therefore σ' is a system state of $\mathcal{M}$.

ζ is a system state over σ. From $\zeta' = \zeta\{v/\text{newobj}\}$ and $\sigma'_{\text{CLASS}}(c) = \sigma_{\text{CLASS}}(c) \cup \{\text{newobj}\}$ we can infer that ζ' is a variable stack over σ'.

Let $\zeta = \langle b_1, \ldots, b_n \rangle$ and $\zeta' = \langle b'_1, \ldots, b'_m \rangle$. We have $n = m$ and

$$\forall w, i : 1 \leq i \leq (n-1) \rightarrow b'_i(w) = b_i(w)$$

by Def. 4.1 [Variable Stack]. Thus, we have validTransition(ζ, ζ').

(vi) [object destruction, $(\sigma', \zeta') = I[\![\text{destroy } e]\!](\sigma, \zeta)]$

By Def. 4.7vi [syntax of object destruction] we have free(destroy e) := free(e).

Let $\zeta = \langle b_1, \ldots, b_n \rangle$ and $x = I[\![e]\!](\sigma, \text{binding}(\zeta))$. By Def. 4.8vi [semantics of object destruction] we have

$$(\sigma', \zeta') := \begin{cases} (\sigma'', \zeta'') & \text{if } I[\![e]\!](\sigma, \text{binding}(\zeta)) \neq \bot \\ (\sigma, \zeta) & \text{otherwise} \end{cases}$$

where $\sigma'' := \sigma$ except

$$\sigma''_{\text{CLASS}}(c) := \sigma_{\text{CLASS}}(c) - \{x\},$$
$$\sigma''_{\text{ASSOC}}(a) := \sigma_{\text{ASSOC}}(a)$$
$$\quad - \{\langle o_1, \ldots, o_n \rangle \mid \exists i : 1 \leq i \leq n \wedge o_i = x\},$$
$$\quad \text{for } a \in \text{ASSOC}$$
$$\sigma''_{\text{ATT}}(a) := \sigma_{\text{ATT}}(a) - \{o_1 \mapsto o_2 \mid o_1 = x \vee o_2 = x\},$$
$$\quad \text{for } a \in \text{ATT}$$

and $\zeta' := \langle b'_1, \ldots, b'_n \rangle$ where $b'_i := b_i \{ v/\bot,$ if $\text{binding}(\zeta)(v) = x \}$.

That $I[\![e]\!](\sigma, \text{binding}(\zeta))$ is well-defined can be shown analogously to step (iii) because $\text{free}(s) = \text{free}(e)$ and is not repeated here. We have $x \in I(t)$.

From the definition of σ' we follow that no dangling links and no dangling attribute references exist in σ'. Therefore σ' is a system state over $\mathcal{M}$. Analogously, all occurrences of x are removed from ζ'. Therefore ζ' is a variable stack over σ'.

We have $n = m$ and

$$\forall v, i : 1 \leq i \leq n \rightarrow \big(b'_i(v) = b_i(v) \ \lor \ b'_i(v) = \bot \big)$$

by the above definition of ζ'. Thus, we have validTransition(ζ, ζ').

(vii) [link insertion, $(\sigma', \zeta') = I[\![\text{insert}(e_1, \ldots, e_n) \text{ into } a]\!](\sigma, \zeta)]$

By Def. 4.7vii [syntax of link insertion] we have $\text{free}(\text{insert } (e_1 \ldots, e_n) \text{ into } a) = \text{free}(e_1) \cup \cdots \cup \text{free}(e_n)$, $\text{associates}(a) = \langle c_1, \ldots, c_n \rangle$, $t_i \leq \text{typeOf}(c_i)$.

Let $x_1, \ldots, x_n = I[\![e_1]\!]\big(\sigma, \text{binding}(\zeta)\big), \ldots, I[\![e_n]\!]\big(\sigma, \text{binding}(\zeta)\big)$.

By Def. 4.8vii [semantics of link insertion] we have

$$(\sigma', \zeta') := \begin{cases} (\sigma'', \zeta) & \text{if } \forall i : 1 \leq i \leq n \rightarrow x_i \neq \bot \\ (\sigma, \zeta) & \text{otherwise} \end{cases}$$

where $\sigma'' := \sigma$ except $\sigma''_{\text{Assoc}}(a) = \sigma_{\text{Assoc}}(a) \cup \big\{ (x_1, \ldots, x_n) \big\}$.

That $I[\![e_i]\!](\sigma, \text{binding}(\zeta))$ is well-defined for $1 \leq i \leq n$ can be shown analogously to step (iii) because $\text{free}(s) = \text{free}(e_1) \cup \cdots \cup \text{free}(e_n)$. Thus, we have $x_i \in I(\text{typeOf}(\text{associates}(a)_i))$.

If $x_i = \bot$ for any i with $1 \leq i \leq n$ then $(\sigma', \zeta') = (\sigma, \zeta)$ and the proposition is fulfilled. Thus, we only need to regard $x_i \neq \bot$ for all i with $1 \leq i \leq n$ in the following. Then we have $x_i \in \sigma_{\text{CLASS}}(\text{classOf}(t_i))$. Then $\sigma'_{\text{Assoc}}(a) = \sigma_{\text{Assoc}}(a) \cup \big\{ (x_1, \ldots, x_n) \big\}$ only associates existing objects of the right classes and, thus, σ' is a system state over $\mathcal{M}$. As $\zeta' = \zeta$ and $\sigma'_{\text{CLASS}} = \sigma_{\text{CLASS}}$, ζ' is a variable stack over σ'. We further have $\zeta' = \zeta$ and therefore validTransition(ζ, ζ').

(viii) [link deletion, $(\sigma', \zeta') = I[\![\text{delete}(e_1, \ldots, e_n) \text{ from } a]\!](\sigma, \zeta)]$

By Def. 4.7vii [syntax of link insertion] we have $\text{free}(\text{delete } (e_1 \ldots, e_n) \text{ from } a) = \text{free}(e_1) \cup \cdots \cup \text{free}(e_n)$, $\text{associates}(a) = \langle c_1, \ldots, c_n \rangle$, $t_i \leq \text{typeOf}(c_i)$.

Let $x_1, \ldots, x_n = I[\![e_1]\!]\big(\sigma, \text{binding}(\zeta)\big), \ldots, I[\![e_n]\!]\big(\sigma, \text{binding}(\zeta)\big)$. That $I[\![e_i]\!](\sigma, \text{binding}(\zeta))$ is well-defined for $1 \leq i \leq n$ can be shown analogously to step (iii) because $\text{free}(s) = \text{free}(e_1) \cup \cdots \cup \text{free}(e_n)$. Thus, we have $x_i \in I(\text{typeOf}(\text{associates}(a)_i))$.

By Def. 4.8viii [semantics of link deletion] we have $(\sigma', \zeta') = (\sigma'', \zeta)$ where $\sigma'' = \sigma$ except $\sigma''_{\text{Assoc}}(a) := \sigma_{\text{Assoc}}(a) - \{(x_1, \ldots, x_n)\}$. As σ is a system state over $\mathcal{M}$ and $\sigma'_{\text{Assoc}}(a) \subseteq \sigma_{\text{Assoc}}(a)$, σ' is a system state over $\mathcal{M}$, too. As $\sigma'_{\text{Class}} = \sigma_{\text{Class}}$ and $\zeta' = \zeta$, ζ' is a variable stack over σ' and we have validTransition(ζ, ζ').

(xi) [operation call $(\sigma', \zeta') = I[\![\,\overline{\omega}(e_1, \ldots, e_n)\,]\!](\sigma, \zeta)]$

By Def. 4.7xi [syntax of operation call] we have $\overline{\omega} : (v_1 : t_1, \ldots, v_n : t_n) \in \overline{\Omega}_{\mathcal{M}}$ with $e_i \in \text{Expr}_{t_i}$ and $\text{free}(\overline{\omega}(e_1, \ldots, e_n)) = \text{free}(e_1) \cup \cdots \cup \text{free}(e_n)$.

Let $x_1, \ldots, x_n = I[\![\,e_1\,]\!](\sigma, \text{binding}(\zeta)), \ldots, I[\![\,e_n\,]\!](\sigma, \text{binding}(\zeta))$. By Def. 4.8xi [semantics of operation call] we have

$$(\sigma', \zeta') = I(\overline{\omega})\Big(\sigma, \zeta, x_1, \ldots, x_n\Big)$$

That $I[\![\,e_i\,]\!](\sigma, \text{binding}(\zeta))$ is well-defined for $1 \leq i \leq n$ can be shown analogously to step (iii) because $\text{free}(s) = \text{free}(e_1) \cup \cdots \cup \text{free}(e_n)$ and is not repeated here. Thus, we have $x_i \in I(t_i)$.

By Def. 4.4 [Operation with side-effects] we have σ' is a system state of $\mathcal{M}$ and ζ' is a system state over σ'.

Let $\zeta = \langle b_1, \ldots, b_m \rangle$ and $\zeta' = \langle b'_1, \ldots, b'_k \rangle$. We have $m = k$ and

$$\forall v, i : 1 \leq i \leq m \rightarrow \big(b'_i(v) = b_i(v) \ \lor \ b'_i(v) = \bot\big),$$

by Def. 4.4 [Operation with side-effects], too. Thus, we have validTransition(ζ, ζ').

(xii) [operation call with result $(\sigma', \zeta') = I[\![\, v := \overline{\omega}(e_1, \ldots, e_n)\,]\!](\sigma, \zeta)]$

By Def. 4.7xii [syntax of operation call with result] we have $\overline{\omega} : (v_1 : t_1, \ldots, v_n : t_n) \rightarrow t \in \overline{\Omega}_{\mathcal{M}}$ with $e_i \in \text{Expr}_{t_i}$ and $\text{free}(v := \overline{\omega}(e_1, \ldots, e_n)) = \text{free}(e_1) \cup \cdots \cup \text{free}(e_n)$.

Let $x_1, \ldots, x_n = I[\![\,e_1\,]\!](\sigma, \text{binding}(\zeta)), \ldots, I[\![\,e_n\,]\!](\sigma, \text{binding}(\zeta))$. By Def. 4.8xi [semantics of operation call] we have $(\sigma', \zeta') = (\sigma'', \zeta''\{v/z\})$ where

$$(\sigma'', \zeta'', z) = I(\overline{\omega})\big(\sigma, \zeta, x_1, \ldots, x_n\big)$$

That $I[\![\,e_i\,]\!](\sigma, \text{binding}(\zeta))$ is well-defined for $1 \leq i \leq n$ can be shown analogously to step (iii) because $\text{free}(s) = \text{free}(e_1) \cup \cdots \cup \text{free}(e_n)$ and is not repeated here. Thus, we have $x_i \in I(t_i)$.

By Def. 4.4 [Operation with side-effects] we have σ'' is a system state of $\mathcal{M}$, ζ'' is a system state over σ'' and – if t is an object type –

$z \in \sigma''_{\text{CLASS}}(\text{classOf}(t)) \cup \{\bot\}$. Thus $\zeta' = \zeta''\{v/z\}$ is variable stack over σ', too.

Let $\zeta = \langle b_1, \ldots, b_m \rangle$, $\zeta' = \langle b'_1, \ldots, b'_k \rangle$, and $\zeta'' = \langle b''_1, \ldots, b''_p \rangle$. We have $m = k$ and

$$\forall v, i : 1 \leq i \leq m \rightarrow \big(b''_i(v) = b_i(v) \ \lor \ b''_i(v) = \bot \big)$$

by Def. 4.4 [Operation with side-effects]. As only the topmost frame in $varstack''$ is modified by $varstack''\{v/z\}$, we have $k = p$ and

$$\forall v, i : 1 \leq i \leq (m-1) \rightarrow \big(b'_i(v) = b_i(v) \ \lor \ b'_i(v) = \bot \big).$$

Thus, we have validTransition(ζ, ζ'').

Induction step:

Given the theorem has already been shown for $s \in$ Stat resp. $s_1, s_2 \in$ Stat, we need to show the theorem for the statements (ii), (ix), and (ix).

(ii) [sequence of statements, $(\sigma'', \zeta'') = I[\![\, s_1; s_2 \,]\!](\sigma, \zeta)$]

By Def. 4.7ii [syntax of sequence] we have

$$\text{free}(s_1; s_2) = \text{free}(s_1) \cup \big(\text{free}(s_2) \ominus \text{bound}(s_1)\big).$$

By Def. 4.8i [semantics of sequence] we have $(\sigma', \zeta') = I[\![\, s_1 \,]\!](\sigma, \zeta)$ and $(\sigma'', \zeta') = I[\![\, s_2 \,]\!](\sigma', \zeta')$.

To show that $I[\![\, s_1; s_2 \,]\!]$ is well-defined we need to show that $I[\![\, s_1 \,]\!](\sigma, \zeta)$ is well-defined and $I[\![\, s_2 \,]\!](\sigma', \zeta')$ is well-defined. We already proved Thm. 4.10 [$I[\![\, s \,]\!]$ is well-defined] for s_1 and s_2. Thus, we need to show that the assumptions of this theorem are fulfilled for s_1 and s_2 in order to apply it transitively. We need to show

$$\forall v, t : v_t \in \text{free}(s_1) \rightarrow \text{val}(\zeta, v) \in I(t) \tag{A.16}$$

and

$$\forall v, t : v_t \in \text{free}(s_2) \rightarrow \text{val}(\zeta', v) \in I(t) \tag{A.17}$$

Proposition A.16 follows directly from the assumption of this theorem

$$\forall v, t : v_t \in \text{free}(s_1) \cup \big(\text{free}(s_2) \ominus \text{bound}(s_1)\big)$$
$$\rightarrow \text{val}(\zeta, v) \in I(t)$$

Proposition A.17 can be shown as follows. From the previous assumption we can infer

$$\forall v, t : v_t \in \big(\text{free}(s_2) \ominus \text{bound}(s_1)\big) \rightarrow \text{val}(\zeta) \in I(t)$$

We insert a case decision (disjunction):

$$\forall v, t : v_t \in \big(\text{free}(s_2) \ominus \text{bound}(s_1)\big) \rightarrow \Big[$$

$$\text{val}(\zeta, v) \in I(t) \wedge \text{val}(\zeta', v) = \text{val}(\zeta, v)$$

$$\vee$$

$$\text{val}(\zeta, v) \in I(t) \wedge \text{val}(\zeta', v) \neq \text{val}(\zeta, v) \wedge \text{val}(\zeta', v) \neq \bot$$

$$\vee$$

$$\text{val}(\zeta, v) \in I(t) \wedge \text{val}(\zeta', v) = \bot \Big]$$

For the first and third part of the disjunction, $\text{val}(\zeta', v) \in I(t)$ follows straightforward. Thus we can infer

$$\forall v, t : v_t \in \big(\text{free}(s_2) \ominus \text{bound}(s_1)\big) \rightarrow \Big[$$

$$\big[\text{val}(\zeta, v) \in I(t) \wedge \text{val}(\zeta', v) = \text{val}(\zeta, v) \rightarrow \text{val}(\zeta', v) \in I(t) \big]$$

$$\vee$$

$$\text{val}(\zeta, v) \in I(t) \wedge \text{val}(\zeta', v) \neq \text{val}(\zeta, v) \wedge \text{val}(\zeta', v) \neq \bot$$

$$\vee$$

$$\big[\text{val}(\zeta, v) \in I(t) \wedge \text{val}(\zeta', v) = \bot \rightarrow \text{val}(\zeta', v) \in I(t) \big] \Big].$$

In the second part of the disjunction, we can infer $\exists t' : v_{t'} \in \text{assigned}(s_1) \wedge \text{val}(\zeta', v) \in I(t')$ by Lem. A.1 [Only variables from the 'assigned' set are modified to non-nil values in the variable stack]:

$$\forall v, t : v_t \in \big(\text{free}(s_2) \ominus \text{bound}(s_1)\big) \rightarrow \Big[$$

$$\big[\text{val}(\zeta, v) \in I(t) \wedge \text{val}(\zeta', v) = \text{val}(\zeta, v) \rightarrow \text{val}(\zeta', v) \in I(t) \big]$$

$$\vee$$

$$\big[\text{val}(\zeta, v) \in I(t) \wedge \text{val}(\zeta', v) \neq \text{val}(\zeta, v) \wedge \text{val}(\zeta', v) \neq \bot$$

$$\rightarrow \exists t' : v_{t'} \in \text{assigned}(s_1) \wedge \text{val}(\zeta', v) \in I(t') \big]$$

$$\vee$$

$$\big[\text{val}(\zeta, v) \in I(t) \wedge \text{val}(\zeta', v) = \bot \rightarrow \text{val}(\zeta', v) \in I(t) \big] \Big].$$

Continuing on the second part of the disjunction, we have $\forall v, t : \exists t' : v_{t'} \in \text{assigned}(s_1) \wedge t' \not\preceq t \rightarrow v_t \notin \big(\text{free}(s_2) \ominus \text{bound}(s_1)\big)$ by Def. 4.7ii [syntax of sequence]. Therefore, we must have $t' \preceq t$ (because $v_t \in$

$\big(\,\mathrm{free}(s_2) \ominus \mathrm{bound}(s_1)\big)\big)$, and therefore $\mathrm{val}(\zeta',v) \in I(t)$.

$$\forall v,t : v_t \in \big(\mathrm{free}(s_2) \ominus \mathrm{bound}(s_1)\big) \rightarrow \Big[$$
$$\big[\,\mathrm{val}(\zeta,v) \in I(t) \ \wedge \ \mathrm{val}(\zeta',v) = \mathrm{val}(\zeta,v) \rightarrow \ \mathrm{val}(\zeta',v) \in I(t)\big]$$
$$\vee$$
$$\big[\,\mathrm{val}(\zeta,v) \in I(t) \ \wedge \ \mathrm{val}(\zeta',v) \neq \mathrm{val}(\zeta,v) \ \wedge \ \mathrm{val}(\zeta',v) \neq \bot$$
$$\rightarrow \ \mathrm{val}(\zeta',v) \in I(t)\big]$$
$$\vee$$
$$\big[\,\mathrm{val}(\zeta,v) \in I(t) \ \wedge \ \mathrm{val}(\zeta',v) = \bot \rightarrow \ \mathrm{val}(\zeta',v) \in I(t)\big]\Big].$$

Thus $\exists x : (v_t,x) \in \mathrm{binding}(\zeta')$ can be followed in all three parts of the case decision, and we now have

$$\forall v,t : v_t \in \big(\mathrm{free}(s_2) \ominus \mathrm{bound}(s_1)\big)$$
$$\rightarrow \ \mathrm{val}(\zeta',v) \in I(t).$$

As we already have $v_t \in \mathrm{bound}(s_1) \rightarrow \mathrm{val}(\zeta',v) \in I(t)$, we can extend the premise of the previous proposition:

$$\forall v,t : v_t \in \mathrm{free}(s_2) \rightarrow \ \mathrm{val}(\zeta',v) \in I(t)$$

which is the proposition to be shown.

(ix) [conditional execution, $(\sigma',\zeta') = I[\![\,\mathrm{if}\ e_1\ \mathrm{then}\ s_1\ \mathrm{else}\ s_2\ \mathrm{end}\,]\!](\sigma,\zeta)]$

By Def. 4.7ix [syntax of conditional execution] we have $\mathrm{free}(\mathrm{if}\ e_1\ \mathrm{then}\ s_1\ \mathrm{else}\ s_2\ \mathrm{end}) = \mathrm{free}(e_1) \cup \mathrm{free}(s_1) \cup \mathrm{free}(s_2)$ with $e_1 \in \mathrm{Expr}_{\mathrm{Boolean}}$. Let $e_2,\ldots,e_n$ denote the expressions in s_1 and s_2. Let $\zeta = \langle b_1,\ldots,b_m\rangle$. By Def. 4.8ix [semantics of conditional execution] we have

$$(\sigma',\zeta') := \begin{cases} I[\![\,s_1\,]\!](\sigma,\zeta) & \text{if } I[\![\,e_1\,]\!](\sigma,\mathrm{binding}(\zeta)) = \mathrm{true} \\ I[\![\,s_2\,]\!](\sigma,\zeta) & \text{otherwise} \end{cases}$$

That $I[\![\,e_1\,]\!](\sigma,\mathrm{binding}(\zeta))$ is well-defined can be shown analogously to step (iii) because $\mathrm{free}(e_1) \subseteq \mathrm{free}(\mathrm{if}\ e_1\ \mathrm{then}\ s_1\ \mathrm{else}\ s_2\ \mathrm{end})$ and is not repeated here. We also have

$$\forall v,t : v_t \in \mathrm{free}(s_1) \rightarrow \ \mathrm{val}(\zeta,v) \in I(t)$$

from $\mathrm{free}(s_1) \subseteq \mathrm{free}(\mathrm{if}\ e_1\ \mathrm{then}\ s_1\ \mathrm{else}\ s_2\ \mathrm{end})$ and

$$\forall v,t : v_t \in \mathrm{free}(s_2) \rightarrow \ \mathrm{val}(\zeta,v) \in I(t)$$

from $\mathrm{free}(s_2) \subseteq \mathrm{free}(\mathrm{if}\ e_1\ \mathrm{then}\ s_1\ \mathrm{else}\ s_2\ \mathrm{end})$.

Thus, the proposition to be shown follows from Thm. 4.10 [$I[\![\,s\,]\!]$ is well-defined] for s_1 and s_2.

(x) [iteration, $(\sigma',\zeta') = I[\![$ for v in e_1 do s end $]\!]]$

By Def. 4.7x [syntax of iteration], we have $e_1 \in \text{Expr}_{\text{Sequence}(t)}$ and free(for v in e_1 do s end) = free$(e_1) \cup \big(\text{free}(s) \ominus \{v_t\}\big)$.

Let $e_2,\ldots,e_n$ denote the expressions in s.

By Def. 4.8x [semantics of iteration] we have

$$(\sigma',\zeta') = I[\![s]\!]\Big(\ldots I[\![s]\!]\big(I[\![s]\!](\sigma,\zeta\{v/x_1\})\{v/x_2\}\big)\ldots\{v/x_n\}\Big)$$

and $\langle x_1,\ldots,x_n\rangle = I[\![e]\!]\big(\sigma,\text{binding}(\zeta)\big)$.

That $I[\![e_1]\!](\sigma,\text{binding}(\zeta))$ is well-defined can be shown analogously to step (iii) because free$(e_1) \subseteq$ free(for v in e_1 do s end) and is not repeated here. Thus, we have $x_i \in I(t)$.

Let (σ_j,ζ_j) denote the intermediate result after the j-th application of $I[\![s]\!]$ such that $(\sigma_{j+1},\zeta_{j+1}) = I[\![s]\!](\sigma_j,\zeta_j\{v/x_j\})$. We have $(\sigma',\zeta') = (\sigma_n,\zeta_n)$.

We infer the propositions to be shown by induction over j.

In the induction basis we have $(\sigma_1,\zeta_1) = I[\![s]\!]\big(\sigma,\zeta\{v/I[\![e_1]\!](\sigma,\zeta)\}\big)$. We can infer

$$\forall w,t' : w_{t'} \in \text{free}(s) \rightarrow \text{val}(\zeta\{v/x_1\},w) \in I(t')$$

as follows by case decision. We start with

$$\forall w,t' : w_{t'} \in \text{free}(s) \rightarrow \big[w = v \ \lor \ w \neq v\big]$$

For the first case $w = v$, it must be val$(\zeta\{v/x_1\},w) \in I(t)$ by Lem. A.1 [Only variables from the 'assigned' set are modified to non-nil values in the variable stack] as Def. 4.7x [syntax of iteration] requires $\not\exists t' : v_{t'} \in$ assigned(s). As Def. 4.7x [syntax of iteration] further requires $\not\exists t' : v_{t'} \in \text{free}(s) \land t \not\leq t'$, it must be $t' \leq t$ and therefore val$(\zeta\{v/x_1\},w) \in I(t')$. For the second case $w \neq v$, it must be val$(\zeta\{v/x_1\},w) = \text{val}(\zeta,w)$ and therefore val$(\zeta\{v/x_1\},w) \in I(t')$ by assumption. Therefore, we have

$$\forall w,t' : w_{t'} \in \text{free}(s) \rightarrow \text{val}(\zeta\{v/x_1\},w) \in I(t').$$

In the induction step we have σ_j is system state of $\mathcal{M}$ and ζ_j is a variable stack over σ_j. Similarly to the induction start, we can infer

$$\forall w,t' : w_{t'} \in \text{free}(s) \rightarrow \text{val}(\zeta_j\{v/x_j\},w) \in I(t')$$

as by case decision, applying Thm. 4.10 [$I[\![s]\!]$ is well-defined] for each interpretation of s. Then $(\sigma_{j+1}$ is system state of $\mathcal{M}$ and ζ_{j+1} is a variable stack over σ_j and validTransition(ζ_j,ζ_{j+1}), and therefore validTransition(ζ,ζ_{j+1}) (transitively).

$\square$

Finally, having proved Thm. 4.10 $[I[\![s]\!]$ is well-defined], we can now prove Thm. 4.11 [Interpretations provided by stat are interpretations for operations with side-effects].

Proof for Thm. 4.11. Let $\zeta = \langle b_1, \ldots, b_m \rangle$, $\zeta' = \langle b'_1, \ldots, b'_p \rangle$, and $\zeta'' = \langle b''_1, \ldots, b''_k \rangle$.

Proof for operation without result value: Given σ is a system state of $\mathcal{M}$, ζ is a variable stack over σ,

$$I\big(\overline{\omega}(v_1 : t_1, \ldots, v_n : t_n)\big) = \lambda(\sigma, \zeta, x_1, \ldots, x_n) \cdot (\sigma'', \uparrow\zeta'')$$

with $(\sigma'', \zeta'') = I[\![s]\!](\sigma, \downarrow\zeta\{v_1/x_1, \ldots, v_n/x_n\})$, and $(\sigma'', \zeta'') = I(\overline{\omega}(v_1 : t_1, \ldots, v_n : t_n)(\sigma, \zeta, x_1, \ldots, x_n)$, we have to show that σ' is a system state of $\mathcal{M}$, ζ' is a variable stack over σ', $m = p$ and $\forall v, i : 1 \leq i \leq m \rightarrow \big(b'_i(v) = b_i(v) \ \lor \ b'_i(v) = \bot\big)$.

By Def. 4.9 [stat], we have

$$\forall w, t : w_t \in \text{free}(s) \rightarrow \exists t' : \big[w_{t'} \in \{v_1, \ldots, v_n\} \ \land \ t' \leq t\big].$$

Thus, all free variables of s are assigned in binding$(\downarrow\zeta\{v_1/x_1, \ldots, v_n/x_n\})$, and by Thm. 4.10 $[I[\![s]\!]$ is well-defined] we have σ'' is a system state of $\mathcal{M}$ and ζ'' is a variable stack over σ''. By 4.10 we also have $k = p + 1$ and $\forall v, i : 1 \leq i \leq k \rightarrow \big(b''_i(v) = b_i(v) \ \lor \ b''_i(v) = \bot\big)$. From $\zeta' = \uparrow\zeta''$ we can then infer $\forall v, i : 1 \leq i \leq m \rightarrow \big(b'_i(v) = b_i(v) \ \lor \ b'_i(v) = \bot\big)$. Thus, ζ' is a system state over σ'.

Proof for operation with result value: Given σ is a system state of $\mathcal{M}$, ζ is a variable stack over σ,

$$I\big(\overline{\omega}(v_1 : t_1, \ldots, v_n : t_n) \rightarrow t\big) = \lambda(\sigma, \zeta, x_1, \ldots, x_n) \cdot (\sigma'', \uparrow\zeta'', y)$$

with $(\sigma'', \zeta'') = I[\![s]\!](\sigma, (\downarrow\zeta)\{v_1/x_1, \ldots, v_n/x_n\})$, $(\sigma'', \zeta'') = I(\overline{\omega}(v_1 : t_1, \ldots, v_n : t_n)(\sigma, \zeta, x_1, \ldots, x_n)$, and $y = \text{binding}(\zeta'')(\text{result}_t)$, we have to show that σ' is a system state of $\mathcal{M}$, ζ' is a variable stack over σ', $m = p$ and $\forall v, i : 1 \leq i \leq m \rightarrow \big(b'_i(v) = b_i(v) \ \lor \ b'_i(v) = \bot\big)$.

We can infer that σ' is a system state of $\mathcal{M}$ and that ζ', ζ'' are variable stacks over σ' analogously to above. Thus, if t is an object type – $y \in \sigma'_{\text{CLASS}}\big(\text{classOf}(t)\big) \cup \{\bot\}$.

$\square$

Appendix B

Project World (Complete)

```
1   model Projects
2
3   enum ProjectSize {small,medium,big}
4   enum ProjectStatus {planned, active, finished, suspended}
5
6   class Company
7   attributes
8     name : String
9   operations
10    hire(w : Worker)
11      begin
12        insert(self, w) into Employs
13        -- TO BE DONE:
14        -- try to activate projects by making the new employee a
             member
15      end
16      pre OnlyNonEmployeesCanBeHired: employees->excludes(w)
17      post Hired: employees->includes(w)
18
19    fire(w : Worker)
20      begin
21        delete (self,w) from Employs;
22        for p in w.projects do
23          delete (p,w) from Member;
24          if not p.missingQualifications()->isEmpty then
25            p.status := #suspended
26          end
27        end
28      end
```

```
29      pre OnlyEmployeesCanBeFired: employees->includes(w)
30      post Fired: employees->excludes(w)
31      post ProjectsStillHappy: projects->forAll(p|
32        p.status = #active implies
               p.missingQualifications()->isEmpty)
33      post NoEmployeeOverloaded:
34        employees->forAll(e|not e.isOverloaded())
35
36    start(p : Project)
37      begin
38        p.status := #active
39      end
40      pre AllPredecessorsFinished:
               p.predecessors->forAll(s|s.status = #finished)
41      pre ProjectSuspendedOrPlanned: p.status = #suspended or
               p.status = #planned
42      pre HasAllQualifications: p.missingQualifications()->isEmpty
43      post ProjectIsActive: p.status = #active
44
45    finish(p : Project)
46      begin
47        for w in p.members do
48          delete(p,w) from Member
49        end;
50        p.status := #finished
51        -- TO BE DONE:
52        -- try to activate further successor projects
53      end
54      pre ProjectIsActive: p.status = #active
55      post ProjectIsFinished: p.status = #finished
56      post NoMoreMembers: p.members->isEmpty
57
58    createWorker(qs : Set(Qualification)) : Worker begin
59        w := new Worker;
60        insert (self,w) into Employs;
61        for q in qs do insert (w,q) into IsQualified end;
62        result := w
63      end
64
65    createProject(n : String, ws : Set(Worker), qs :
          Set(Qualification), s : ProjectSize) : Project begin
66        p := new Project;
67        insert (self, p) into CarriesOut;
68        for w in ws do insert (p,w) into Member end;
```

```
69        for q in qs do insert (p,q) into Requires end;
70        p.status := #active;
71        p.size := s;
72        p.name := n;
73        result := p
74      end
75
76   constraints
77     inv OnlyOwnEmployeesInProjects:
78       employees->includesAll(projects.members->asSet)
79   end
80
81   class Worker
82   attributes
83     nickname : String
84     salary : Integer
85   operations
86     isOverloaded() : Boolean =
87       let active = projects->select(p|p.status = #active) in
88         active->select(p|p.size=#big)->size * 2 +
89         active->select(p|p.size=#medium)->size > 3
90   constraints
91     inv notOverloaded: not isOverloaded()
92   end
93
94   class Project
95   attributes
96     name : String
97     size : ProjectSize
98     status : ProjectStatus
99   operations
100    missingQualifications() : Set(Qualification) =
           requirements->select(q|
101      not members->exists(m | m.qualifications->includes(q)))
102    isHelpful(w : Worker) : Boolean =
           missingQualifications()->exists(q|w.qualifications->includes(q))
103   constraints
104     inv AllQualificationsForActiveProject: status = #active
            implies missingQualifications()->isEmpty
105   end
106
107
108   class Qualification
109   attributes
```

```
110    description : String
111  end
112
113  class Training < Project
114  end
115
116  association CarriesOut between
117   Company[1]
118   Project[0..*] role projects
119  end
120
121  association Employs between
122   Company[0..1] role employer
123   Worker[1..*] role employees
124  end
125
126  association IsQualified between
127   Worker[0..*] role workers
128   Qualification[1..*] role qualifications
129  end
130
131  association Member between
132   Project[0..*] role projects
133   Worker[1..*] role members
134  end
135
136  association Requires between
137   Project[0..*] role projects
138   Qualification[1..*] role requirements
139  end
140
141  association Prerequisite between
142    Project[0..*] role predecessors
143    Project[0..*] role successors
144  end
145
146  association Trains between
147    Training[0..*] role trainings
148    Qualification[1..*] role trained
149  end
```

List of Figures

List of Tables

Index